D1110243

100 THINGS WASHINGTON FANS SHOULD KNOW & DO BEFORE THEY DIE

Adam Jude

TRIUMPH BOOKS

Library of Congress Cataloging-in-Publication Data

Names: Jude, Adam, author.
Title: 100 things Washington fans should know & do before they die / Adam Jude.
Other titles: One hundred things Washington fans should know and do before they die
Description: Chicago, Illinois : Triumph Books LLC, [2017]
Identifiers: LCCN 2017016999 | ISBN 9781629373416
Subjects: LCSH: University of Washington—Football—Miscellanea. | Washington Huskies (Football team)—Miscellanea.
Classification: LCC GV958.U5865 J84 2017 | DDC 796.332/6309797772—dc23 LC record available at https://lccn.loc.gov/2017016999

This book is available in quantity at special discounts for your group or organization. For further information, contact:

Triumph Books LLC
814 North Franklin Street
Chicago, Illinois 60610
(312) 337-0747
www.triumphbooks.com

Printed in U.S.A.
ISBN: 978-1-62937-341-6
Design by Patricia Frey
Photos courtesy of AP Images unless otherwise indicated

To Ashley

Contents

Foreword

There was no doubt about it: I was always going to be a Husky. I never wanted to be anything else. The Don James Era was in full effect when I was growing up in Puyallup, Washington. I was 11 years old when the Huskies went down to Miami and shocked the Oklahoma Sooners in the 1985 Orange Bowl. It was a fun time to be a young Huskies fan.

As I got older, I went to summer camps at U-Dub in junior high and in high school I went to Washington games with fellow Puyallup Vikings Billy Joe Hobert, Tom Gallagher, and Joe Kralik. We all dreamed of one day wearing the purple and gold. Those three guys signed and had solid careers with the Huskies, and I was very fortunate and blessed to get that opportunity from Don James, too.

I was the scout team quarterback on the 1991 national championship team. That Husky defense was the best I've ever seen. They didn't care that I had that little red (no-contact) jersey on. They welcomed me to college football the only way they knew how. They hit me; they hit me hard. They let me know who was boss.

But it was awesome practicing against those guys every single day. Going up against Steve Emtman, Donald Jones, Jaime Fields, Dave Hoffmann, Chico Fraley, Tommie Smith, and Dana Hall certainly helped me in my development as a college quarterback. Those names just roll off the tongue because they were all such great players, and it was such a great team.

And then you just think about that offensive line and those two tackles, Lincoln Kennedy and Siupeli Malamala. I mean, those guys were monsters. And then you look at Beno Bryant, Jay Barry, and Napoleon Kaufman running behind them, and Mario Bailey making plays out wide. The competitive fire and spirit of Billy Joe

Hobert that year has been underappreciated through the years. It was a tight team, a tight unit.

We had an amazing freshman class in 1991, too. We told ourselves, "You know, we're going to go 60–0 here. We're not going to lose a game." That's honestly how it felt in my mind.

Playing at U-Dub was an incredible experience for me. Certainly, we had some highs and some lows as a program after the '91 season, but going through some of those trials and tribulations taught me so much and helped me survive for more than a decade in the National Football League.

Since 2010 I have joined Bob Rondeau as the color analyst for gameday broadcasts and in 2013 I returned to the program as director of external relations after being a major gifts officer during the stadium campaign from 2010 to 2013. It's a fun time to be a Husky again. Just as Don James won the right way three decades ago, Chris Petersen is doing it the right way here again. Inside the program there's an incredible sense of accountability. You can feel it. You feel a great sense of obligation and opportunity to do your job and do it well—whether you're a player, whether you're an administrator, whether you're an equipment guy. The head coach has set the standard. *This is how to do it. Your role is to follow.* And you don't want to let that coach down. It was that way with Coach James, and it's that way again with Coach Petersen.

There is no doubt about it. The Huskies are back on the map, and I am honored and excited to be part of the program once again.

—Damon Huard

1 The Dawgfather

After a restless night's sleep, Don James awoke at 6:30 AM on January 2, 1992 in a 14th-floor suite at the Anaheim Marriott. It had been just 12 hours since James' Washington Huskies completed a perfect season with a thorough dismantling of the Michigan Wolverines in the Rose Bowl, and yet the coach and his wife, Carol, spent much of that night and early morning anxiously awaiting results from the final tabulation of the college football coaches' poll.

There was reason to fret: the Miami Hurricanes, who also completed a 12–0 season on New Year's Day, had already been declared the national champion in a vote of media members for the Associated Press poll. (It was the closest vote in the history of the wire service poll with Miami receiving 1,472 votes to claim No. 1; the Huskies received 1,468 points to finish No. 2.) As dawn approached on January 2, results from the CNN/*USA TODAY* coaches' poll had yet to be announced, and James believed that the delay was a bad omen for Washington. "We didn't get it," he said to Carol. "Nobody's got to nerve to call and give us the news."

Finally, at 6:41 AM the phone rang. It was Bob Roller, an advertising executive representing the coaches' poll, and he had good news. Washington, he told James, was No. 1 in the coaches' poll—the Huskies were national champions.

James cried at the press conference later that morning. "It's just a great day in the life of a football coach," he said. "I'm emotional now...It's so difficult to express the feelings I have for these kids. For them to not get a piece of this would have been a tragedy."

The Huskies' perfect 1991 season had a perfect ending for the most successful coach in UW history. He was affectionately nicknamed "the Dawgfather" and, to this day, more than two decades after his abrupt resignation as head coach, Don James remains synonymous with the dominance that the Huskies had when they reigned over the Pacific-10 Conference for much of his 18 years as head coach. "When all is said and done, Don James has no peers," said Don Heinrich, the Huskies' All-American quarterback from the 1950s who later became close with James. "He has taken a school that plays in the rain and brought it to a national power and success in bowl games. It gives him the recognition of what kind of coach he is. He ranks with the great ones. I equate him with Bear Bryant, who, in my opinion, was the top banana."

Funny story about James and Bryant, Alabama's Hall of Fame coach. In the 1960s, when James was an assistant coach at Florida State and Bryant was in the middle of his reign at Alabama, they had a chance meeting at the Miami airport one day. "We were walking at the Miami airport, and Don turned to me [and whispered], 'Carol, there's Bear Bryant,'" Carol recalled in a 2016 interview. "And as we got closer to him, he saw us and said, 'Well, hi there Don James, how are you?' And he shook his hand. And they talked for a couple minutes, and when he walked away he said, 'Carol, I think I've arrived in coaching.'"

It was a seminal moment for the young coach. Some three decades later, James received the Bear Bryant Award as college football's Coach of the Year after leading the Huskies to that perfect season in 1991. "When he got that award," Carol said, "it was really meaningful to Don. It meant a lot to him."

And yet James was not the first choice to become the UW coach in 1974. He wasn't the fourth choice either. The search to find the successor to longtime coach Jim Owens lasted nearly a month. It was December of 1974, and UW athletic department administrators considered about 120 candidates for the job. That list was whittled down to about a dozen serious candidates, a handful of whom were brought to Seattle for interviews.

California Bears coach Mike White and former Green Bay Packers coach Dan Devine were among those who turned down UW's initial offers. The 41-year-old James, who had just completed his fourth season in his first head coaching job at Kent State, was largely unknown in the Northwest. When Don and Carol arrived in Seattle to formally interview for the job on December 20, 1974, the marquee at Husky Stadium greeted them with the message: "Welcome Don Jones." Oops.

Warren Moon puts his arm around coach Don James after the 1978 Rose Bowl, one of six Rose Bowls that James helped the Huskies reach. (AP Images)

Don was offered the job two days before Christmas. A few days after the holiday, James flew from Ohio out to Seattle. A couple weeks later, Carol, their three children, and the family dog—a half-poodle/half-schoodle mix named Barbie—followed him. "I am extremely excited about coming," James told *The Seattle Times* after his hiring. "I am honored that I've been chosen."

Born in the football hotbed of Massillon, Ohio, James was a quarterback and defensive back for Massillon High, leading the school to two state championships. It was in Massillon where Don and Carol had met at the local fireman's festival. They were both born in December 1932; she is 26 days older—"and he never let me forget it," she said.

They were practically inseparable from then on, attending the University of Miami (Florida) together. He was the star quarterback, she was the cheerleader. At Miami, James set five passing records and was named the team's top scholar-athlete before graduating in 1954.

He was an assistant coach at Florida State, Michigan, and Colorado before landing his first head coaching job at Kent State in 1971. James' first team at Kent State included future Hall of Fame linebacker Jack Lambert, current Alabama coach Nick Saban, and future Missouri coach Gary Pinkel. "Coach James was my coach, my mentor, and my friend, and there probably isn't anyone who influenced my life more than he did because of his leadership and the example that he set but also professionally as a coach," Saban said. "Our program today still reflects many of the things that we did and that I learned from Coach James when I first got into this profession, which he inspired me to get into this profession by asking me to be his graduate assistant at Kent State."

At UW James had a 12–14 record through four games in the 1977 season. That's when things took a sudden turn, and Warren Moon and the Huskies won six of their next seven games to claim the Pac-8 Conference championships and earn the first of James' six trips to the Rose Bowl. In Pasadena UW defeated Michigan 27–20. In the 1980s UW won more games (84) than any other Pac-10 team. "It was a special time and a special place, and he was really a special person," said Joe Steele, a UW running back from 1976 to 1979.

The Huskies' dominant 1991 team might be the best in conference history and was led by All-Americans Steve Emtman, Mario Bailey, and Dave Hoffmann. In 1992 James led UW to its third consecutive Rose Bowl berth, where the Huskies lost a rematch to Michigan 38–31. It was the last game James would coach.

On perhaps the darkest day for Washington football—August 23, 1993—the Pac-10 announced a two-year bowl ban and scholarship reductions after a scandal involving several UW players receiving money for little or no work done in Los Angeles. Feeling betrayed, James resigned the same day in protest. "We had done so much for the league," James told *The Seattle Times* in 2006, "and rather than regard us as family, they went after us because we were so good. It wasn't the NCAA. It was the Pac-10 and our administration."

The qualities former players hold long after their time with the Huskies are the integrity, humility, and perseverance James preached above all. "I met him when I was 18 years old. He had a profound impact on my life," Pinkel said. "Coach James was a huge influence on my life, personally and professionally; I wanted to coach because of Don James. He was my idol. He was my mentor. The values he taught included hard work, ethics, determination, perseverance, integrity, teamwork, and he was one of the most successful men with the most humility that I've ever met in my life. There were invaluable lessons that applied to my life when coaching kids for the last 36 years."

James died from the effects of pancreatic cancer in October 2013. He was 80 years old.

"He was a special man and meant the world to me," Saban said. "There aren't enough words to describe not only the great coach he was, but how much he cared for people and the positive impact he made in the lives of everyone he came in contact with. Coach James was my mentor and probably did more than anybody to influence me in this profession."

2 The Greatest Setting in College Football

Likely no one has been to more games at Husky Stadium than Jim Lambright, who was involved in 386 total games for the Washington Huskies as a player, assistant coach, and head coach.

In the fall of 1957, Lambright was a sophomore at Everett High School when he attended his first game at Husky Stadium. He went to the game with a couple buddies but without tickets. As they tried to sneak in from one corner of the venue, they encountered a chain-link fence surrounded by barbed wire. It was no deterrent: they maneuvered around a small opening in the wire and arrived inside the stadium.

Nearly six decades later, Lambright couldn't recall the opponent or the score that day. But he knew the Huskies won and he knew he was hooked. "I remember looking around, being big-eyed, mouth open," Lambright said. "It was unbelievable."

Many, many more who have entered the "The Greatest Setting in College Football," as UW calls it, have surely felt the same.

Built in 1920 for $600,000—it was initially named Washington Field—Husky Stadium has been Seattle's iconic venue for nearly a century. On a warm September afternoon, the views from the top of the bleachers—with Lake Washington's Union Bay just a long punt away from the east end zone, the Cascades beyond that, the Space Needle and the Olympic mountains toward the west, and Mount Rainier to the south—are simply wondrous. "I'd put it out there by itself as the grandest view in all of sports," said Keith Jackson, the longtime ABC college football announcer. "I've hit most of the major stadiums in the world and I don't remember one that offers that."

In 2013 UW completed a $280 million overhaul to the stadium—a long-overdue renovation that put Husky Stadium on par with any program in the ever-expanding facilities race around college football. The two-story, 83,000-square-foot football operations center, built in as part of the west end of the stadium, offers ample space for players and coaches to train, study, recover, and relax. The building's amenities—from a hot tub to a two-seat barber's room adjacent to the locker room shaped like a "W"—were designed to help with the all-important goal of attracting the attention of high-profile recruits. "When recruits come in here, I don't know where else they're going to go in the country and see better," then-UW coach Steve Sarkisian said.

Some 36,000 cubic yards of concrete were used in the new construction, and the renovation featured 93 luxury suites and 447 total bathrooms.

History surrounds Husky Stadium. For the record, it was Bob Abel, the UW quarterback and student body president, who scored the first touchdown on the dirt-covered field at Husky Stadium on November 27, 1920 before a crowd of 24,500. Abel scored on a 63-yard return of a blocked field-goal attempt. (UW wound up losing to Dartmouth 28–7.)

Two presidents gave speeches at Husky Stadium. In fact, on July 27, 1923, president Warren G. Harding made his final speech in front of a crowd of 25,000. He died of a heart attack six days later in San Francisco. Nearly 70 years later, on July 21, 1990, former president Ronald Reagan opened the Goodwill Games with a short speech before a crowded stadium on a sweltering evening. Husky Stadium was the site of the opening and closing ceremonies of the Goodwill Games; it also hosted the games' track and field competition, where 33 stadium records were set.

Charles Lindbergh, during a barnstorming tour in 1927, buzzed the stadium before landing at Sand Point Naval Air Station. During World War II, a number of military-themed events also were held there. UW graduations are an annual event at Husky Stadium, too.

"It's got a great history," said Tom Porter, co-author of the 2004 book *Husky Stadium: Great Games and Golden Moments.*

The stadium's first expansion was completed in 1937, increasing capacity to 40,000. Capacity was increased again—to 55,000—in 1950 when the south side upper deck was built in 1950 but not without skepticism. Only 30,245 attended the Huskies' season opener that September, and many were fearful that the south stands would collapse. Those who stayed home missed Hugh McElhenny running for 177 yards in the Huskies' 33–7 victory against Kansas State. It was also the first Band Day, featuring high school marching bands from around the state, which has long been one of the more popular traditions at Husky Stadium.

Working in the old Husky Stadium press box could feel like a thrill seeker's paradise, especially when the crowd got the place shaking. The press box, which looked like a vintage camper trailer, hung from the south end roof high above the field. "I learned to put on layers of clothing in case the weather changed," said Jackson, who early in his illustrious broadcasting career called UW games for 10 years for Seattle's KOMO radio. "And I learned if the game got exciting, things would shake and to expect my chair to start to move—otherwise I might have wanted to carry a parachute."

When filled to capacity—now set at 70,083—Husky Stadium is one of the loudest places in college football. That was evident when the Huskies hosted Boise State on August 31, 2013, for the first game after the massive renovation. Washington won 38–6 before a crowd of 71,963.

3 The 1991 National Championship Team

Washington's 1991 defense is generally acknowledged as the best in the history of the Pac-10/Pac-12, and there's a good case to be made that it's among the best ever in college football. As a whole the UW team that would go on to rout Michigan in the Rose Bowl and claim a share of the national championship is viewed by some as the best in conference history.

The Huskies, however, hardly looked the part early one September evening.

Before celebrating their perfect march to a national championship, the Huskies found themselves surrounded by 76,304 hostile fans clad in red at Memorial Stadium in Lincoln, Nebraska, on September 21, 1991. Ranked No. 9 in the nation, the Nebraska Cornhuskers had taken a 21–9 lead late in the third quarter in their highly anticipated nonconference game before a national television audience. The Huskies' fourth-quarter comeback that day would define their season and become a seminal moment for the program. "It's a big victory, to beat a team like Nebraska at home," UW coach Don James said after the Huskies' 36–21 victory. "They don't lose very many at home...We had adversity and fell behind and then when we fumbled the punt and fell further behind—that's a time when a team can hang it up and quit. But it was a great fourth quarter for us."

Led by quarterback Billy Joe Hobert, running back Beno Bryant, and that mauling defense, the Huskies scored 27 unanswered points to close out the game, including 20 points in the fourth quarter. Bryant, who lost a costly fumble earlier, scored on a 15-yard touchdown run with 19 seconds left in the third to cut UW's deficit to 21–16. After a UW defensive stand, Hobert found Orlando McKay on an eight-yard touchdown pass that put the Huskies ahead for the first time 22–21 with 11:20 remaining in the game.

On Nebraska's next possession, UW linebacker Jaime Fields forced a fumble recovered by Paxton Tailele for Washington. That set up Hobert for a short touchdown run to make it 29–21. UW tailback Jay Barry closed the door with an 81-yard touchdown

Who's No. 1?

More than 25 years later, the debate rages on: Washington or Miami? In 1991 the Huskies finished 12–0 and were crowned national champs by a vote of college football coaches. The Hurricanes were also 12–0 and were crowned national champs by a vote of college football media members.

There was, of course, no national championship game in that era, so both sides had to settle for a share of the championship. Many have asked aloud over the years what would have happened if UW and Miami did have a chance to settle the debate on the field. "We would've whipped them. It would not have even been close," said Ed Cunningham, UW's center and captain in 1991 and now an ESPN college football analyst. "I'll stick with that. But who knows? I do know this: I have been around the game for a long time...and it's hard to say that this [Washington] team, even as an insider, wasn't one of the best of all time. We were so good and we had so many great players that were playing within a good system that it's hard to think we wouldn't have run roughshod in a playoff that year. We were pretty damn good."

run to push the lead to 36–21. "These kids are really special," Keith Gilbertson, UW's offensive coordinator, said after the game. "When you get down 21–9 in the heart of Big 8 country and you come back like we did, hey, that's special."

The Huskies finished with a staggering 618 yards of total offense, including 335 rushing.

"That was just as good an ass kicking as you could have in the second half," said UW center and captain Ed Cunningham. "It was the varsity against the freshmen. I think that's what gave us our swagger, maybe...We came into hallowed ground, and their fans hated us when we got here, and they gave us a standing ovation when we left. We started to figure out we were pretty good."

Legendary Nebraska coach Tom Osborne was impressed, noting UW's defense "is one of the best defenses we've seen over the years."

The superlatives continued to roll in for the Huskies defense throughout the 1991 season, which culminated in a 34–14 thumping of Michigan in the Rose Bowl and completed the Huskies' 12–0 season. Washington was voted the national champion in the coaches' poll.

"I can't imagine a better football team than the University of Washington," Michigan coach Gary Moeller said. "Their defense is even better than I thought it was."

The Huskies outscored opponents by an average of 41.2 to 9.6 points, and the 1991 team remains in the discussion as the best in conference history and one of the best ever in the sport.

"That is as fine a Pac-10 team as I've ever seen," Tom Hansen, executive director of the Pac-10 Conference, said after the Huskies' win. "And that goes back to the USC teams of the 1960s and 1970s, teams that had athletes who were clearly dominant players. Washington has a great, great defense and an offense that is more versatile than most people think."

4 Purple Reign: 1985 Orange Bowl

The score between No. 2 Oklahoma and No. 4 Washington was tied 14–14 with just more than 14 minutes remaining in the 1985 Orange Bowl when Oklahoma's Tim Lashar kicked what appeared to be a go-ahead 22-yard field goal. Instead, the kick was wiped off because of an illegal procedure penalty. But those operating the "Sooner Schooner"—a covered wagon powered by two white ponies, which served as Oklahoma's mascot—were oblivious to the penalty flag, and the wagon raced onto the field, as it did to celebrate Oklahoma scores. The Schooner got stuck in a muddy patch and drew another penalty, a 15-yarder for unsportsmanlike conduct, against the Sooners. That meant Lashar's re-kick was from 42 yards, and it was blocked by UW safety Tim Peoples. It was a wacky moment in a wild two-week buildup in Miami, all of which serve as sidenotes to one of the greatest games in UW history.

Lashar would actually give Oklahoma a 17–14 lead with a 35-yeard field goal a few minutes later, but UW quarterback Hugh Millen—who came in to replace starter Paul Sicuro earlier in the fourth quarter—led the Huskies on a 74-yard drive capped by his 12-yard touchdown pass to his old Roosevelt High School teammate, Mark Pattison, to give the Huskies the lead with 5:42 left.

An interception by linebacker Joe Kelly set up Rick Fenney's six-yard touchdown run for the final score in the Huskies' 28–17 victory. Running back Jacque Robinson was named the game's MVP after rushing for 135 yards against an Oklahoma defense that had yielded an average of 68 rushing yards all season. The trick for UW's offense was a trapping blocking scheme designed to negate Tony Casillas, Oklahoma's All-American defensive tackle and the

No. 2 pick in the 1986 NFL Draft. The trap worked time and again.

With Barry Switzer as its coach and Brian Bosworth as its popular freshman linebacker, Oklahoma had the swagger coming into the matchup. Switzer openly campaigned for his team to be voted No. 1 if the Sooners beat Washington. But Don James had a dominant defense of his own, and the "Purple Reign" Huskies had spent four weeks during the 1984 season ranked No. 1 in the AP poll. They missed out on a Rose Bowl berth following their late-season loss at USC.

One joint team event during the Orange Bowl buildup was a cruise on Biscayne Bay. Players drank an "Orange Bowl special" concoction offered up by the hospitality crew, and a scuffle eventually broke out between the two teams. It was broken up before becoming an all-out brawl, but the Huskies felt disrespected, which helped fuel their upset days later. "Before the game people treated us like we were some kind of strange creatures from the Great North Country, like we still hunt with bow and arrows," Pattison said after the game.

The Huskies ended the 1984 season with an 11–1 record but were bitterly disappointed to finish No. 2 in the poll behind BYU, which was crowned national champion. BYU had finished 12–0, but UW had played a much more difficult schedule, which included a victory at No. 3 Michigan early in the season. "I've always been opposed to a playoff and voted for a mythical national champion, so I really wasn't in a position to complain," James told *The Seattle Times*' Bob Condotta more than 20 years later. "But I thought we were better [than BYU]. A lot better."

With or without the national championship, the '84 team remains one of the greatest in school history. "The '91 team, based on how they beat everybody, you have to say they're the best team in Husky history," linebacker Joe Kelly said. "But that '84 team—we'd line up against anyone, on any alley, any field. We had some players, man."

5 Return to Glory: 2016 Pac-12 Champs

For the first time in 16 years, the Huskies were relevant again on the national scene and so too was the Apple Cup. In the 109-year history of their in-state rivalry, Washington and Washington State had never played a game with more significance than their 2016 showdown in Pullman.

The winner would claim its first Pac-12 North championship. For the Huskies a berth to the College Football Playoff remained on the line this time, too. The stakes were great. The drama peaked. And then, *womp-womp*, the sixth-ranked Huskies went out and eliminated all intrigue with a furious first-quarter dismantling of the No. 23 Cougars. Washington built a 28–3 lead by the end of the first quarter and cruised to a 45–17 victory—the Huskies' third consecutive blowout of Washington State under third-year coach Chris Petersen.

The rout was one of many in the Huskies' breakthrough 2016—a trend that continued a week after the Apple Cup against No. 9 Colorado in the Pac-12 Championship Game. True freshman safety Taylor Rapp returned an interception 35 yards for a touchdown on the first snap of the third quarter, the highlight in another defensive gem for the Huskies, who pulled away from the Buffaloes for a 41–10 victory. That gave UW its first conference championship since 2000 and just its second 12-win season in school history. "This is crazy. I'm speechless right now," UW left tackle Trey Adams said during an on-field celebration at Levi's

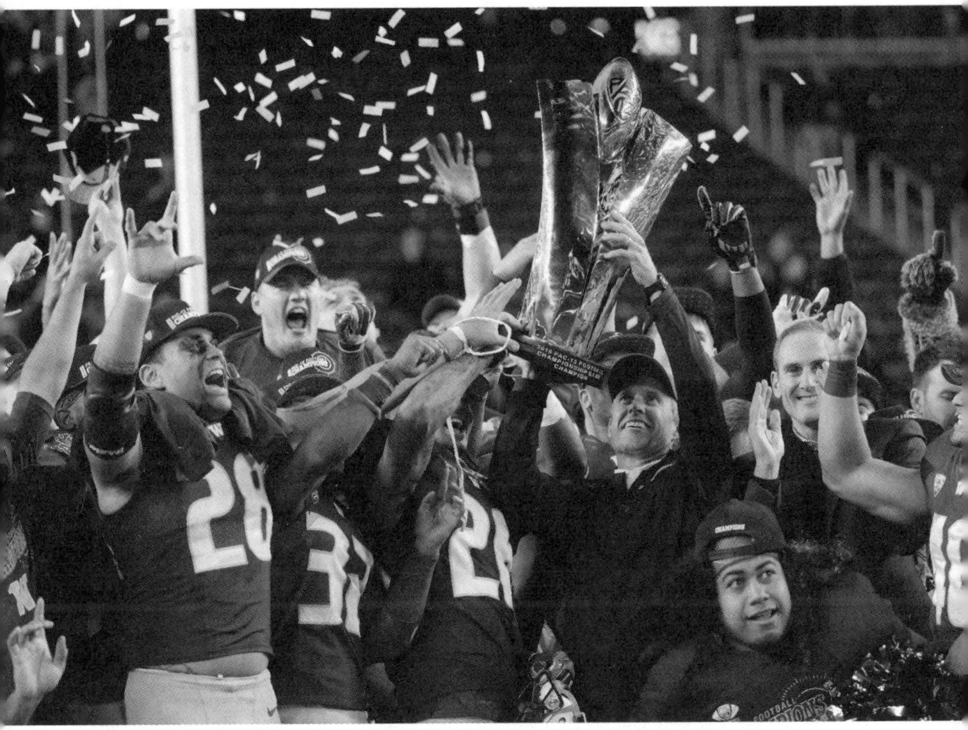

The Huskies celebrate defeating Colorado 41–10 in the 2016 Pac-12 Championship Game. (AP Images)

Stadium in Santa Clara, California, while confetti rained down on the Huskies. "This is what we all came here for."

And this was their reward: a College Football Playoff berth and a date with No. 1 Alabama. Back in the summer, as the anticipation about the season escalated, Petersen did his best to ignore the expectations of a team that was coming off a 7–6 finish in 2015. "The hype means nothing. The hype almost sets us back. The hype almost hurts us in terms of what we're trying to do," he said. "I really think that. That's a negative. Except for, I get college football—and I want our fans to be excited about it. I get that. But everything else…"

Turns out, the hype was warranted.

The Huskies opened the season by routing their first three opponents by a combined 148–30—and would finish the season with the Pac-12's top-ranked scoring offense and top-ranked scoring defense. Sophomore quarterback Jake Browning tied the Pac-12 record with 43 touchdown passes and finished sixth in the Heisman Trophy voting, the second best finish in school history (behind Steve Emtman in 1991).

Forming UW's most productive wide receiver tandem ever, John Ross III had 17 touchdown receptions, and Dante Pettis had 15. They each had multiple touchdown catches in the Huskies' historic 70–21 thumping of rival Oregon in early October. Myles Gaskin (1,373 yards, 10 touchdowns) and Lavon Coleman (852 yards, seven touchdowns) were a formidable 1–2 punch out of the backfield, helping the Huskies set a school record with 41.8 points per game.

All-American safety Budda Baker led one of the nation's best defensive secondaries, and the UW defense led the nation with 33 takeaways. The "Death Row" defense set the tone in UW's 44–6 rout of No. 7 Stanford in late September, a game in which the Huskies had eight sacks in front of a raucous Husky Stadium crowd for a Friday night primetime game on ESPN.

Washington fans had been starved for a return to national prominence, and they got it when the Huskies were awarded one of four berths to the national playoffs. The Huskies knew that getting matched up against No. 1 Alabama wouldn't be easy, and it certainly wasn't. Washington took a 7–0 lead in the first quarter when Browning found Pettis in the corner of the end zone at the Peach Bowl in Atlanta.

But Alabama's top-ranked defense held UW's offense in check after that, and the Crimson Tide went on to a 24–7 victory, ending the Huskies' magical season one game short of the national championship game. "We talked about how the bar has been moved, and they get that," Petersen said. "So they got a taste of it, and that's awesome. I think that can change your mind-set. But it's not like when we go back to work, we're the same team. It's a balance between knowing that they can do special things if we kind of go back to our humble roots of starting over."

6 1960 Rose Bowl Upset

The Huskies' first Rose Bowl victory also stands as one of the most resounding upsets in the history of the venerable New Year's Day game. Going into the 1960 game, the Big Ten conference had enjoyed a stranglehold on Rose Bowl matchups against the Pacific Coast Conference, winning 13 of 14 games since the Big Ten-PCC pairing was formally established in 1946. As such, the Wisconsin Badgers, the 1959 Big Ten champions, were a 6.5-point favorite against the Huskies.

In just his third season as the Washington coach, 32-year-old Jim Owens led a young UW squad to its first Rose Bowl appearance in 16 years and then built a gameplan to take advantage of UW's athleticism against the plodding Badgers. It worked to perfection. The Huskies humbled the Badgers 44–8, a victory meaningful for not only Washington, but also for the greater perception of football out west. "Whatever ways there are to whip a football team, the Huskies used all of them on the 1959 champions of the Big Ten," wrote *The Seattle Times*' Georg N. Meyers.

Before a sold-out crowd of 100,809 in Pasadena—among those in attendance was 92-year-old Frank Griffith, the captain of the first UW football team in 1888—junior quarterback Bob Schloredt, backs George Fleming and Don McKeta, and a stout offensive line led the Huskies' stunning outburst. McKeta scored the game's first touchdown on a six-yard run, and then Fleming kicked a field goal and returned a 53-yard punt for a touchdown on the final play of the first quarter, giving UW a 17–0 lead before Wisconsin even managed a first down. Fleming returned three punts for 122 yards, had a 65-yard reception, and also kicked a 36-yard field goal and five extra points.

The Huskies' 36-point victory is one of the most lopsided in Rose Bowl history. "We read all week what a weak, little line we had," McKeta said. "We ought to show our appreciation by taking those guys out and buying them anything they want to eat."

Schloredt, UW's All-American quarterback who was blind in his left eye, completed 4-of-7 passes for 102 yards, including a 23-yard touchdown to Lee Folkins, and he rushed 21 times for 81 yards and a score. Schloredt shared the game's Most Outstanding Player honors with Fleming; a year later, in leading UW to an upset of No. 1 Minnesota, Schloredt was again named the game's Most Outstanding Player, becoming the first person to win that award twice at the Rose Bowl.

George Fleming

George Fleming, a running back and kicker, was one of the biggest stars on the Huskies' back-to-back Rose Bowl teams in 1960 and 1961. He was named co-MVP after the Huskies' stunning upset of Wisconsin in 1960, when he scored a touchdown and kicked a field goal. A year later he kicked a 44-yard field goal, the longest in Rose Bowl history at the time, in UW's victory against Minnesota. "I was saying to myself, 'Did this really happen?'" Fleming said. "And not only did my dream came true, amazingly I was able to go a second time."

Fleming was even more accomplished during a long public service career. He served 22 years in the Washington State Legislature, was elected to the House of Representatives in 1968, and then became the first African American to serve in the State Senate in 1970. He championed legislation benefiting minorities, women, and the elderly.

Owens had a 6–13–1 record in his first two years as the UW coach, and few expected his young team to make such a historic march in 1959. He didn't start a single senior in the Rose Bowl; instead, UW had a lineup of 10 juniors and one sophomore. In a raucous locker room, Schloredt, Fleming, and McKeta were lifted on teammates' shoulders, and Owens was hoisted in celebration, too. "I'm on top of the world," Owens said. "I felt beforehand our boys would win it if they prepared themselves, and they did."

7 Another Rose Bowl Stunner

Hoisted on his players' shoulders after their upset of Wisconsin at the Rose Bowl, Jim Owens lifted the Huskies to greater heights a year later in their return to Pasadena. Washington would later claim its first national championship for its 17–7 upset of No. 1 Minnesota at the Rose Bowl on January 2, 1961—a win that cemented Owens' legacy as one of the preeminent coaches in UW history. "I can't say anything except that now we're No. 1," Owens said. "This season was more of a satisfaction than last year. We sneaked up on 'em last year. This time everybody was trying to bushwhack us."

The Gophers, 8–1 in the regular season, had been voted No. 1 in the final Associated Press poll, which during this era was released before bowl games were played. But the Huskies' convincing victory against Minnesota gave them ample reason to claim the national title years later. "I still can't believe it," UW captain Don McKeta said. "Our hillbillies have come out of the woods and won two Rose Bowls in a row."

The Helms Foundation was one of the few polls to conduct a postseason vote in that era and it chose the Huskies as the national champion. Decades later, in 2007, UW held a banquet to honor the 1960 team and officially recognized it as the national champs. "Most of us felt we were national champs after we won that game because we beat the No. 1 team and we were in the top five or six at the time, and the other teams ahead of us had worse records and didn't have as good a two years as we did," said Bob Schloredt, the Huskies' All-American quarterback, referring to the team's 20–2 mark over the 1959 and '60 seasons. "So we felt we were national champs. But we never got a big award ceremony or anything like that. But they didn't do a lot of those things in those days, so what can you say?"

As they had done to Wisconsin a year earlier, the Huskies stunned Minnesota early, jumping out to a 17–0 lead in the first half. Unlike their rout of the Badgers, though, the Huskies faced a mighty fight in the second half against the Gophers. Statistically, Minnesota had the edge in first downs (14 to UW's 11), yards (253 to 193), and offensive plays (67 to 46). But the Huskies defense stopped the Gophers three times on fourth downs and intercepted Gophers quarterback Sandy Stephens three times. "I guess I read the newspapers too much about the Gophers," UW defensive end Pat Claridge said. "We found out they're human and we do pretty well against humans."

To get back to the Rose Bowl, the Huskies had to eke out three one-point victories during the 1960 regular season and do it without their All-American quarterback, Bob Schloredt, who broke his collarbone early in the season. Schloredt returned for the Rose Bowl and threw a four-yard pass to Brent Wooten for the Huskies' first touchdown early in the second quarter. Later in the quarter, he broke free for a 31-yard run deep into Minnesota territory, setting up his own touchdown run, a one-yard plunge to extend UW's lead to 17–0 at halftime.

Greatest Collegiate Prank of All Time

It's been called the greatest prank in the history of college athletics and it happened during a halftime performance by Washington's cheer team at the 1961 Rose Bowl. Chalk up a major win for California Institute of Technology.

A small group of Caltech students engineered the hoax by creating 2,232 individual instruction cards and covertly replacing the flip cards that had been created by the UW cheerleaders. When fans went to hold up the cards during the halftime performance, they spelled out "CALTECH."

The game was being broadcast to some 30 million viewers on NBC, and the game's announcers laughed when they recognized the hoax. Museumofhoaxes.com lists the "Great Rose Bowl Hoax" No. 1 on its list of all-time college pranks. "It was one of those classic moments when a prank comes together instantly, perfectly, and dramatically," the website wrote.

UW star wingback George Fleming, co-MVP of the previous year's Rose Bowl, was stellar again. He returned a first-quarter punt 17 yards to help set up his own field goal, a career-best 34-yard conversion to give the Huskies a 3–0 lead. On Minnesota's next series, Fleming made a sensational one-handed interception of Stephens. The Huskies' unsung hero was little Ray Jackson, a 177-pound fullback who had a team-high 60 yards rushing on 13 carries and a 12-yard reception.

Don McKeta, a team captain in both Rose Bowl victories, preserved the victory late in the fourth quarter with two defensive stops on successive plays to halt a promising Minnesota drive. On the first play, McKeta burst through the line and hit Stephens for a 13-yard loss at the UW 19-yard line. On the next play, Minnesota faked a field goal with Stephens lofting a pass toward the end zone—only to see McKeta step in and intercept the pass at the 1-yard line. "We raised the bar for Husky football and football on the West Coast," McKeta said. "The Big Ten dominated the West

Coast in the Rose Bowl for years and years and years. We came along and changed everything."

8 Too Much Tui

As a senior in 2000, Marques Tuiasosopo led Washington to a rousing defeat of Purdue in the Rose Bowl. For that and more, he is revered as one of the best quarterbacks—if not the best—in school history. For many Washington fans, surely one of the lasting impressions of "Tui" is his performance on Halloween eve 1999, when he turned in one of the most impressive games by a college quarterback ever—and did it all while playing through a painful bruise on his backside.

In a 35–30 upset of No. 25 Stanford at Husky Stadium, Tuiasosopo threw for 302 yards and rushed for 207 to become the first quarterback in NCAA Division I-A history with a 300/200 game. What makes the performance all the more unfathomable was that Tuiasosopo had to leave the game in the first quarter to seek treatment in the UW locker room after absorbing a significant hit on the game's second play. The bruised hip/buttocks left him limping the rest of the game. "It was the most amazing thing I've ever seen a football player do," UW wide receiver Dane Looker said. "What he pulled off today was miraculous—just one of the greatest performances I've ever been a part of."

After getting treatment Tuiasosopo returned to the game, but Looker and other teammates wondered at halftime if their captain would be able to make it back onto the field for the second half. "Tuiasosopo's performance was one of the greatest by a quarterback. Ever. Anywhere," wrote Steve Kelley, the columnist for *The*

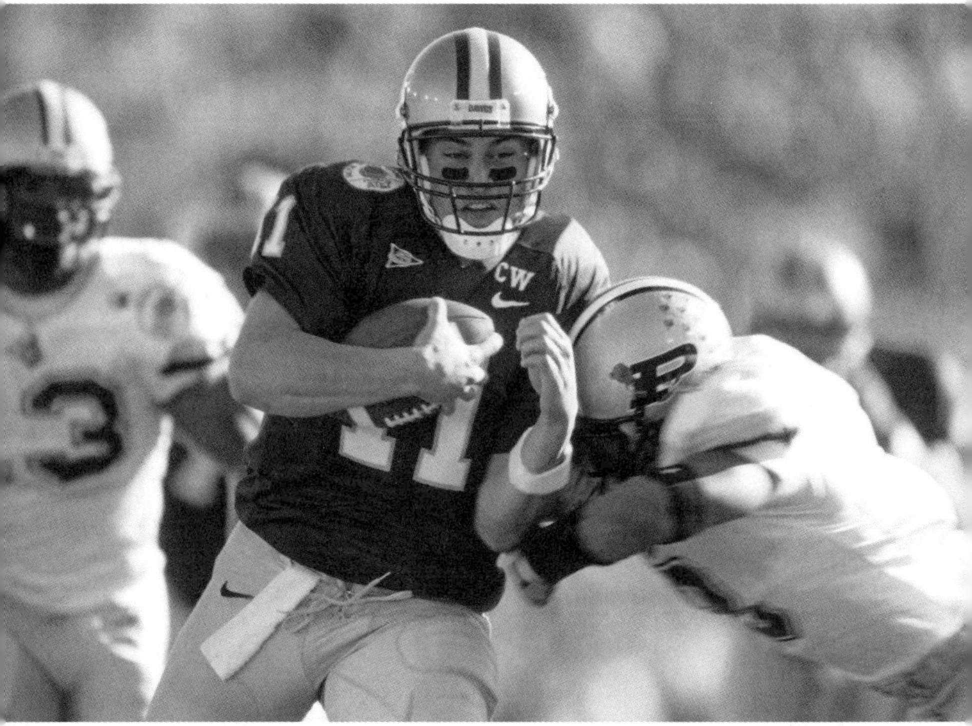

In addition to his amazing performance against Stanford in 1999, Marques Tuiasosopo rumbled through the Purdue defense to cap the 2000 season with a Rose Bowl victory. (AP Images)

Seattle Times. "The fact he barely could walk between plays made it a performance for the ages."

Tuiasosopo's gutsy effort sparked the Huskies to a second-half rally. Stanford led 23–12 early in the third quarter before UW scored 23 unanswered points to take control. His 509 yards of total offense shattered Cary Conklin's 10-year-old school record for total offense (419). "I was surprised by him way back in eighth grade when he would pull out some amazing stuff," said fullback Pat Conniff, a friend of Tuiasosopo's since middle school. "Over the years, though, nothing he does surprises me. He's a great ballplayer. It's a privilege to watch him play and to play with him. It just seems like he pulls something new out every week. He does something special whenever he needs to."

The son of former Seahawks defensive lineman Manu Tuiasosopo, Marques, at 6'2" and 225 pounds, looked less like a typical quarterback and more like a rugged linebacker. In fact, as a star at Woodinville High, Tuiasosopo was courted by many college recruiters to play defense. One of those recruiters was Colorado coach Rick Neuheisel, who several years later would wind up coaching Tuiasosopo at UW. "We wanted to be very upfront with Marques and his father," Neuheisel said in 2000. "I told them, 'We'll give Marques a chance at quarterback, but if that doesn't work out, we would love to have him play safety or linebacker.'"

After narrowing his list to California, UCLA, and UW—all three schools said they'd let him play quarterback—Tuiasosopo eventually chose his hometown Huskies. "Around junior high and high school, I started to really like the Huskies—the toughness that they brought and their attitude and the mentality that they played with," Tuiasosopo said. "As far as being a quarterback for the Huskies, I felt a responsibility. I didn't want to be the guy that let the level or standard of play slip. I would watch old films and watch guys like Mark Brunell and Billy Joe [Hobert] and Damon Huard and watched Brock [Huard] for two years and say, 'Hey, I want to uphold the standard of play here.' That was a personal goal of mine."

9 Moon's Miracle: The 1975 Apple Cup

On a cold, soggy afternoon in Seattle on November 22, 1975, the Huskies and Cougars combined for 11 fumbles, helping Washington State build a 27–14 lead with three minutes remaining. That's when thousands of soaked fans began to file out of Husky Stadium. Those that stayed saw one of the most improbable finishes in Apple Cup history.

The Cougars were driving deep into UW territory, facing a fourth and 1 at the Huskies' 14-yard line, wanting another first down to seal the victory. Instead, UW senior safety Al Burleson intercepted WSU quarterback John Hopkins and returned it 93 yards for a touchdown, cutting UW's deficit to 27–21 with two minutes, 47 seconds left and starting a miracle comeback. "It was easy," Burleson said. "After I got past the first guy, I knew nobody was going to touch me."

UW's defense got a quick stop, giving Warren Moon and the Huskies offense one more possession with 1:58 remaining. Moon, a sophomore playing that day in place of ill senior starter Chris Rowland, heaved a long pass toward freshman wide receiver Spider Gaines, who had gotten behind the WSU secondary. Moon's pass was underthrown, and several WSU defenders were in position to intercept it. But the ball deflected away from WSU's Tony Heath, and Gaines reached out to grab it and then ran free for a 78-yard touchdown to tie the score at 27–27. "That ball hit the defender's shoulder pads," said Gaines, a standout sprinter in high school. "The other defender crashed into him, and the ball fell into my hands. I knew nobody was going to catch me."

Steve Robbins then kicked the extra point to give the Huskies the 28–27 victory. *I don't believe it*, Don James thought to himself.

A sweet turnaround it was for Moon, who was booed for much of the second half while completing just three of his first 21 passes. His 22nd was the most memorable of his collegiate career. It was, James said, "the most bizarre finish" in his coaching career. "No, I've never seen anything quite like that. I had to admit to the players that things looked a little dim at one point."

The victory gave James a winning record (6–5) in his first season as the Huskies' coach and the program its first winning season in three years. "What a way to end the season," Burleson said. "I'm very happy for Coach James. I think he had a good system. Not taking anything away from [Jim Owens], but I've never seen a staff that knows so much about the game."

Years later, James recalled it as the wildest Apple Cup he'd been involved in. "I remember the stands were empty," he said, "and 95 [million] people have told me they were there and saw it."

10 Chris Petersen Comes Aboard

One of the last questions of Chris Petersen's first press conference as the University of Washington head coach cut right to the point. "You going to beat Oregon?" he was asked.

Petersen chuckled. "We have to start that already?"

That was in December 2013—just a few days after Petersen had been formally announced as the Huskies' successor to Steve Sarkisian, who had left abruptly for USC. Petersen had interviewed for the job at USC and many other head coaching jobs during his unprecedented run of success at Boise State. He rebuffed every opportunity to leave the Broncos—until the Washington job.

Turns out, Petersen all along had been eyeing the Huskies. Petersen had spent six years at Oregon as the wide receivers coach under then-head coach Mike Bellotti. Before Bellotti retired in 2009, he had mentioned to Petersen about the possibility of returning to Oregon as the head coach someday. "He said he wasn't as excited about that," Bellotti said, "but the Washington job was one that had always intrigued him."

Petersen left Boise after eight wildly successful seasons. He was 92–12 with two undefeated seasons and two BCS bowl victories. His .885 winning percentage there was the best of any coach at a Football Bowl Subdivision (formerly Division I) school with eight years of experience, and he was the only two-time winner of the Paul "Bear" Bryant Award, given to the nation's top coach, at the time UW hired him.

Why Washington? "People keep asking me, 'Why now? You've been at Boise for so long,'" Petersen said. "And the two things that keep coming to mind [are] timing and fit. It was just time. I think every place kind of has a shelf life. Sometimes that's very short, sometimes that's very long, sometimes it's in between. It was just time. We'd done some really good things there. And for me to take the next step as a coach, as a teacher, as a person, to grow—I needed to take that next step out of that comfort zone over there."

Like Don James—with whom Petersen has often been compared—Petersen wasn't UW's first choice. After Sarkisian's departure the Huskies initially turned to former Seattle Seahawks coach Jim Mora, a walk-on defensive back at UW in the early 1980s. Mora, however, opted to stay at UCLA, agreeing to a six-year contract extension.

So as the Huskies turned an eye toward Idaho, their first call was to a 69-year-old financial adviser with a bum hip. "Would Petersen be interested?" Skip Hall was asked. Hall had worked alongside James for 12 of Washington's "Camelot Years," as Hall calls them, in the 1970s and '80s. Then after a stint as Boise State's coach from 1987 to 1992 and another stop on the staff at Missouri, Hall settled back in Boise as a financial planner. Hall's family and Petersen's family attended church together in Boise. He remains close to both the UW and Boise programs.

At home recovering from a recent hip surgery, Hall relayed the question to the Boise State coach. He reported back to the Huskies that Petersen would "definitely" like to speak to the Huskies. "And it took off from there," Hall said. "He's the right man for the job. I think it's a great fit. I spent 18 years with Don James. The characteristics, the qualities, the leadership…that's Coach Pete's philosophy. It's the same philosophy Coach James had. There's such a parallel there. Of all the coaches I know in the country, I wouldn't put anybody in front of Coach Pete."

A native of Yuba City, California, Petersen was a coach's son. His father, Ron, spent 22 years as a football coach at the high school and junior college level in northern California. Even as he became a star quarterback for the Yuba City High Honkers, Petersen never intended to follow his father into coaching. "He was the typical coach's kid who gets exposed to all those things, so it was second nature to him," Ron Petersen said. "[But] he didn't want to have 18 to 22-year-olds determining his happiness. So he said he was not going to coach."

As the quarterback at the University of California-Davis, Petersen was named the Northern California Athletic Conference Player of the Year and was the top-rated Division II quarterback in the nation as a senior. After a deal to play in the Canadian Football League fell through—the Montreal club he was supposed to play for folded—Petersen instead returned to UC-Davis to finish his degree in psychology. One of his Davis coaches, Bob Foster, persuaded him to coach the freshman team, and an elite coaching career began to blossom.

Since that 1987 season, Chris Petersen has been a part of only one losing season (3–9) in his career. That was in 1992, when he was the quarterbacks coach on Paul Hackett's staff at Pittsburgh. Since then he hasn't coached a team located east of the Mountain Time Zone, and many believe UW could be Petersen's last coaching stop. "He really is a unique guy and a special guy—a guy that's just trying to be better all the time," former Boise State coach Dan Hawkins said. "That's what he's all about: to get better all the time. He's a real stickler for details. He's an awesome friend, always been great to me, and he just totally gets it...He's special."

After a bumpy start—which included a 45–20 loss at Oregon in his first season—Petersen got the program back into the national relevance in 2016. The biggest statement came when Petersen led the Huskies to a 70–21 victory at Oregon, signaling a dramatic shift of power in the Northwest.

11 Steve Emtman

The first time it happened, Steve Emtman was a senior defensive lineman at Cheney High School. He had chased down the quarterback from Spokane's East Valley High for a sack. He then stood and began what would become his signature celebration: he leaned back, raised both arms, and looked skyward, "as if paying tribute to some sort of mythical gridiron god of lost yardage," *The Seattle Times*' Dick Rockne poetically wrote.

"It wasn't really a planned thing," Emtman said of that first celebration. "It just happened."

It continued to happen over and over and over during Emtman's illustrious career with the Washington Huskies. Oh, those poor Pac-10 quarterbacks.

His sack celebration was captured in one of the iconic photos of Washington's perfect 1991 season. There's Emtman standing over Arizona's fallen quarterback, George Malauulu, with his arms raised and index fingers pointed to the sky. And that happened *twice* with Emtman sacking Malauulu on each of the game's first two plays. "When can a defensive lineman be more interesting to watch than a running back, more dominant than a quarterback, stronger than a pickup truck, and more relentless than the IRS? When it's Steve Emtman," wrote Blaine Newnham, columnist for *The Seattle Times* that day.

After that game in early October, someone mentioned to Emtman the idea of him as a Heisman Trophy candidate. The 6'5", 285-pound defensive end scoffed at the notion. "The Heisman Trophy?" he said. "Hey, that's a joke."

Hardly.

Two months later Emtman was the first Washington player invited to New York for the Heisman Trophy ceremony. Michigan wide receiver Desmond Howard won in a landslide, and Emtman finished fourth—the highest finish ever for the Huskies and the best by a defensive player since Oklahoma's Brian Bosworth finished fourth in 1986.

An All-American and future College Football Hall of Famer, Emtman was the Pac-10's Defensive Player of the Year and also received the Outland Trophy as the nation's best interior lineman and the Lombardi Award as the nation's best defensive lineman, making him the most decorated player in UW history. After receiving the Lombardi Award, Emtman said: "I'm really in awe right now. This is the greatest award of my life. It's the greatest moment of my life."

A few weeks after the awards circuit, Emtman and the Huskies defeated Michigan 34–14 in the Rose Bowl to complete their 12–0 season and capture a piece of the national championship. Emtman played in that Rose Bowl despite missing three practices earlier that week while battling the flu. Three days before the game, he had spent eight hours in the hospital, where he was given fluids—electrolytes, vitamins, antibiotics, and glucose. "Everything we could find," Dr. Bill Scheyer, the team's doctor, said with a grin.

It worked. In his final collegiate game, Emtman was named the Rose Bowl's co-MVP along with quarterback Billy Joe Hobert.

And to think most folks never thought Emtman would wind up at UW. Growing up on his family's 2,000-acre cattle ranch in Eastern Washington, Emtman was initially, and naturally, drawn to Pullman. In January of 1988, he made his recruiting trip to Washington State and hung out that weekend with WSU star quarterback Timm Rosenbach. He nearly announced his commitment to the Cougars that weekend. "Everyone thought I'd go to WSU," Emtman said, "and I guess at one point, I did too. But I wanted to see if the U might not be too big. Everyone was sure it would overwhelm me—everyone but me."

The next weekend he then made his visit to Seattle and enjoyed his time on the UW campus, falling in love with the Huskies' new weight room. He got back to Cheney and then called UW offensive coordinator Gary Pinkel at 2:00 in the morning to tell him he had chosen the Huskies. "Hardly anyone at home believed me," Emtman said.

WSU coach Dennis Erickson was said to be especially stunned at Emtman's reversal.

"I think what got him," UW recruiting coordinator Dick Baird said, "is that people said he wouldn't be able to play over here. He basically said, 'Don't tell me I can't play for Washington.'"

Baird had studied Emtman's high school film closely. "What you want to know is how badly a person wants to be a great player," Baird said. "Watching Steve Emtman, it just jumps off the videotape. This guy is thrashing around, doing anything he can to get to the ball carrier. On offense he's blocking his guy until he's got him drilled to the ground. To me, Steve Emtman epitomizes what a defensive football player is all about. The kid is tenacious, and he burns to be a great player. He has a great work ethic."

Emtman was selected No. 1 overall by the Indianapolis Colts in the 1992 NFL Draft. Injuries derailed his pro career. He blew out both knees and ruptured a disc in his neck and then retired at age 27 after six NFL seasons. "I'm a competitor and I wish things would have been different," he said in a 2011 ESPN interview. "I wish I had stayed healthy. When I was healthy, I think I did okay. It wasn't like I didn't perform at all. Yeah, there's frustration. Any athlete who sets out to set a higher standard, if you don't reach it, it's frustrating. As you get older, though, you look back on it and you go, 'I don't question my work ethic or my effort to be good.' I just didn't achieve everything I wished to achieve."

In 2006 Emtman was voted into the College Football Hall of Fame. "I've coached with and against a lot of great players, but I've never seen in all my years a more dominant lineman," longtime UW coach Keith Gilbertson said. "I put him on the same level as offensive guys like Reggie Bush and Marcus Allen—so extraordinary that they are the best on their team, league, and nation."

To this day he deserves to be on the short list as the most dominant defensive player in conference history. "You go to the weight room," UW defensive line coach Randy Hard said in 1991, "and watch the younger players lift. When you talk about, 'Give me an Emtman effort,' they know what you mean. He has set standards for dedication, unselfishness, and hard work here."

12 The Father of Husky Football

The influence Jim Owens had on University of Washington football would be difficult to overstate. His larger influence on West Coast football was almost as important. "He brought football alive in Seattle," said Bobby Monroe, a UW fullback from 1960 to 1962. "The community was ready for it. They grasped it wholeheartedly."

Owens was just 29 years old, the youngest head coach in UW history, when he took over in 1957. He pleaded with Seattle reporters to not print his age. He promised to bring stability to a UW program that had churned through four coaches in six years and was on NCAA probation.

Despite chances to go elsewhere, he stayed for 18 years, leading the Huskies to three Rose Bowls and a piece of the mythical 1961 national championship. He had a 99–82–6 record at UW and was part of the inaugural Husky Hall of Fame in 1979. When he was the coach, Owens lived across Lake Washington from Husky Stadium. Many admirers figured he simply walked straight across to work.

To honor his contributions to the program, UW dedicated a statue of Owens outside Husky Stadium in 2003. "Coach Owens is the father of Husky football," said Don McKeta, the star running back on UW's back-to-back Rose Bowl teams in the '60s.

Owens had served two-and-a-half years with the Naval Air Corps during World War II and he treated Husky practices as rigid boot camps. It was a brutally tough style Owens had learned while coaching under legendary coaches Bud Wilkinson and Bear Bryant. Owens was an All-American wide receiver at Oklahoma under Wilkinson and then spent six years on Bryant's staffs at Kentucky and Texas A&M. (The 1954 training camp at Texas A&M inspired the book *The Junction Boys.*)

That toughness helped reshape the national perception of the West Coast, which had lost 13 of 14 to the Big Ten in the Rose Bowl before Owens' arrival in Seattle. "We were a bunch of guys you didn't want to fool around with," McKeta said.

The Seattle Times columnist Bud Withers wrote in 2009 that the Huskies "were simply the baddest, most feared team on the West Coast for the first half of [Owens'] 18 years here."

Owens earned the admiration of opponents, too. "He was always the total definition of a gentleman," former Washington State coach Jim Sweeney said. "He was the same, win or lose, just a wonderful guy and a hell of a good friend."

During the social revolution of the 1960s, racial turmoil hit the Washington locker room, and Owens would admit decades later that he should have handled aspects of the program differently then. At one point in the late '60s, he had demanded a McCarthy-style loyalty pledge from players—and the few black players who refused were suspended. "Looking back," Owens said in 2003, "I wish we had done some things different. I mean this from the bottom of my heart. I never intended them any disappointment and apologize for any pain that occurred."

Owens died on June 8, 2009, at his home in Bigfork, Montana, at age 82. "What can you say about Jim?" McKeta said. "I can't put it in words. Just like in your life, when you meet somebody that was so dominant, who does so much to create a positive image in your life, and you try to emulate that guy. I think Jim was that to a lot of people."

13 Dobie's Perfect Decade

As he stalked the sideline, Gilmour Dobie famously puffed cigars while wearing a black trench coat over a three-piece suit and a black derby pulled down to his eyebrows. He was a militant man who demanded perfection. Incredibly, that's what he got during his nine-year run as Washington's head coach from 1908 to 1916.

Washington's record over that time was 59–0–3.

A century later Washington's 64-game unbeaten streak from that era remains the longest such streak in NCAA Division I football history. (UW had tied Idaho 0–0 in the final game of the 1907 season and then won their first game of the 1917 season, following Dobie's departure.)

That unbeaten run included a stretch of 40 consecutive victories, a mark that still stands as the second best streak in major college football. (Oklahoma won 47 games in a row from 1953 to 1957.)

Nicknamed "Gloomy Gil" because of his pessimistic outlook, Dobie was actually "negative only when it suited his needs," wrote Lynn Borland, Dobie's biographer. The son of Scottish immigrants, Dobie had a difficult childhood. His mother died when he was four, and his father died when he was eight. Dobie was orphaned and later indentured out to four families as a child laborer. Despite the rough upbringing, he went on to become an honorable mention All-American at Minnesota, playing quarterback and end, and earned a law degree.

Dobie didn't lose a game in the first 13 seasons of his coaching career, which began with two undefeated seasons at Minneapolis South High School and then two more undefeated seasons at North Dakota Agricultural (now North Dakota State). As great as he was in nine seasons at Washington, Dobie achieved even greater fame during his 16 seasons at Cornell, which claims national titles in three straight 8–0 seasons from 1921 to 1923.

In an era with coaching legends such as Knute Rockne, John Heisman, and Glenn "Pop" Warner, Dobie was as good as any. In 2016 the website SportsonEarth.com ranked Dobie the 40th best coach in college football history, four spots ahead of Lou Holtz and just two spots behind Pete Carroll. Dobie finished his 33-year career with a record of 182–45–15. "He was held in the highest respect and admiration by the men over whom he held his mailed fist because he was fair and honest," said William "Wee" Coyle, a star quarterback for UW in that era. "He was a natural leader of men."

After Dobie's death in December 1948, Coyle wrote about his coach and "The Spell of Gil Dobie" in a 10-part series published by *The Seattle Times*. Coyle began his UW football career as a freshman in 1908, the same year Dobie had arrived in Seattle. Coyle knew nothing about Dobie but thought quite highly of his own talents coming out of Seattle's Broadway High School, where one of his teammates, Penny Westover, had also joined the UW squad. "[As] far as football was concerned, we stood just about at the head of the class," Coyle wrote. "Just one day on the practice field convinced us that the tall, angular genius was the boss. He quickly brought us to our senses, and we became as docile as babes in arms."

Dobie was tough on his players. Boy, was he tough. "Under Dobie," Coyle wrote, "nothing was done right, no raw recruit nor even a veteran could perform as he demanded. We couldn't pass, we couldn't run, we couldn't kick, we couldn't tackle, we couldn't block—in fact, to use his own words, 'You are the dumbest, clumsiest, rankest collection of so-called football excuses I have ever seen.'"

In 1915 Washington went 7–0–0 and outscored opponents 274–14. That included a 72–0 shellacking of California, "a pivotal game in West Coast football history that signaled to every western school it would have to upgrade its programs or be flogged by

Dobie's teams," Borland wrote. "Washington cast such a long shadow over the league that other members grew discouraged and dissolved the Big 6. That led to the birth of the Pacific Coast Conference, the predecessor of the Pac-12."

Late in the 1916 season, a scandal rocked the football program and ultimately hastened Dobie's departure from UW. Seven Washington players had been called up by the National Guard, including star tackle Bill Grimm. Upon his return from basic training, Grimm was suspended by the university for cheating on a history exam. To protest the suspension, Grimm's teammates went on a strike. Dobie and university president Henry Suzzallo were at odds over the strike, and on December 8, 1916 they made a "dual announcement" that Dobie would "retire." *The Seattle Times* wrote that UW was losing a coach "with a record unequaled in the annals of American intercollegiate football."

Suzzallo issued a statement: "It has become quite apparent that Mr. Dobie and I disagree as to the functions of a university coach. He has not accepted in practice the obligation to be a vigorous moral force as well as an excellent technical instructor. In such a disagreement, it is natural that we cannot utilize Mr. Dobie. Every part of the university organization must cooperate toward one end, character building."

Dobie's firing, Borland wrote, "set off a near-riot. A thousand Dobie supporters marched on his house late one night in a pounding December rainstorm."

Standing on his front porch, Dobie addressed the crowd: "Kings, presidents, and statesmen have been greatly honored, but I know that they could have felt no greater honor than the honor I feel has been bestowed on me tonight." A few years after his death, Dobie was part of the inaugural class enshrined into the College Football Hall of Fame in 1951.

14 The King: Hugh McElhenny

Any list of Washington's all-time great running backs has to start with Hugh McElhenny. A few years before Elvis became the King of Rock and Roll, McElhenny became the King of college football on the West Coast.

In what still stands as the most dominant rushing performance in school history, McElhenny raced 84 yards for a touchdown on his final carry of the 1950 Apple Cup, completing one of UW's most lopsided victories over the Cougars 52–21 in Spokane. McElhenny's 296 yards and five touchdowns—on just 20 carries—still stand as the Huskies' single-game rushing record. (During that same game, UW quarterback Don Heinrich completed 17 passes to break the national record with 134 completions in a season.)

McElhenny is the only Washington player in both the College Football Hall of Fame and the Pro Football Hall of Fame. He was an All-American for the Huskies in 1951, and his 100-yard punt return for a touchdown against USC that season remains the stuff of legend. It was Frank Gifford, himself a future Hall of Famer and noted broadcaster, who had punted the ball for USC that day. "I was supposed to get the ball in the corner. Well, I did all right, but the King took it there, right on the goal line," Gifford recalled years later. "He started down the sideline, and all of a sudden there was only one man—me—between him and the goal line. He left me flat on my face and ran 100 yards for a touchdown."

At 6'1" and 195 pounds, McElhenny was considered an enormous halfback in that era—a larger-than-life figure in Seattle. "I was a movie star up there," McElhenny told *The Seattle Post-Intelligencer* in a 2004 interview. "The people made you feel that

An All-American in 1951, Hugh McElhenny is the only Washington player in both the College Football Hall of Fame and the Pro Football Hall of Fame. (AP Images)

way. It got to my head. I don't know if I took advantage of it...or didn't take advantage of it enough."

It's true, he confessed years later, that he actually took a pay cut when he left the Huskies to play in the NFL. In an era when NCAA enforcement was more lax, UW boosters supported McElhenny and his wife, Peggy, with about $10,000 a year. (As a rookie with the San Francisco 49ers, he made about $7,000 a year.) "I got a check every month, and it was never signed by the same person, so we never really knew who it was coming from," he said. "They invested in me every year. Peg and I made more in college than I made in pro ball. When I look back, it was funny."

One of McElhenny's favorite pieces of memorabilia is a plaque presented to him by Chicago Bears fans. "To the most respected opponent the Bears ever faced," an inscription on the plaque reads. "If everyone played the game like Hugh McElhenny, wouldn't it be beautiful?"

McElhenny went on to score 60 touchdowns and account for 11,375 yards in 13 NFL seasons. McElhenny invented the screen pass while playing with Y.A. Tittle, Joe Perry, and John Henry Johnson in the so-called "Million Dollar Backfield." His No. 39 jersey is retired by the San Francisco 49ers, and he was inducted into the Pro Football Hall of Fame in 1970 and the College Football Hall of Fame in 1981.

15 All I Saw Was Purple

An uncomfortably hot afternoon it was for the 72,617 fans basking in 92-degree heat at Husky Stadium on September 22, 1990. It's likely USC's Todd Marinovich has never been so uncomfortable on a football field either.

Washington punished USC's celebrated quarterback, holding him to 7-of-16 passing for 80 yards and two interceptions. The Huskies stunned the fifth-ranked Trojans 31–0. Afterward, Marinovich uttered the famous words that came to define this era of UW defensive dominance:

"All I saw," he said, "was purple."

"I've never been shut out in my life," he added. "It's pathetic. I'm embarrassed. We never did anything to shut the crowd up. The only thing that Washington did that was a little different is that they showed blitz every time. I saw purple. That's all I saw. No numbers, no faces, just purple."

Inspired by Friday night speeches from Washington legends Nesby Glasgow and Hugh McElhenny, the Huskies ended USC's 20-game conference winning streak in a game that was "as important as any" victory during Don James' first 16 years at UW, wrote Dick Rockne of *The Seattle Times*. The Huskies had lost four in a row to the Trojans, who went to three consecutive Rose Bowls from 1987 to 1989. The statement win in 1990 served as a seismic shift in power from Los Angeles to the Northwest. "We mashed them right from the start," UW offensive lineman Dean Kirkland said. "I was darn tired of losing to USC. They're a good bunch of athletes, but they're real arrogant. Today was our turn."

Washington tallied 410 yards while limiting USC to seven first downs and 163 yards—just 28 of them rushing. The rushing total was USC's lowest since 1982 and its first-down total its lowest since 1962. "It was an attack attitude, and they had confidence in what they were doing," said USC defensive coordinator Jim Lambright, who would later become a head coach of the Huskies. "They believe they can make things happen."

By halftime Washington led 24–0 and held the Trojans to minus-6 yards rushing. "The look in their eyes kind of stunned some of us," UW receiver Mario Bailey said years later. "We knew we were good, but we didn't know we were that good yet."

UW senior running back Greg Lewis had 219 yards of total offense—120 yards rushing and 99 yards receiving. The victory also served as a coming-out party for UW sophomore quarterback Mark Brunell, who had completed just 35 percent of his passes for 216 yards in UW's two lackluster victories to start the season. Against USC Brunell was 12-of-23 for 197 yards and a touchdown and he added several key runs to earn player of the game recognition.

"I don't think there's any question that when you beat a USC, you start believing in yourself," James said. "And it was a real thorough defeat. For us to beat that team like that, the one thing it gave us was confidence. It was a great lift."

16 Napoleon Kaufman

In the fall of 1990, the idea was to pair running back Napoleon Kaufman, one of the fastest players ever to play for the Huskies, with offensive tackle Lincoln Kennedy, one of the biggest players to ever play for the Huskies.

Kennedy, already an established starter for UW at the time, served as the host for Kaufman's official recruiting visit to Seattle.

And what a tandem it was. "He was the biggest man I had ever seen in my life," Kaufman said a couple years later. "I thought he would be big and mean, but he was nice and laid back. We related to each other, respected each other. He took me around everywhere."

One place they visited was Husky Stadium—just the two of them on the turf together one night. Kaufman ran for imaginary touchdowns, envisioning himself scoring real ones for the Huskies on Saturdays. A year later, he was doing just that.

Running behind Kennedy and UW's stout offensive line, Kaufman scored four touchdowns as a 5'9", 170-pound freshman reserve running back on the Huskies' 1991 national championship team. "In terms of instinct and natural ability to run the football at a similar stage, Napoleon is the best I've seen," Matt Simon, UW's veteran running backs coach, said during Kaufman's freshman season.

At Lompoc High on the central California coast, Kaufman was one of the greatest prep running backs in state history, scoring 86 touchdowns in three seasons. His average scoring play covered 34 yards. He was a high school All-American and also won multiple California state championships on the track (in the 100 and 200-meter sprints). "Napoleon is something in the open field," Dick Barrett, Kaufman's high school coach, once said. "He has speed, balance, eyes in the back of his head."

In 1992 "Nip" took over as Washington's featured running back and rushed for 1,045 yards—the first sophomore in UW history to break the 1,000-yard mark. By 1993 he was the Huskies' biggest star and a bona fide Heisman Trophy candidate. In 1994, after turning down the NFL and opting to return to UW for his senior season, he became UW's all-time leading rusher with 4,106 yards—a mark that still stands more than two decades later. His record for career all-purpose yards (5,832) stands, too.

The Oakland Raiders made Kaufman the 18th overall selection in the 1995 NFL Draft. He played his entire six-year pro career for the Raiders, leading the NFL with 5.8 rushing yards per attempt in 1996 and setting the franchise single-game record with 227 yards against the Denver Broncos in 1997.

Still in the prime of his career, he retired from the NFL in 2001 to pursue a career as a Christian minister. Two years later he opened his own nondenominational church near Oakland. He's preached all over the world. "This is what I do," Kaufman told *The Seattle Times* in 2011. "When I gave my life to God, I really, really meant it. I'm still in shock...I'm still in a position where I'm saying, 'Is this really happening?' I've got a beautiful wife. I've got beautiful kids. I don't drink. I don't smoke. I don't cuss. I'm faithful to my wife, to my kids. I have God in my heart. I've forgiven people. I love people. Is this real?"

17 Lincoln Kennedy

To anyone who would ask, Lincoln Kennedy proudly shows off the bling on his mammoth right hand. "I only brought one of my Rose Bowl rings," he said with a smile on a beautiful August afternoon in 2015. He has two more Rose Bowl rings back home in Arizona. Better yet, on his index finger is a bigger ring with the number "1" at its center. It's his 1991 national championship ring.

The best offensive lineman in University of Washington history, Kennedy was back at Husky Stadium in a new role as an analyst for the Pac-12 Networks. He used the word "ecstatic" many times to describe his feelings about the renovated stadium—and about the future of the program under Chris Petersen. "This," he said, standing on the Husky Stadium sideline, "is remarkable. They got me up here, a kid from San Diego, once upon a time. It's hard to put in words. I'm extremely excited to be here. This is fun. This is fun, beautiful facility. I love the excitement around the young guys. Coach Pete gave me a moment to chat with them earlier during the walk-through. It's like a proud papa coming home, a proud alum coming home. This is great. You can't beat this."

After spending time with Petersen and some players that day, Kennedy was confident the program would again return to the level it was when he was an All-American in the early '90s.

"One thing that resonates here that you don't have at every program—you've got history," he said. "And when this place is rocking, greatest seat in the house. When we had this place rockin', it was the hottest ticket in town."

Kennedy was a big part of that—the biggest, in fact. When he arrived from San Diego as a 16-year-old in 1988, Kennedy was the largest freshman ever for the Huskies—6'7" and 344 pounds. And, to think, he was never much interested in sports as a kid. He played the trumpet in the high school band and sang in the choir and joined the drama club. And he majored in drama at UW, too. He loved having the "creativity to be someone else—to act and show off in front of people," he said in 1991.

Not until his sophomore year of high school did football enter the picture for Kennedy, who played on the junior varsity team that year. "I didn't even know he was playing sports when he told us to come to his game," his mother, Hope, said. "We thought he was going to play in the band as usual. I said, 'Sure, we'll be there. What's so special?' I thought maybe he was going to do a solo. He said, 'No, mom, I don't play in the band anymore. I play football.'"

As a junior, Kennedy finally joined the varsity team—but missed the first four games because there were no shoes big enough for him. "He needed a size 17," said John Shacklett, Kennedy's coach at Morse High. "We finally went to the San Diego Chargers, and they helped us get some."

As a senior Kennedy finally started to realize some of his vast potential, and scholarship offers started pouring in. Four years later he was an All-American left tackle for a national championship team. Soon after that the Atlanta Falcons selected him with the ninth pick in the first round of the 1992 NFL Draft. He was a three-time Pro Bowl selection and was the starting left tackle for the Oakland Raiders in Super Bowl XXXVII.

In 2015 he was inducted into the College Football Hall of Fame. "You know what, it really is a dream come true," he said later that year. "You think about all the time and all the sweat I had on this field, to see it taken to that step, I never truly imagined it would happen. I just have a lot of fond memories of playing this game, especially in this uniform up here [with the Huskies]. So now it becomes synonymous with football history."

18 Sonny Sixkiller

The idea of wearing the jersey number featured in his popular name had never occurred to Sonny Sixkiller. "It might seem like it always made sense for me to wear the No. 6 given my name. But believe it or not, I had never worn No. 6 until I got to the University of Washington," the quarterback wrote in his 2002 memoir, *Sonny Sixkiller's Tales from the Huskies Sideline*.

"At my high school, quarterbacks wore No. 12 and No. 15, so that's what I wore. And I didn't even wear No. 6 as a freshman at UW. I think I was either 10 or 11. I just never thought about wearing No. 6, even though it seems obvious now because of my name. But it was John Reid, who was then the sports information director at UW…who convinced the UW coaches that I should wear No. 6. What a great move that was."

The number change coincided with Sixkiller's sudden rise as the Huskies' starting quarterback in 1970 and a major shift in UW offensive philosophy. And that's no wonder, considering a quarterback like Sixkiller could chuck it. Running a wishbone offense, the Huskies faltered to a 1–9 finish in 1969. With Sixkiller emerging as a sophomore in '70, Jim Owens moved to a more open passing attack, and the Huskies improved to 6–4 that season. Sixkiller became an instant star in Seattle and later an iconic one for the Huskies during a career that saw him break more than a dozen school passing records.

Sixkiller's first varsity start came against Michigan State at Husky Stadium in September 1970. In a stunning twist for an Owens team, on the Huskies' first snap of the game, Sixkiller threw a 15-yard pass to tight end Ace Bulger. "The crowd went nuts," Sixkiller recalled. "Coach Owens had a reputation for being a three-yards-and-a-cloud-of-dust-kind of guy. But here we were throwing the ball one play into the season."

A few plays later, he threw his first touchdown pass to split end Ira Hammon from about 30 yards, and the Huskies would go on to beat Michigan State 42–16—the most points UW scored since the opening game of the 1960 season. UW had 598 yards of total offense, the most since the end of World War II, and Sixkiller passed for 276 yards and three touchdowns. A new era of Husky football was born. "I still get chills sitting here thinking about it all these years later," he wrote.

Sixkiller completed an impressive 186-of-362 passes for 2,303 yards and 15 touchdowns his first season. As his profile grew, so too did the curiosity about his name and heritage. Born in Tahlequah, Oklahoma, and a member of the Cherokee Nation, Sixkiller was a baby when his family moved to Ashland, Oregon. At Ashland High he was a three-sport standout and at 5'11" and some 155 pounds, he was lightly recruited as a quarterback.

Upon Sixkiller's emergence as the star quarterback in Seattle, writers seemed to go out their way to describe his exploits in cliché battle phrases and, worse yet, racist tones. One writer described him as "the most celebrated redskin since Crazy Horse." "I was dumbfounded," Sixkiller told *Sports Illustrated* for a 1971 cover story. "One guy asked if people gave me any trouble over my name—like I'm supposed to get mad and stab 'em in the back or set a trap for 'em. Jeez."

"All my life, people have been jumping on that name," he told the *Los Angeles Times*. "I have no idea where it came from. I've asked my dad. He doesn't know. His dad handed it to him…I'm just trying to prove that I'm not somebody they keep on the roster just because of a spectacular name."

That was hardly the case. Sixkiller was, and remains, one of the most popular figures in program history. He inspired a best-selling record called "The Ballad of Sonny Sixkiller," a "6 Killer" T-shirt line, and a "6 Killer Fan Klub." He also appeared in the Burt Reynolds movie *The Longest Yard* in 1974, playing the part of a Native American quarterback.

19 Warren Moon

Don James was only a few months into new job as the Washington Huskies' head coach when he made a trip to Los Angeles to personally finalize the recruitment of a star junior college quarterback. During a visit to Warren Moon's home, James made a call to his wife, Carol, with some good news. "Don called me on the phone,"

Carol recalled in a 2016 interview. "So he's being real casual... and I said, 'So does that mean maybe Warren is going to come here?' And he said, 'Oh, I think maybe.' I can't remember exact wording...but that was a big get."

The biggest "get" of the coach's career, James would later call it. "Warren Moon," he said, "was probably the most significant player I ever brought into our program."

After a year at West Los Angeles Junior College, Moon arrived in Seattle in late August 1975 and won the starting quarterback job just 18 days later. He went on to lead the Huskies to the 1977 Pac-8 Conference championship and the program's first Rose Bowl berth since 1964, but it was hardly smooth sailing in his first two seasons in Seattle.

Moon was the Huskies' first black quarterback, which came at a time when coaches throughout the sport balked at the idea of having a black quarterback. The Huskies went 6–5 in 1975 and 5–6 in '76, and fans at Husky Stadium often voiced their displeasure at the quarterback situation. Decades later, Moon has said, fans would approach him, grown men would be crying, asking for forgiveness for their unruly behavior during his time at UW. "Those were some bittersweet days," Moon said during a 2006 interview with *The Seattle Times*. "I learned a lot about people. I learned about how tough I was. And I learned a lot about adversity and success."

James, of course, stuck by Moon. "He would tell Warren: 'All they have to do is come look at the film and they'll see why you're starting,'" Carol James recalled.

The payoff came in 1978. After a 1–3 start to the season, Moon and the Huskies went to Oregon and crushed the Ducks 54–0. From there, the Huskies won seven of their final eight games of the season, including an upset of No. 4 Michigan 35–15 in the Rose Bowl. Moon was the conference's Player of the Year and the Rose Bowl MVP.

Over the years, Moon remained close to UW—one of his dearest friends is basketball coach Lorenzo Romar—and even funded a scholarship for quarterback Keith Price. Another black quarterback from Los Angeles, Price set the UW record with 75 touchdown passes from 2010 to 2013.

Moon made his mark in the NFL, too, but not before overcoming more stigmas about black quarterbacks. He refused to switch positions, as many had suggested he do, and was passed over in the 1978 NFL Draft. "Reading defenses, understanding schemes, being the face of a franchise—there were just a lot of people in pro

Other Noteworthy NFL Quarterbacks

Warren Moon, a Pro Football Hall of Famer, is the gold standard, but the list of Huskies quarterbacks to play in the NFL is impressive. In 2012 *The Wall Street Journal* compiled a list of career NFL quarterback starts by a school since 1970, and at the time Washington came in second behind Purdue.

Among former Huskies, Moon has the most starts in the NFL with 203. Chris Chandler is second with 152 NFL starts and he remains the only former Huskies quarterback to start a Super Bowl, having led the Atlanta Falcons there in 1998. Mark Brunell is third on the list with 151 NFL starts, and most of those came with the Jacksonville Jaguars. In a 17-year pro career, the left-handed Brunell threw for 32,072 yards, 184 touchdowns, and 108 interceptions.

Steve Pelluer, the 1983 Pac-10 Offensive Player of the Year, is fourth on the list with 30 NFL starts. Before Troy Aikman's rise, Pelluer was the starting quarterback for the Dallas Cowboys during Tom Landry's last game in his Hall of Fame coaching career. Damon Huard started 27 NFL games and won one Super Bowl ring as Tom Brady's backup with the New England Patriots in 2002. Another former Patriots quarterback, Hugh Millen started 25 games in his 10-year pro career. He threw for 3,073 yards, nine touchdowns, and 18 interceptions for the Patriots in 1991 and then started seven games the next year before New England drafted Washington State product Drew Bledsoe in 1993 to supplant him.

football who didn't think we could do that," Moon told *The New York Times* in 2016. "I never wanted anyone to think this stuff bothered me. Everyone in the freaking place is booing you, and you got 10 guys in the huddle who are watching your eyes to see if it's bothering you. So you do your best De Niro, even if inside it's killing you. I internalized a lot of stuff I had to deal with in therapy later in my career."

Shunned by the NFL, he went to Canada instead, leading the CFL's Edmonton Eskimos to five straight Grey Cups. He finally got his shot in the NFL when the Houston Oilers signed him as an unrestricted free agent in 1984. He was the NFL MVP in 1990 and in a 17-year NFL career threw for 49,325 yards, 291 touchdowns, and 233 interceptions. At the time of his retirement in 2000, his pass attempts, completions, passing yardage, and total offense totals all ranked third all time in the NFL, and his touchdown total was fourth. He was a first-ballot selection into the Pro Football Hall of Fame in 2006.

20 George "Wildcat" Wilson

It is regarded as one of the greatest Rose Bowl games ever played, and Washington halfback George Wilson was the greatest to play in that 1926 game.

Consider this: with Wilson in the game, the heavily favored Huskies built a 12–0 lead against Alabama in the first half. Wilson had an interception, a 36-yard run out of a punt formation, threw a 20-yard touchdown pass, and had 10 tackles on defense—all before halftime.

Famed sportswriter Damon Runyon, on hand for the game, wrote that Wilson was "one of the finest players of this or any other time." Runyon also noted that Wilson might have been playing with broken ribs.

Wilson was then knocked unconscious in the second quarter and had to be carted off the field on a stretcher. With Wilson out, Alabama—led by quarterback Pooley Hubert and running back Johnny Mack Brown, who both would be inducted into the College Football Hall of Fame—scored all 20 of its points in the third quarter to take a 20–12 lead.

In the fourth quarter, Wilson returned and scored on a 27-yard touchdown run, cutting Washington's deficit to 20–19. But the Huskies wouldn't get any closer.

Washington was the nation's highest scoring team in 1925—with victories by margins such as 108–0, 59–0, 56–0, 64–2, and 80–7—and thus entered the Rose Bowl as the overwhelming favorite in an era when southern football didn't have near the stature as in other regions. The upset of UW put Alabama football on the map, and the NCAA retroactively crowned the Crimson Tide its first national champion that year. "Washington was undoubtedly one of the greatest football teams I have ever seen, and I am filled with much gladness that we won," Alabama coach Wallace Wade said. "The fact that the crowd at the game gave our team such wonderful support made the triumph a still more joyous one. The people here have been mighty courteous to all of us, and I as well as the rest of the party certainly appreciate it."

Wilson, a three-time All-American, had also led the Huskies to the 1924 Rose Bowl—a 14–14 tie with Navy. The Everett High School alumnus would become one of just three Husky football players to have his number (33) retired, and his 38 career touchdowns remain the school record (a record tied by Bishop Sankey in 2013).

Wilson was inducted into the College Football Hall of Fame in 1951. He had a vagabond professional career following his time at UW, notably helping the Providence Steam Rollers win the National Football League championship in 1928. Wilson then dabbled in professional wrestling.

21 Don Heinrich

From the perspective of a modern-day football enthusiast, the statistics for Don Heinrich's final game in a Huskies uniform hardly jump off the page. The quarterback's passing numbers in the 1952 Apple Cup included a mere seven completions on 16 attempts for 145 yards with no touchdowns and one interception.

Consider, though, that the forward pass was still something of a novelty of the era. Consider also that the game was played in a 25-degree chill—hardly ideal conditions for throwing a football—two days after Thanksgiving at Spokane's Joe Albi Stadium. And finally, consider the significance of those seven completions, which gave Heinrich a total of 137 completions in his senior season to break his own national passing record (of 133 completions) from 1950. Impressive, indeed. Oh, and the Huskies beat the rival Cougars 33–27 on that cold November day, capping one of the most accomplished careers in Washington history.

For a while, however, Heinrich's availability for that 1952 Apple Cup was very much in doubt. Earlier that month Heinrich had been drafted by the Army. He had previously served in the Army Reserve, and as war raged in Korea, Congress had earlier that year enacted the Reserve Forces Act, requiring him to report to Joint Base Lewis-McChord near Tacoma on November 24. He needed to secure a three-day weekend pass from the Army just to play in Huskies' final game that season. And two days after his record-setting finish for the Huskies, he was in a private's uniform to begin his Army career.

Heinrich was a two-time All-American for the Huskies and set nearly every school passing record in 1949, '50, and '52. A shoulder injury kept him out in 1951, and he completed 335 passes out of 610 attempts for 4,392 yards, records that stood for more than 20 years until Sonny Sixkiller arrived at UW.

Heinrich was inducted into the College Football Hall of Fame in 1987 and was named the quarterback on the Huskies' centennial team in 1990. Before coming to UW, Heinrich had already built a legendary reputation as one of the best prep players in Washington state history, a reputation cemented when the 6'0", 165-pound quarterback led Bremerton High to a 19–14 victory against Ballard in the 1947 state championship game. After the game *The Seattle Times*' Jim Duff wrote "that anything said about Don Heinrich is an understatement."

"Don was something special in the huddle," Jim Wiley, a teammate of Heinrich at Bremerton and UW, said years later. "He had the knack of making everybody feel he was important. After a half dozen or so plays in a game, he would start asking the linemen questions: 'Okay, what have you got to tell me? Who've you found that's soft?'"

After his sensational UW career, Heinrich played eight seasons in the NFL, helping the New York Giants reach three championship games and winning the NFL championship in 1956. During his time in New York, Heinrich split quarterback duties with Charlie Conerly. "Vince Lombardi was the offensive coordinator at the time and he would start Heinrich and then replace him with Charlie Conerly," said Giants running back Frank Gifford, the NFL's Most Valuable Player in 1956 and a close friend of

Heinrich. "It was a frustrating arrangement, but neither quarterback complained, and Don and Charlie became close friends."

After his playing career ended, Heinrich remained around football as coach and broadcaster. He was an NFL assistant coach with the Giants, Los Angeles Rams, Dallas Cowboys, New Orleans Saints, Pittsburgh Steelers, and San Francisco 49ers. In 1976 he became the color analyst on the radio broadcasts of Seattle Seahawks games and he later worked as an analyst for the Huskies. He also worked for HBO to call two world boxing championship fights.

Heinrich remained close to UW football throughout his life and even had a hand in helping Don James land the Huskies' coaching job in December 1974. Earlier that year Heinrich and James, then the coach at Kent State, had met during the buildup to the Pro Football Hall of Fame ceremonies, and when the UW coaching job came open, Heinrich called UW athletic director Joe Kearney to recommend James. "His was the first name to pop into my mind," Heinrich said. "I mentioned this to a number of people. I told Kearney he should look at James very carefully."

In turn, more than 17 years later, at around 8:00 AM on January 2, 1992, James rang Heinrich. The UW coach wanted the former UW quarterback to be one of the first to hear the news that the Huskies had claimed a share of the 1991 national championship. Heinrich had been battling pancreatic cancer and was unable to attend the Huskies' Rose Bowl victory against Michigan the day before. "He said, 'You're part of this,' which, of course, is a nice thing to say," Heinrich said. Less than two months later, on February 29, 1992, Heinrich died at age 61.

22 Whammy in Miami

In leaving a day early for their cross-country trip, the idea was for the Huskies to have a little extra time to acclimate to the thick air in Miami. The vaunted Miami Hurricanes, led by future NFL stars Warren Sapp and Ray Lewis—and a future pro wrestler/actor in Dwayne "The Rock" Johnson—seemed to have plenty of advantages against Washington going into Week 3 of the 1994 season, and UW coach Jim Lambright hoped the extra day would at least give his players a chance to get comfortable in South Florida's crippling humidity. "It's very rare I'm not able to sleep," UW fullback Richard Thomas said, "but as I tossed and turned in the Miami heat [the night before the game], I knew something great might happen."

He was right. What followed that Saturday afternoon in sweltering 86-degree heat at the Orange Bowl was the most memorable nonconference victory in UW history, and Thomas had a big hand in it. He took a short screen pass from Damon Huard and went 75 yards for a touchdown early in the third quarter, the start of a 22-point outburst over a four-minute stretch to turn the Huskies' 14–3 halftime deficit into a 25–14 lead.

No. 17 Washington would outscore No. 6 Miami 35–6 in the second half en route to a stunning 38–20 victory. "I feel great now, but I'm sure that 10 years from now I'll feel even better," Huard said. "It's something I'll remember for the rest of my life."

The Hurricanes hadn't lost a game at the Orange Bowl in nine years—a 58-game home winning streak that still stands as the NCAA record—and they came into the game as 14-point favorites against the Huskies.

Three years earlier the Huskies and the Hurricanes, each 12–0, had shared a piece of the national championship; UW claimed the coaches' title, and Miami claimed the Associated Press one. Earlier in the week, Miami coach Dennis Erickson joked that the losers of this matchup should give back their '91 championship rings. "I'm really sort of sick," Erickson would say after the Huskies' victory. "I've never been around a game like that, what happened in the second half."

The victory was especially gratifying for Lambright, who was in his second season as the UW head coach. Washington was serving its second year of a two-year postseason ban handed down by the then-Pacific-10 Conference, and many players and coaches viewed the trip to Miami as their showcase game of the year. "No game has meant more to me," Lambright said afterward.

In the first half, Miami had success in slowing down the Huskies' star running back, Napoleon Kaufman. But the extra attention the Hurricanes paid to Kaufman helped spring Thomas loose on the game-changing touchdown. Thomas took the pass from Huard near the line of scrimmage, cut inside, evaded two shoestring tackle attempts, and broke free with Kaufman coming in near the end of the run for a punishing block on a Miami defender.

Kaufman finished with 80 yards—65 in the second half—on 28 carries and on his last carry he broke Joe Steele's UW career rushing mark of 3,091 yards. A historic day, indeed.

"To me," Kaufman said, "it was a perfect game, my best game. It was a tough game, and I made tough yards. I also showed I could catch, that I could block, that you'd better believe if I need to run the entire field to make a block for Richard Thomas, I'm going to do that, too."

UW cornerback Russell Hairston followed Thomas' touchdown with a 34-yard interception return for a score. On the ensuing kickoff, Tony Parrish forced a fumble, setting up another touchdown for the Huskies—this a most unusual one. Huard fumbled near the goal line, and in the mad pileup that followed, UW offensive lineman Bob Sapp wound up with the ball in the end zone. Officials huddled and after several tense moments credited Sapp with the touchdown. During an interview after the game, it was Sapp who spread the word of the "Whammy in Miami," a phrase coined in a celebratory locker room by longtime UW staffer Abner Thomas.

Huard had 217 yards passing and put the finishing touches on the win when he dove into the end zone for a seven-yard touchdown late in the fourth quarter. "I could have laid there forever. Dig a grave," Huard said. "It's the greatest feeling I've ever had in my life."

23 2001 Rose Bowl

Late in the third quarter of the 2001 Rose Bowl, Washington's star quarterback, Marques Tuiasosopo, was tackled onto his right shoulder and had to leave the game, exiting to the locker room. Clinging to a three-point lead, the Huskies turned to backup quarterback Cody Pickett, who had taken all of two snaps during the 2000 regular season.

Pickett then took just three snaps against Purdue before Tuiasosopo, missing the first snaps of his illustrious Huskies career, came hustling back onto the field to start the fourth quarter. Eight plays later, he threw an eight-yard touchdown pass to receiver Todd Elstrom to push the Huskies' lead to 10 points, helping Washington hold on for a 34–24 victory against Purdue. Tuiasosopo's shoulder injury, UW coach Rick Neuheisel said after the game, "would have put a lot of other guys out of the game."

Tuiasosopo earned the game's Most Valuable Player award in leading the Huskies past Drew Brees and the Boilermakers for UW's first Rose Bowl win in nine years. In his final game in a UW uniform, Tuiasosopo ran 15 times for 75 yards and a touchdown and completed 16-of-22 passes for a 138 yards and a touchdown. "What a ride," Neuheisel said, encapsulating a wild 11–1 season that featured five fourth-quarter comebacks and put the Huskies in a three-way tie (with Oregon and Oregon State) for the Pac-10 championship. "You come from behind as many times as we did...something about your belief in one another caused that to happen."

The Huskies won an emotional Rose Bowl in part by keeping the ball away from Brees, Purdue's All-American quarterback (and future NFL MVP) who orchestrated the nation's most prolific offense. After Purdue forged a 17–17 tie early in the third quarter, the Huskies held the ball for 23 minutes, 29 seconds in the second half, finishing with 245 yards rushing. Brees was 23-of-39 passing for 275 yards and two touchdowns, and UW's defense held Purdue to a season-low 351 yards of total offense. "We threw a lot of blitzes at him," UW safety Hakim Akbar said. "He couldn't get any rhythm the whole game."

UW's Willie Hurst scored on an eight-yard touchdown run to make it 34–17 with 7:25 left. The victory was the Huskies' eighth straight, and they would finish the season ranked No. 3 in the AP poll, their highest finish since their 1991 national championship season.

An emotional scene played out in the Huskies' locker room before the start of the 2001 Rose Bowl when Washington safety Curtis Williams, paralyzed on the field during a game two months earlier, spent about 10 minutes visiting with teammates, who wore Williams' initials on their jerseys. Williams was transported to the Rose Bowl from his rehabilitation center in Santa Clara, California, and watched the game from a suite in the press box. A senior from

Fresno, California, Williams had been paralyzed from the neck down on a helmet-to-helmet hit during UW's victory against Stanford on October 28, 2000. He died in May 2002 at age 24.

24 2002 Apple Cup

It took two decades, but Washington got its revenge against Washington State during the 2002 Apple Cup. This rendition of the annual rivalry game was perhaps the craziest one ever.

Knocked out of contention for a Rose Bowl berth in 1982 and 1983 after getting upset by WSU, the Huskies wiped away both the third-ranked Cougars' national championship and Rose Bowl dreams with a stunning 29–26 triple-overtime victory in Pullman on November 23, 2002.

Controversy still lingers about the game's finish. On the final play, Washington defensive end Kai Ellis batted down a backward pass from WSU quarterback Matt Kegel and then fell on top of it. Officials deliberated about whether Kegel's pass was a lateral—and after about a minute they ruled it indeed was. That gave the Huskies possession, ending the game on the spot, and setting off a wild UW celebration. "They were thinking of holding their red roses in the air," UW defensive end Ellis said. "And we really spoiled their fun."

Some in the crowd of 37,600 at Martin Stadium threw bottles and other debris at the Huskies, and WSU coach Mike Price left the field fuming over the final call. "It was a pass," Price said. "The ball was knocked backward, but it was a batted pass. It's an unforgivable mistake as far as I'm concerned. It's too bad that they take away from the kids. Both teams fought so hard to win this game.

It's ugly, as far as I'm concerned, to see it end that way. I'm not going to let go of this one for a long time."

Worse for the Cougars, star quarterback Jason Gesser had left the game in the fourth quarter, which pressed Kegel into action. That helped start a comeback for UW, which trailed 20–10 with 4:41 left. Huskies quarterback Cody Pickett threw a seven-yard touchdown pass to Paul Arnold with 3:13 left to get the Huskies within three points. Nate Robinson, the future basketball star, then intercepted Kegel to set up John Anderson's 27-yard field goal to tie the score with 15 seconds left and force overtime.

In the first two overtimes, both teams kicked field goals. The Cougars were barely able to move the ball with Kegel at the helm. "Once Gesser was out, we knew we had an advantage over Kegel," UW linebacker Ben Mahdavi said.

The win would represent Rick Neuheisel's last game as the UW coach and also wrap up the mythical "Northwest Championship" that Neuheisel had contrived earlier in the month to help spark the Huskies' three consecutive victories against Oregon State, Oregon, and WSU to end the regular season. "This is the greatest feeling I've ever had in my life," UW tackle Khalif Barnes said. "This to me is better than the Rose Bowl win [in 2001] the way this team has shown so much character, pride, and charisma in coming back."

25 Sailgating

On its own Husky Stadium stands as one of the great venues in college football. What makes the experience of a gameday truly special for Washington fans, particularly on a warm September afternoon, is the picturesque landscape that surrounds campus, including Lake Washington adjacent to the stadium.

Tailgating is a popular ritual throughout the country. For many Husky fans, the pregame festivities have a unique twist at UW. Husky Stadium and Tennessee's Neyland Stadium are the two venues in major college football that can be directly accessed by boat, and "sailgating" at Husky Harbor is a particularly unique pastime at UW. "At how many tailgate settings does one get to walk past the *lily pads*?" Chuck Culpepper of *The Washington Post* wrote in 2016.

Other Pregame Options

In addition to the sailgating experience, fans can enjoy more traditional pregame festivities around Husky Stadium. RV tailgating is especially popular in the main parking lot just north of Husky Stadium. Space is limited, and RV parking spots must be reserved in advance through the UW ticket office. Call 206-543-2200.

The RAM Restaurant & Brewery, located a few blocks north of the stadium at U-Village, is a popular restaurant for pregame gatherings. A few blocks farther north, the Duchess Tavern is typically overflowing with fans before games.

The Link light rail system, which opened at Husky Stadium before the 2016 season, provides another transportation option to games. Those traveling from the south can park at Sea-Tac airport and use the light rail to UW games.

Washington fans sailgate prior to the Huskies' 44–6 victory against Stanford in 2016. (AP Images)

A number of local restaurants and charter companies offer popular group rides with boats leaving from various locations around Puget Sound heading for Husky Stadium early on gamedays. The Lake Washington harbor can accommodate boats up to about 100 feet, and upwards of 100 boats will moor there on warm gamedays. Once there, fans can partake in the typical tailgating experience—food, drinks, and football on TV (or on streaming devices)—with a few extra splashes of fun. For boats moored out on the bay, UW provides roundtrip water taxi rides to the docks (for $8 per person). No reservation needed. You simply flag down the taxi when it's nearby.

26 Rick Neuheisel's Abrupt Exit

In June of 2003, two and a half years after Rick Neuheisel led the Huskies to a Rose Bowl victory, the Washington football program was rocked when it was revealed Neuheisel was under NCAA investigation for his involvement in college basketball gambling pools. Acting on an anonymous tip, two NCAA investigators and one from the Pac-10 conference interviewed Neuheisel after he put up $5,000 and won some $20,000 in an auction format pool on the 2002 Men's Basketball Tournament. Such pools are against the rules of the NCAA, which prohibits gambling on college athletics by its players, coaches, and other personnel. "I never in my wildest imagination thought I was breaking an NCAA rule," Neuheisel said after the investigation became public on June 4. "Obviously, that would be the furthest thing I would ever want to do. I just thought I was participating in a social event with my neighbors."

He was fired a week later in part because he had initially lied about his involvement in the basketball pool. "Rick's actions have left me little choice and have seriously undermined his ability to continue as head football coach," UW athletic director Barbara Hedges said at a press conference. In February of 2003, Neuheisel had also lied to Hedges about his interview with the San Francisco 49ers about their head coaching vacancy, which she also cited as cause for his firing. "It's a serious issue betting on college sports," she said. "But it's also a serious issue not being honest about it."

Neuheisel had a 33–16 record in four seasons as the UW coach. Almost immediately after being hired in January 1999, Neuheisel ran into trouble with the NCAA when five UW coaches were found to have improperly made visits to recruits. Neuheisel's legacy is the 2000 season, when he led the Huskies to an 11–1 record, a victory against Purdue in the Rose Bowl, and a No. 3 national ranking. That season was also marred by the legal troubles of a handful of players, including star tight end Jerramy Stevens, as later documented by *The Seattle Times*' 2008 "Victory and Ruins" series about that 2000 season.

UW's play also had slipped on the field in Neuheisel's final two years, when the team finished 8–4 in 2001 and 7–6 in 2002, losing bowl games each year. Neuheisel's abrupt departure started a tailspin for the program, which didn't have another winning season until 2010 and bottomed out with a winless 2008 campaign under Tyrone Willingham.

Neuheisel later sued UW and the NCAA over his firing and ultimately received a $4.5 million out-of-court settlement. "I know it's been a rough couple of years for everybody involved," Neuheisel said in 2008 during his first season as the coach at UCLA. "To those who think I'm responsible, all I can say is I'm sorry you feel that way. But it's time to move forward and think about the future."

27 Knocking Off USC

For the first 10 minutes, as No. 3 USC ran up and down the field in building a 10–0 lead, it appeared nothing had changed. Pete Carroll's Trojans, a college football dynasty in the 2000s, had previously defeated the Washington Huskies 56–0 during UW's winless 2008 season, and it looked like the result might be something similar less than a year later at Husky Stadium.

Instead, in a stunning turnaround, quarterback Jake Locker led the Huskies on a wild comeback to upset the Trojans 16–13 on September 19, 2009, for the program's most significant win since the 2001 Rose Bowl. "Hands down, this is the greatest day I've ever experienced," UW linebacker Donald Butler said. "I'll be telling it to my children, to my grandchildren. I'll be talking about this day for a long time."

Butler was part of a UW defense that forced three USC turnovers and held the Trojans to only one field goal over the game's final 50 minutes. Then in the final four minutes and with the score tied at 13–13, Locker led the Huskies on a 10-play, 63-yard drive. He converted on third and 15 by throwing a 21-yard pass to Jermaine Kearse. On Locker's final play, he found Kearse for another 19-yard gain. The quarterback was hit late on the play, too, and the roughing-the-passer penalty moved the ball to the Trojans' 8-yard line.

That set up Erik Folk for the game-winning 22-yard field goal with three seconds remaining. Moments later, a delirious crowd joined the team on the Husky Stadium turf in celebration. "That's when it really hit me, the implications of what we'd just done," Locker said. "It was crazy."

Amid the pandemonium UW's first-year head coach, Steve Sarkisian, couldn't find his mentor, Carroll, for the traditional postgame handshake. "Hopefully," Sarkisian said, "it sends a message of where we're headed and what we're trying to do."

"The Huskies didn't just send a message," wrote Jerry Brewer, *The Seattle Times* columnist. "They stamped it on the foreheads of everyone who paid attention. They enabled their deprived, resilient fans to transform their years long frustration into a wild celebration."

In his introductory press conference as the UW coach, the 35-year-old Sarkisian had promised it wouldn't take long to turn around the program. "I firmly believed that," he said. "Some people in the world, maybe outside of our own little domain, thought that was just press conference-speak. But when you get around our kids, when you get around our coaches, I firmly believe that it's not going to take us very long."

28 Montlake Jake

At his heart, Jake Locker will always be just a kid from Ferndale, and for leading the resurrection the UW football program, "Montlake Jake" will forever have a place in the hearts of Husky fans. Locker's decision to return to UW for his senior year in 2010—at a time when some said he would have been the No. 1 pick in the NFL draft had he left school a year early—was the catalyst that got the Huskies back to the postseason just two years removed from the winless 2008. "It's been some frustrating years," Locker said after the Huskies' 19–7 win against Nebraska in the 2010 Holiday Bowl, the final game of his college career. "But to go out this way, to see this program off this way, this is the experience I came back for."

A star at small-town Ferndale near the Washington-Canada border, Locker was already anointed "the Savior" before even arriving at UW in 2006. He redshirted that season and was the Pac-10 Freshman of the Year in 2007. But he battled a number of injuries throughout four fractured years as the Huskies' starter. He broke the thumb on his right (throwing) hand four games into the 2008 season and sat out the rest of the year, helplessly watching as the program reached its nadir, going 0–12 and leading to the firing of coach Tyrone Willingham.

With a healthy start under new coach Steve Sarkisian, Locker led the Huskies to an upset of No. 3 USC early in the 2009 season,

2010 Holiday Bowl

Making their first postseason appearance in eight years, the Huskies stunned No. 16 Nebraska 19–7 in the 2010 Holiday Bowl. The victory gave the Huskies (7–6) their first winning season since 2002 and came just a few months after the Cornhuskers had embarrassed UW in Husky Stadium 56–21. "We got spanked pretty good in Washington," UW linebacker Cort Dennison said. "And everybody wrote us off."

In their rematch in San Diego, UW's defense shut down Nebraska's vaunted rushing attack. Chris Polk rushed for 177 yards, and Jake Locker closed out his UW career with another milestone victory. "I really can't believe two years ago we were an 0–12 team," Polk said.

which ended just short of a bowl game as UW finished 5–7. Despite the lure of millions of dollars from the NFL, Locker didn't spend much time deliberating his future, announcing his intention to return for his senior season just two weeks after the end of the season. "I made that decision because of a lot of things," he told *The Seattle Times* in 2010. "I get my degree. I spend another year in college with friends that I will be friends with the rest of my life and get to experience another season of college football, which I have said time and time again is the greatest sport in America at any level…I am happy with the decision I made. I don't regret it, I won't ever regret it, and I won't second-guess my decision, no matter what happens."

Locker played through more injuries his senior season—notably a broken rib—but left a wonderful legacy at Washington. He trailed only Cody Pickett in career passing yards (7,639), attempts (1,147), completions (619), and touchdown passes (53) and he remains the all-time leader in rushing yards by a quarterback (1,939).

The NFL money was still there for him in 2011, too, when the Tennessee Titans made him the No. 8 pick in the first round.

Injuries continued to mount during his four-year pro career, and he retired in 2015 at age 26. "A lot of people wonder and were surprised by his decision," Locker's father, Scott, said of the retirement. "But in dealing with Jake, it always comes back to he goes where his heart leads him. And for whatever reason, this seemed like the time to dedicate his time to his kids and his family and his life like that. And at this time, it didn't include being a football player."

Locker retired back home to Ferndale with his wife, former UW softball player Lauren Greer, and their two children. "When I go back there, I'm who I am," Locker said in 2010. "And I haven't changed since I lived there. I'm still the same person, still enjoy the same things. When I'm there, it's not 'Jake, the Washington quarterback.' It's just 'Jake.' I enjoy that."

29 Cold-Blooded Isaiah Thomas

Isaiah Thomas had played nearly every minute of every game for three consecutive days at the 2011 Pac-10 Tournament, and here the Huskies were asking for more still from their dynamic 5'9" point guard. Thomas, as he so often did at Washington, delivered when it mattered most. In one of the biggest shots in school history, he hit a step-back, fadeaway jumper just inside the three-point line to lift the third-seeded Huskies to a 77–75 overtime victory against top-seeded Arizona, giving Washington its second straight conference tournament championship.

Teammates mobbed Thomas at midcourt of the Staples Center in Los Angeles and then hoisted him on their shoulders in celebration. "Biggest shot of my life," Thomas said. "It's the biggest stage, national TV, Pac-10 Tournament championship game, overtime. Everybody is watching. I'll never forget this as long as I live."

Thomas scored a season-high 28 points on 10-for-16 shooting to go with seven assists, five rebounds, and two steals against Arizona. In three tournament games, he played 123 out of a possible 125 minutes—including 45 minutes in the championship game, an effort that netted him the tournament's Most Outstanding Player award for a second consecutive year. "I needed some air," Thomas said. "I needed to breathe a little bit. I was tired. I'm tired now. I'll sleep on the plane and I'm sure I'll sleep good tonight."

Thomas' clutch shots were nothing new. At Curtis High School in University Place, he scored 51 points in a state tournament semifinal game, a performance that has taken on legendary status over the years. In late March 2011, Thomas declared for the NBA draft, saying leaving UW was "the hardest thing I've done in my life."

He certainly left behind an impressive legacy. "The only thing I want to be known as is a winner," Thomas said. "You can hate on my basketball game, you can say what you want about anything in my life or anything on the basketball court, but I came here and won basketball games with my teammates and coaching staff."

Still, his size was a hurdle for some NBA executives. "Before I got to high school, they said I was too short to play high school," Thomas said prior to the 2011 NBA Draft. "Before I got to college, they said I would never do the things I did in college that I've done the past three years. So that's not the issue with me. I feel like the NBA is going back to smaller guards."

And yet there were 59 players—*59*—selected before Thomas in the 2011 NBA Draft. That year he was the very last player drafted, a slight that has motivated him throughout his blossoming career. Drafted by the Sacramento Kings, Thomas was traded to the Phoenix Suns in 2014, where he was used in a reserve role. Through all the frustrations early in his NBA career, he said he never lost confidence. "I think that's the difference between me and other people," Thomas said. "Some people's opportunity comes, and they waste it because they're not ready for that moment. I remember Jason Terry always telling me, 'Opportunity doesn't go away; it goes to somebody else.' You just gotta be ready for that moment. To this day I've always been ready for the moment that came my way."

In February of 2015, Thomas was traded to the Boston Celtics for next to nothing and in his first full season as the Celtics' starting point guard he blossomed into a bona fide superstar, averaging 22.2 points and 6.2 assists per game and making his first All-Star Game—the shortest player in NBA history to do so.

He was selected to the All-Star Game again in 2017. "Not to be cocky, but I feel like I'm the best player in the world," Thomas said. "That's just the work I put in, and if you don't feel like that, then you're cheating yourself."

For Huskies fans Thomas' emergence as one of the most clutch fourth-quarter players in the NBA, of course, comes as no surprise. During the 2016–17 season, he was averaging 10.1 fourth-quarter points—midway through the season—the most of any NBA player over the previous 20 years. (By comparison, Kobe Bryant's best fourth-quarter scoring output was 9.5 points during the 2005–06 season.) "I want to embrace that moment of the fourth quarter," Thomas says. "The fourth quarter isn't for everybody. It's tighter situations, it means a little more, and the game is usually on the line a little more in that fourth quarter. The great players embrace those moments."

30 Brandon Roy

At the height of his NBA career, Brandon Roy came back to the University of Washington in January 2009 to attend his first Huskies basketball game since his remarkable senior season in 2006. Special circumstances surrounded his return: the retirement of his No. 3 jersey. A sold-out crowd stood and chanted "B-Roy" during his introduction before the game against USC. Roy's was just the second jersey hung in the rafters at Hec Edmundson Pavilion, following the retirement of Bob Houbregs' No. 25. "It's such a moment for me," Roy said. "For me, that just says how special it is and how these people really view me at Washington. I'm just happy that I'm able to continue to make people proud."

By then, Roy was an All-Star guard for the Portland Trail Blazers and far removed from his days earning $11 an hour working as forklift driver in a Seattle shipyard. At that point—not long after his graduation from Seattle's Garfield High—Roy's basketball future was in limbo as he prepared to retake the SAT exam he needed to pass to get into UW. "It made me see the other side of life," Roy said of working at the shipyard. "It made me realize I have a chance to do something special and I need to take advantage of it."

After working weekdays from 8:00 AM to 2:00 PM at the shipyard, Roy would go home and study for the exam. Ultimately, not only did his SAT score improve enough to gain him admittance into UW, but it also improved so drastically that the NCAA flagged the result and ordered him to retake the test, which he passed.

Oregon, Gonzaga, and Arizona had all recruited Roy, but he opted to stay home and play for a dormant UW program. "The biggest thing that made me want to go to Washington was how bad

Perhaps the best NBA player Washington ever produced, Brandon Roy goes up for a dunk against Seattle Pacific in 2004. (AP Images)

all those programs talked about Washington," Roy said. "It almost made me defensive...It definitely made me want to help bring Washington back because that's where I'm from."

Coming out of high school, Roy had put his name in the NBA draft. He would back out of the draft and enroll at UW, becoming the rare star who stayed in college for four years while helping the Huskies advance to the NCAA Tournament's Sweet 16 in his final two seasons.

"He's just a great, great example of someone in today's age, who really did things the right way," UW coach Lorenzo Romar said.

The 2004–05 season was one of Washington's greatest. A knee injury had kept Roy out for the early portion of that season, and upon Roy's return, Romar used the versatile guard as the Huskies' sixth man in a dynamic lineup that featured Nate Robinson, Will Conroy, Bobby Jones, and Tre Simmons. The Huskies won the Pac-10 Tournament title and earned the program's first No. 1 seed in the NCAA tournament. After victories over Montana and Pacific in the first two rounds, the Huskies were upset by fourth-seeded Louisville in the Round of 16.

After again toying with the NBA draft, Roy returned for his senior season and turned in one of the greatest seasons in school history. He averaged 20.2 points, 5.6 rebounds, and 4.1 assists. He was named the Conference Player of the Year and was UW's first first-team AP All-American since Houbregs in 1953.

A star on the court, Roy was just as popular off it. Fans in Seattle and Portland were drawn to his humble, unassuming nature. "He'll talk to anyone," UW forward Jon Brockman said. "We can call him anytime we want to and talk to him. He's just a normal guy."

The sixth overall pick in the NBA draft, Roy was a landslide winner of 2006–07 Rookie of the Year. Just as he had done by resuscitating the Washington program, Roy was a catalyst for a

Portland franchise eager to move on from its destructive Jail Blazers era. "I called him Oprah one time because everything he touched turned to gold," Trail Blazers coach Nate McMillan said. "When he first came here, we probably needed him more off the floor than we did on the floor—and he knew it," McMillan said. "He allowed the organization to use him in that way. He became the face—this clean-cut guy who can play, who becomes an All-Star—but also off the floor, people liked him. That doesn't come along very often."

Described as "an old-school artist," Roy was a crafty player with a well-rounded game. He was a two-time member of the All-NBA team and was selected to three All-Star games. Roy averaged 20.2 points, 5.0 assists, and 4.6 rebounds in his first four seasons for Portland, and Hall of Fame guard Clyde Drexler—the most celebrated player in Portland history—once told Roy he expected him to break all his franchise records. "It caught me off guard," Roy said. "I was like, 'Break his records? The greatest Blazer of all time? Me?' That has never even been a thought of mine. For me, I can't even put that in words. As a kid playing basketball, I never thought I would be considered as a top player in a franchise. Humble is not a good enough word to describe how that made me feel. I would have to look in a dictionary for a word to describe it."

Roy's career, however, was cut short by degenerative knee injuries—which necessitated six surgeries—and in 2011 he announced his retirement at age 27. "This is a very difficult and painful day," Roy said.

Back in Seattle, Roy took his first head coaching job at Nathan Hale High School in 2016, helping the team to a No. 1 national ranking. Roy's prized player was Michael Porter Jr., who originally committed to Washington before enrolling at Missouri after Romar was fired.

31 "Hook" Houbregs

Introduced to it by Washington coach Tippy Dye, Bob Houbregs needed only a couple months to master the hook shot in the early 1950s. Even six decades later, it's safe to say no Huskies player has inflicted more harm on opponents than Houbregs did with his hook.

John Wooden was once quoted as saying that "Bob has a hook shot better than George Mikan."

Mikan was the NBA's first great center of that era, and Houbregs' nickname, appropriately so, was "Hook." With that shot he led the Huskies to heights never reached before—or since. "The only thing better than his basketball was him as a person. Everybody liked Bob Houbregs," said UW teammate Frank Guisness. "He had the best hook shot I ever saw and I saw a bunch of them in my career—using no backboard and way out."

Indeed, Houbregs' hook wasn't what you see in today's game—short jumpers in the lane or modified layups. No, the 6'7" Houbregs would unleash his hook from just about anywhere, sometimes from even beyond the modern-day three-point line. "I shot a lot of hooks," he said. "And then I'd fake the hook shot and drive to the basket for lay-ins...It was kind of a silly shot to take, but they went in."

A graduate of Seattle's Queen Anne High School, Houbregs is one of the Huskies' all-time greats. As a senior in 1952–53, he averaged 25.6 points a game, was named the national Player of the Year, and led the Huskies to their first—and only—Final Four appearance. Washington was 24–6, 25–6, and 28–3 in Houbregs' three varsity seasons, including a 15–1 mark in the Pacific Coast Conference in his final season. Matched up against Seattle

University's Johnny O'Brien, a fellow All-American, Houbregs scored 45 points on 20 field goals—both NCAA Tournament records—in a blowout victory against the Chieftains in the Western Regional semifinals in 1953. "Like I tell people, I was proud to hold Bob to 45 points," O'Brien joked. "He had a great hook shot, and we decided to overplay him to his right hand and force him to the basket so he couldn't get that shot. Unfortunately, our off-side forward couldn't get around to him quickly enough. It turned into a gym rat game, and they were better than us."

Houbregs scored 1,774 points during his three years with the Huskies—in that era freshmen weren't allowed to play varsity—a record that stood for 31 years. His No. 25 jersey hangs in the rafters at Hec Edmundson Pavilion, and he was the first Huskies player to have his number retired. "Having my number retired means more than anything else to me," said Houbregs, who also pitched and played first base for the UW baseball team. "I enjoyed my four years there, three years on varsity. I was fortunate to make great friends and teammates. We enjoyed practicing, we enjoyed the games, and we had a lot of fine moments on the floor and away from the floor."

The second overall pick in the 1953 NBA Draft by the Milwaukee Hawks, Houbregs played for four teams over five years before retiring from the NBA because of a back injury. He returned to Seattle and served as the general manager of the NBA's SuperSonics in the franchise's early days from 1970 to 1973. Houbregs was inducted into the Naismith Memorial Basketball Hall of Fame in 1987. He's also a member of the Husky Hall of Fame (1979 induction) and the Canadian Basketball Hall of Fame (2000). He died in May 2014 at age 82. "He was a special player," UW coach Lorenzo Romar said. "But the thing that most impressed me with him was his humility and the person that he was. Boy, he was a really solid man."

32 Super Mario

Just weeks after collecting his Heisman Trophy, Michigan's Desmond Howard was the hyped wide receiver entering the 1992 Rose Bowl. By the end of the New Year's Day game, though, Washington senior Mario Bailey was the celebrated one. He made sure of that when he made a diving catch in the end zone off a 38-yard touchdown pass from Mark Brunell. Bailey then got up and did the Heisman pose, mimicking the same pose Howard had made a month earlier against Ohio State. "Mario Bailey struck the Heisman pose for one reason: he's the best receiver in America," Huskies center Ed Cunningham said.

Bailey finished with six receptions for 126 yards and a touchdown in the Huskies' 34–14 victory against Michigan. UW's defense, meanwhile, shut down the Heisman winner, limiting Howard to a season-low one catch. "I just wanted to prove to everybody that there is another receiver," Bailey said after the game.

Coming out of Seattle's Franklin High School, Bailey was told he was too small to play major college football. Several years later he would finish his collegiate career as one of the most exciting offensive players in school history. "My size has never worried me," said Bailey, who was listed at 5'9" and 165 pounds as a UW senior. "I don't think it makes a difference. If you can catch the ball, run, and take the hits, you can play the game."

He set the then-Pac-10 record with 18 touchdown receptions during UW's run to the national championship in 1991. He was named the league's Co-Offensive Player of the Year that year and was a consensus All-American. His 30 career touchdowns also still stand as the school record. "When people told me I couldn't play Pac-10 football, it just made me go out and work that much harder," Bailey said.

As a junior Bailey had two touchdown catches in the Huskies' Rose Bowl victory against Iowa on New Year's Day 1991. As a pro he played in the NFL for the Houston Oilers and New York Jets, becoming one of the most decorated players in NFL Europe and a fan favorite for the Frankfurt Galaxy from 1995 to 2000. He caught more passes than anyone in NFL Europe history. In 2016 he returned for his second stint as the head coach at Franklin, his alma mater, saving a program on the brink of folding.

33 Iron Man

Chuck Carroll's career at Washington is the stuff of legends. In an era when players played both offense and defense, it is said that Carroll missed a mere six minutes of action in three years as the Huskies' star running back and linebacker, earning him the nickname "Iron Man."

After a Washington loss at Stanford in 1928, president-elect Herbert Hoover, a Stanford alumnus in attendance, said of Carroll: "That man is the captain of my All-America team."

After the game Carroll was carried off the field...by *Stanford* players. "These old eyes have never seen a greater player," famed Stanford coach Pop Warner said.

Born on August 13, 1906, in Seattle, Carroll was a local icon. A graduate of Seattle's Garfield High, Carroll played three years for the Huskies from 1926 to 1928, following in the footsteps of 1925 All-American halfback George Wilson. As a Huskies senior in 1928, Carroll scored 17 touchdowns, a school record that stood until Corey Dillon came along in 1996. Carroll led the Pacific Coast Conference in scoring and was named to 12 All-American teams in 1928.

At age 94, Carroll was asked about the appeal of football for him during a 2001 interview. "I loved it," he said. "You'd stand behind the line of scrimmage, and it was either him or you."

Carroll's No. 2 is one of three numbers retired by the UW football program, and he was inducted into the College Football Hall of Fame in 1964. After earning his law degree from UW in 1932, he would become a King County prosecutor in 1948 and served in that role for 22 years. "He was really a giant of his era both in the sports and legal arenas," King County prosecutor Norm Maleng said after Carroll's death at age 96 in June 2003.

34 Oh, What a Night!

They came in waves. At first, just a handful of students from the Dawg Pack leapt over the rail and onto Husky Stadium's west end zone. Then they kept coming…and coming…and coming. The students swarmed around Washington players and coaches at midfield and then all over the field, bouncing and dancing and posing for selfies left and right in celebration of the Huskies' most impressive victory in more than a decade.

In the first showdown of top 10 teams in Husky Stadium in 19 years, the No. 10 Huskies never gave Stanford a chance on September 30, 2016. Washington stunned the reigning conference champion 44–6 in their Friday night showcase event nationally televised on ESPN. "That was one of the coolest things I've ever been a part of," UW sophomore quarterback Jake Browning said after escaping the celebratory swarm.

In his nationwide introduction, Browning led UW on to touchdowns on its first two possessions, and the Huskies sacked Stanford quarterbacks six times in the first half en route to a 23–0 halftime lead. They did so before the largest—and rowdiest—crowd at Husky Stadium in six years that had an announced sellout of 72,027. The building shook like it hadn't in years. "What a night," UW coach Chris Petersen said, "that truly was the greatest setting in college football."

For members of UW's 1991 national championship team—on hand for a 25-year anniversary tribute—it must have felt familiar. The Huskies' defense finished with eight sacks and shut down Heisman Trophy favorite Christian McCaffrey (12 carries, 49 yards) by beating Stanford at its own game—with a smashing, bruising brand won at the line of scrimmage.

UW's offensive line didn't allow a single sack of Browning, and sophomore running back Myles Gaskin rushed for 100 yards and two touchdowns in a thorough dismantling of the preseason Pac-12 favorites. The victory signaled UW's return to national prominence. Two days later the Huskies jumped to No. 5 in the Associated Press Top 25, their highest ranking since the end of the 2000 season. "We did a very good job of showing the nation that we can play, too," UW receiver John Ross said.

35 Huskies Make Their Point

Eight days after knocking off No. 7 Stanford, Jake Browning and the No. 5 Huskies went on the road and put their stamp on another historic victory for the program. The final score was Washington 70, Oregon 21. The Ducks' 12-year reign in the rivalry was completely, emphatically, dramatically over on October 8, 2016. Boy, was it over. In signaling a changing of the guard in Northwest supremacy, the Huskies did something no opponent had ever done in Eugene's Autzen Stadium—scoring 70 points and doing so with an assassin's precision.

As stunning as the Huskies' sudden return to power was, Oregon's fall from grace was equally so. The loss continued a tailspin for the Ducks—much to the delight of Washington fans everywhere. It had been 14 years since the Huskies were last able to celebrate a victory in Eugene. "I'd have to look down to see Cloud Nine," UW offensive lineman Kaleb McGary said after the game. "This was personal—a lot more than just player to player, program to program. This was for UW. This was incredible. This was absolutely incredible."

Browning was the catalyst, finishing with a school-record eight total touchdowns—that's right, eight—including six passing touchdowns, also a school record, to put him in the middle of the Heisman Trophy chase at the season's halfway point. Browning finished with 304 yards passing. Three of his touchdown passes went to John Ross, and two went to Dante Pettis, including an in incredible one-handed grab while being held by an Oregon defender in the right corner of the end zone. Sophomore running back Myles Gaskin added 197 yards rushing and a touchdown as UW piled up 682 yards of total offense. "We'll take a win no matter what," Browning said, "but yeah, it's kind of cool. Seventy-seven would've been cool, too. The more points you can score, the better."

Browning had the game's seminal moment when on his first touchdown run he pointed at an Oregon linebacker as he crossed the goal line. "The Point" drew a taunting penalty after the score, and Browning later apologized for the act. "That's not me," he said. But, well, by then the Huskies had made their point.

As part of the team's standard punishment for personal-foul penalties, Browning later had to do 500 push-ups at practice. Showing support for their quarterback, teammates had volunteered to do the push-ups for him. "Everybody raised their hand and told him we'd do something with him. So that's how everyone felt about it," cornerback Kevin King said a few days later. "We stand behind Jake. When we have a quarterback like that, he's just a fighter. Things like that, he's not a cocky guy; we all know his character. He just got caught up in the moment. For us, that's exciting to see. That was a good thing for us to see: that he's having that attitude. That's somebody you want to be leading you."

The Huskies' win came 22 years after the most celebrated play in Oregon history—"the Pick" against Damon Huard and the Huskies at Autzen Stadium in 1994. "I think that's going to be a picture [of Browning] that's going to be around forever in terms of this Oregon-UW battle," King said. "They talk about 'the Pick?' Nah, they're gonna talk about the finger wag."

36 Bob Schloredt

When Bob Schloredt was in the second grade, a playmate dropped a firecracker into a bottle. The ensuing explosion sent shattered bits of glass flying, one piece searing Schloredt's left eyeball, leaving him legally blind for the rest of his life. "I don't notice it," he would say years later. "I can't remember seeing any other way."

Schloredt never used the disability as an excuse, and it never seemed to bother the quarterback much during his Hall of Fame career with the Huskies. When Schloredt was a senior, a year after leading the Huskies to a monumental upset against No. 1 Wisconsin in the 1960 Rose Bowl—a victory that would years later give UW ample reason to claim a national championship—*Sports Illustrated* dispatched a reporter to Seattle to profile the "one-eyed" quarterback. Schloredt is the only Huskies player to ever appear on the cover of the magazine and did so for its October 3, 1960 issue. "The fact that he is a one-eyed quarterback on one of the best college teams in the country is a source of amazement to almost everybody but Schloredt himself," Alfred Wright wrote for *SI*.

Schloredt arrived at the University of Washington late in the summer of 1957 just weeks before Jim Owens' first season as the Huskies head coach. As a little-known freshman from Gresham, Oregon, Schloredt was one of 11 quarterbacks—yes, 11—on the roster to start that season, and he wound up splitting time with Phil Borders, a popular local star from Ballard High School, as quarterback of the freshman team. In that era everyone was expected to play on both sides of the ball. "Of course, we were not all going to play quarterback," Schloredt said in a 2015 interview. "Obviously, you played both ways."

By mid-September 1958, Schloredt and Borders had settled into a three-man competition alongside Bob Hivner, a junior college All-American from Southern California who wound up getting most the quarterback snaps that fall. It was a young team. Of the 27 players who played in the season-opening 14–6 victory against San Jose State, 15 of them were making their varsity debuts, and UW finished the year with a 3–7 record. Schloredt's most notable contributions that season came as a defensive back and punter.

It wasn't until his junior year in 1959 that Schloredt would start to make his mark as one of the Huskies' all-time great quarterbacks. Unlike All-American Don Heinrich, who a decade earlier became one the finest passing quarterbacks in college football history up to that point, Schloredt was a physical runner who threw only on occasion.

In the 1959 opener against Colorado, Hivner broke a finger in his throwing hand, opening the door for Schloredt, a 200-pound dual-threat quarterback who proved to be just about the perfect fit for Owens' Split T offense. All Schloredt did was go on to earn All-American honors, lead UW to back-to-back Rose Bowl victories, and become the first player to win two Rose Bowl MVP awards.

Schloredt had more rushing attempts (253) and yards (782) than any Huskies quarterback up to that point; the latter record would stand until Dennis Fitzpatrick broke it in 1974. (Jake Locker now owns the school rushing record for a quarterback with 1,939 yards rushing.) "Bob is a really fine athlete," Owens told Wright for the *SI* story, "and he can do just about everything on the football field well. First of all, he likes the contact part of it. There isn't a harder tackler on the team, and I could use him as a linebacker if I had to. He's big and strong, and although he isn't unusually fast, he's a very good runner. He's improved his passing terrifically and he's a very fine kicker. He may not have any one great specialty, but I'll tell you that if I were a pro coach I'd hire him just to have him on my team."

Schloredt was also a standout defensive back for the 1959 defense that still ranks among the best ever at UW, having allowed just 73 points in 10 games. "It was a helluva time—a great time to start a tradition at Washington," Schloredt said. "It was an experience and a half, I tell ya."

And not only did Schloredt put together one of the most accomplished careers in school history, he helped recruit another all-time great to UW. After his playing career, Schloredt spent 11 years on Owens' coaching staff and he helped bring Sonny Sixkiller to Seattle.

37 The Huards

It wasn't a given that Brock Huard would follow his older brother to the University of Washington. While Damon Huard had established himself as the Huskies' starting quarterback in the mid-1990s, Brock was the star quarterback at Puyallup High School, playing for his father, Mike. Recruited by many of the nation's top programs, Brock had an open mind, and for a while, it appeared he might be leaving for another Pac-10 school, UCLA.

Some timely family advice ultimately kept him close to home for college. "Damon and my dad both said if you want to lay down roots here, if you want to be part of this community, you could go win the Heisman Trophy at UCLA, but you're not coming back here," said Brock, the Gatorade National Player of the Year in 1995. "You're just not going to have that kind of connection to the community. You're going to be a UCLA guy in a purple-and-gold town. There was some real wisdom in that."

Brock became a Husky. He redshirted during the 1995 season, Damon's last as the Huskies' starter. Damon had always wanted to be a Husky and he had come to UW four years earlier during the program's peak. He was a redshirt during the Huskies' 1991 national championship season. "There was no doubt," Damon said. "I had always dreamed of being a Husky. To stay in my own backyard, it was a dream come true for a young guy."

Brock Huard (right) would succeed his brother, Damon (left), as quarterback for the Washington Huskies before playing for the Seahawks in the NFL. (AP Images)

Damon, however, endured a rocky collegiate career after the program was put on NCAA probation and coach Don James resigned in protest. But Damon did help lead the Huskies to one of the most notable regular-season wins in school history—the "Whammy in Miami" in 1994—and he helped the Huskies to a share of the 1995 Pac-10 championship with USC.

Damon had also finished his UW career as the program's career leader in passing (5,692 yards) and touchdown passes (34)—records his little brother would break just a few years later. Brock was a three-year starter for the Huskies and held 20 school records by the end of his career in 1998. Notably, he left UW with 51 touchdown passes and 5,742 passing yards in 30 games.

Brock's most memorable throw came in the opener of the 1998 season at No. 8 Arizona State. Trailing 38–35 with two minutes remaining, Huard threw a pass on fourth and 17 to tight end Reggie Davis for a 63-yard touchdown, lifting the 18th-ranked Huskies to a 42–38 victory.

"Two years ago we had a drive to win the game and we blew it," Huard said after the game. "Tonight we just scored. This was the greatest game I have ever been a part of."

The Huskies, though, would stumble in '98 to a 6–6 finish, the program's first non-winning season in 23 years, prompting the school to fire head coach Jim Lambright. Huard left UW with a year of eligibility remaining and wound up being selected by the Seattle Seahawks in the third round of the 1999 NFL Draft.

By then Damon was entering his third season as a backup to Dan Marino with the Miami Dolphins. In 2001 Damon signed with the New England Patriots and served as the backup to Drew Bledsoe, whose injury that season opened the door for a young Tom Brady to take the reins. (Damon recalled in an ESPN interview years later that a confident Brady told him after just two NFL starts: "I'm going to be a great one. I'm going to be one of the best at this game.") With Brady and the Patriots, Damon won two Super Bowl rings.

Damon had his best years with the Kansas City Chiefs, leading the team to the playoffs in the 2006 season. In all, Damon played 10 NFL seasons, throwing for 6,303 yards and 33 touchdowns. Brock played six seasons in the NFL—four with the Seahawks and two as Peyton Manning's backup with the Indianapolis Colts.

Post-football, the brothers settled back in the Seattle area. In 2013 Damon was named the UW football program's director of external relations. He works alongside longtime play-by-play voice Bob Rondeau as the Huskies' radio color analyst and he teamed with Marino to start a winery in a Seattle suburb called Passing Time. The release of their 2012 cabernet sauvignon, one wine writer noted, "turned heads from Seattle to Miami and was considered among the most remarkable Washington wines of the year."

Brock also transitioned into broadcasting after his playing days. In 2009 he paired with Mike Salk as a co-host of the *Brock and Salk* morning show on 710 ESPN Seattle. Brock also works for ESPN as a college football analyst for games and in-studio shows. "I never would have said to you, 'Boy, I want to be John Madden someday,'" he said. "But now that I'm in it, it fits my nature and my personality really well...I absolutely love it."

Damon is a regular guest on *Brock and Salk*, and the brothers remain close—and close to the Huskies. "They have unbelievable brotherly love, and that goes to the closeness of the Huard family," Rondeau said. "I'm not surprised either of them is doing as well as they are. They are not shy about working hard."

38 The Billy Joe Hobert Scandal

To this day you will find some ardent Washington supporters who will tell you that Billy Joe Hobert is the best quarterback to ever play for the Huskies. They point to his undefeated record in 17 games as the Huskies' starting quarterback—and then to his cocksure leadership on the Huskies' 1991 national championship team. Of course, opinions have always been divided about Hobert, perhaps the most controversial figure in UW history. "He's just such a rascal...but a good rascal," Don James said of Hobert.

Hobert, then a redshirt sophomore, got the job as the Huskies' starting quarterback only after veteran Mark Brunell suffered a serious knee injury during a spring practice in April of 1991. Suddenly, a team with designs on a national championship turned to a young quarterback from Puyallup.

All Hobert did was put together one of the most efficient seasons by a UW quarterback. He completed 60 percent of his passes (173-of-285) for 2,271 yards with 22 touchdowns, then a school record, plus 10 interceptions and five rushing touchdowns in 1991.

In one of the biggest wins in program history, at Nebraska early in the 1991 season, Hobert helped the Huskies rally from a 21–9 deficit by scoring 27 unanswered points and amassing 618 total yards in a 36–21 victory. Hobert was 23-of-40 for 283 yards that day, and his eight-yard pass to Orlando McKay early in the fourth quarter gave the Huskies the lead for good.

"It was the biggest thrill of my life playing against Nebraska," Hobert said.

Hobert was raw and, at times, reckless. "I am brash," Hobert said in '91, "but I'm not the arrogant piece of crap that people might think I am."

He was named the Offensive Most Valuable Player of UW's victory against Michigan in the Rose Bowl to cap the perfect season. But things unraveled for Hobert and the Huskies 10 months later when *The Seattle Times* reported that the quarterback had received a $50,000 loan from an Idaho businessman. Hobert spent the money during a three-month spree on cars, guns, expensive stereo equipment, golf clubs, and wild weekends in which he lavished "hundreds of dollars" on friends. The loan was an NCAA violation in part because Hobert didn't have a plan to repay it. He was suspended immediately from the team and left campus within a few days. His college career was over. "It wasn't the smartest thing I did because I ended up blowing it," he said at the time, "and now I've got all the bills and nothing to show for it."

Hobert's loan set off a Pac-10 Conference investigation. The conference found a "lack of institutional control" over how cash was handled during recruiting visits, and the following summer, the program was placed on two years' probation. James resigned in protest—a dynasty ended.

Even though a number of players were implicated in various violations, Hobert took the brunt of the blame from many around the program. He received death threats soon after. He later admitted he also blamed himself for James' resignation. "He doesn't owe me an apology. That's not the case," James said in a 2002 interview. "I resigned because of what the league did to us. I don't think he did one thing that was an NCAA violation."

The Oakland Raiders drafted Hobert in the third round of the 1993 NFL Draft, and he bounced around the league over the next eight years, playing for four different teams and never quite living up to the potential many saw in him.

39 Sound the Siren

When the Huskies score at home, everyone hears about it.

In the closing moments of the Huskies' victory against rival Washington State in the 2015 Apple Cup, UW senior linebacker Travis Feeney ran up a handful of steps in Husky Stadium's west end zone, where the Husky Marching Band's "sound the siren" machine sits in the front row. As students around him counted down the final seconds, Feeney hit the siren when the timer struck zero—sending out a celebratory blare throughout the stadium.

The siren—a World War II vintage air-raid siren that was once attached to a building at a Navy ammunition depot in nearby Bremerton—has become a staple at Husky Stadium, ringing out whenever the Huskies score.

University of Washington band director Bill Bissell has been credited with introducing the siren at Husky Stadium in the early 1970s. Bissell lived in Bremerton near the old Naval Ammunition Depot. After the depot closed in 1959, some teenagers apparently took the siren off one of the buildings and kept it as a keepsake, often playing it around small-town Bremerton.

Hearing the siren around town, Bissell, who died in 2001 at age 70, thought it would make a great addition to Husky Stadium and made a deal with the teens, offering them free tickets to UW games in exchange for the siren. Bissell got permission from then-athletic director Mike Lude, and the siren has been wailing at games ever since.

The siren is stored in the stadium and cared for by the band's dedicated "Siren Team."

"It's also used for commencement and a few special events," said Brad McDavid, UW's current band director. "People have asked if they could borrow it for a tailgate party, or longtime fans have asked to use it for a birthday party."

40 Dillon's Spartan Effort

Corey Dillon never needed much time to leave a lasting impression. He spent only one season on Montlake—long enough to make him one of the most memorable running backs to don a Huskies uniform. And he needed only one quarter on a cold November day in 1996 to put together one of the most stunning performances in UW history.

Dillon set NCAA records for one quarter by rushing for 222 yards and four touchdowns in the first quarter of the Huskies' 53–10 victory against San Jose State at Husky Stadium on November 16, 1996. He also had an 83-yard touchdown reception in the first quarter, giving him 305 total yards—also an NCAA record for a quarter.

UW running backs Terry Hollimon (148 yards) and Maurice Shaw (100) joined Dillon in rushing for 100 yards against San Jose State, the first time the Huskies ever had three backs hit the century mark in the same game. "It is a tremendous compliment to Corey and our offense," UW coach Jim Lambright said. "The volumes of running backs that have run in NCAA history, and no one has ever had a bigger quarter."

There's more: on the same day against San Jose State, the 6'2", 220-pound Dillon also set four Washington records, finishing the season as the school's single-season record-holder for most rushing yards (1,695), most all-purpose yards (2,356), most rushing touchdowns (24), and most total touchdowns (25). "Corey Dillon really surprised me," San Jose coach John Ralston said. "I knew he was strong, but I didn't think he was that quick. He just ran by some people. He'll make an outstanding pro back."

A graduate of Seattle's Franklin High, Dillon spent a brief time in the San Diego Padres minor league system and then was out of football and working as a janitor the year after graduating high school. He then spent two years at junior colleges in Utah and Kansas, working toward becoming academically eligible. He then came home to join the Huskies. "It came down to where I might want to live for the rest of my life," Dillon said, "where I might have a family, playing in front of your people. From that standpoint this was the best choice for me."

Dillon opened the '96 season as Rashaan Shehee's backup. But Shehee injured his ankle in early October, opening the door for Dillon's sensational run to close out the year. During one stretch he had seven consecutive 100-yard rushing games. "When I grew up playing on the back streets as a kid, I was a receiver," he said. "Even at Franklin I weighed 195 pounds and I was a slasher. But now, well, now I don't have time to run around people. My main focus is to run through them."

Dillon was selected by the Cincinnati Bengals in the second round of the 1997 NFL Draft. Later acquired by the New England Patriots, he ran for 1,635 yards during the 2004 season en route to helping them win the Super Bowl.

41 1990 Rebirth

Doubt had started to creep in around Don James in the late 1980s, and the Huskies coach could feel it. After going 6–4–1 during the regular season in 1987, Washington had settled for a trip to the Independence Bowl that year; things got worse in 1988, when the Huskies dropped to 6–5 and missed out on a bowl berth for the first time in nine years. "There was talk that James, despite all he accomplished at Washington—two victories in three Rose Bowls and beating Oklahoma in the 1985 Orange Bowl—was losing it," *The Seattle Times*' Dick Rockne wrote.

That doubt dissipated at the outset of the new decade. The Huskies, ranked as high as No. 2 late in the season, jumped back into the national championship picture in 1990, won the Pac-10 conference championship, and returned to the Rose Bowl for the first time since the 1981 season.

"If you're ever buried, it's nice to come back to life," James said after the Huskies' 46–34 victory against Iowa in the Rose Bowl. "There were a few people shoving dirt on the grave. But that's the fun part of it. And I haven't known any coaches who have been around a long time who haven't had some tough years. You have to keep working. You have to believe in what you're doing and not get real excited about criticism."

The Huskies never gave Iowa much of a chance in the Rose Bowl. Washington cornerback Dana Hall returned a blocked punt 27 yards for a touchdown to give UW a 10–0 lead in the first quarter. After a slow start, sophomore quarterback Mark Brunell heated up in the second quarter, running in for a five-yard touchdown and then throwing a 22-yard strike to Mario Bailey to extend the Huskies' lead to 33–7 at halftime.

Brunell added another touchdown run—of 30 yards—and another touchdown pass to Bailey—from 31 yards—in the second half, tying a then-Rose Bowl record with four total touchdowns. Brunell was named the Player of the Game. "To tell you the truth," Brunell said, "I didn't think I was having an MVP kind of game. But I'm very proud to have won the award…I just know I can get a lot better. I want to be respected as much as a passer as I am a runner. In fact, I think I can be a better passer than a runner."

Greg Lewis, UW's star running back, returned from knee surgery to rush for 128 yards on 19 carries. Lewis had injured himself in a loss to UCLA on November 10. He had arthroscopic surgery three days later. "I was pleasantly surprised," James said of Lewis' performance.

The Huskies finished the season 10–2 and were ranked fifth in the final AP Top 25 poll.

Looking back, James likened the win against Iowa to his first Rose Bowl victory against Michigan in 1978. That win had also erased some doubts about his coaching ability after back-to-back seasons of 6–5 and 5–6 and a 1–3 start in 1977. "People were pretty sure that I couldn't coach," he said. "So I think that is why this one compares mostly with the first one."

The Rose Bowl triumph on New Year's Day 1991 set the stage for the Huskies' greatest achievement to come. "The goal is to be back next year," UW offensive coordinator Gary Pinkel said, "and be undefeated when we get here."

42 Back on Top: 1992 Rose Bowl

A year after beating Iowa in the Rose Bowl, the Huskies were back in Pasadena. This time the stakes were greater than they'd ever been for Washington football, and the outcome produced the most significant victory in program history. There wasn't much drama on the field. No. 2 Washington had its way with No. 4 Michigan, rolling to a 34–14 victory to cap a perfect 12–0 season for the Huskies.

The next morning, the coaches' poll vote was announced, and UW earned a share of the national championship with Miami. "I know I couldn't have asked for anything more," Don James said after the game. "Not just today, but for the entire season. We played better today than we ever had; as a program we've never accomplished anything quite like this game or this season. We took apart a very, very good football team in the Rose Bowl. To do what we did against them, I think that says a lot for our players. We have a great football team."

It was—what else?—UW's defense that stole the show in the Rose Bowl. As they had done all season to opposing quarterbacks, Steve Emtman and the Huskies hounded Michigan's Elvis Grbac, who had led the nation in quarterback efficiency rating during the regular season. Grbac completed a season-low 13 passes—on 26 attempts—for 130 yards and one touchdown and one interception against the Huskies. "He was panicking because the rush was on," UW safety Shane Pahukoa said. "He would look at Desmond Howard right away and panic."

The Huskies sacked Grbac six times. Michigan had allowed just six sacks all season before the Rose Bowl. So dominant was UW's defense that, over the course of seven Michigan drives in the middle of the game, the Huskies yielded just three first downs and a total of 55 yards on 26 plays. "I'm not sure Elvis Grbac ever knew what we were doing," said Jim Lambright, UW defensive coordinator. Grbac himself conceded that Washington was the "best team I've ever played by far."

After a scoreless first quarter, UW quarterback Billy Joe Hobert scored the first touchdown on a two-yard run. Michigan answered with a Grbac touchdown before the Huskies got two field goals from Travis Hanson to take a 13–7 halftime lead. Hobert threw both of his touchdown passes in the second half, and both went to tight ends—the first to Mark Bruener from five yards and the second to Aaron Pierce from two yards. Mark Brunell came in and threw a 38-yard touchdown pass to Mario Bailey in the fourth quarter to extend the Huskies' lead to 34–7.

Hobert and Emtman shared the game's MVP honors. The Huskies' dominance was complete, and it was perfect. "It's fantastic," UW center Ed Cunninghan said afterward. "I guess I'm relieved more than anything...At one point you could see the frustration on their faces. They didn't even know how to slow us down."

43 From Sundodgers to Dubs

For the first 30 years of Washington athletics, the university hadn't settled on an official mascot. For a time Indians had caught on and then Vikings, but neither seemed to fit. Some publications simply referred to UW as the "purple and gold." In 1920 the Associated Students of the University of Washington voted to introduce Sundodger as the school's mascot. The name was adopted by the publication, *Washington Alumnus*, which featured a smiling figure named Sunny holding an umbrella.

Sundodgers didn't last long. Many took the name as a negative connotation to Seattle's weather, and by 1921 the university set out to find another new mascot. A name committee of alumni, staffers, students and coaches—including basketball coach Clarence Edmundson and football coach Enoch Bagshaw—came up with Husky, feeling it represented virility, faith, strength, fairness, and courage.

During halftime of a basketball game on February 3, 1922, Robert Ingram, captain of the football team, introduced the new mascot name to the crowd, which "received a big ovation," *The Seattle Times* wrote. "Immediately the students' bleachers shook with a newly conceived 'growl' yell which ran: 'Gr-r-r-r-r! Washington Husky! Washington Husky! Gr-r-r-r-r!'"

The name received unanimous ratification from the Big "W" Club and the Press Council at the university. Soon, the first live mascot, an Alaskan Malamute named "Frosty," was adopted by the Sigma Alpha Epsilon fraternity. UW uses the Husky breed, the Alaskan Malamute, because it is the largest and strongest of all Husky breeds. The new pup lived with his fraternity brothers and attended football games "with great enthusiasm," as the university's official website recounts. Frosty was a social dog who often roamed the neighborhoods around campus. "An understanding taxi cab company agreed to escort the social butterfly home free of charge when he was found wandering," the website notes.

Frosty was followed by Frosty II in 1930. After World War III, "Wasky" was adopted in 1946, followed by Wasky II, Ski, Denali, King Chinook, Regent Denali, Sundodger Denali, King Redoubt, Prince Redoubt, and Spirit. The current mascot is Dubs, who took the reins in 2009.

44 The Miraculous Interception

You couldn't script a more bizarre sequence, a stranger twist of events. The Huskies scored two touchdowns in 18 seconds to pull off a 36–33 victory against Arizona on October 10, 2009—a win as improbable as any in the history of UW football.

Mason Foster had a hand in perhaps the unlikeliest play you'll ever see—thanks to the fortuitous foot of Arizona receiver Delashaun Dean. A pass from Arizona's Nick Foles deflected first off Dean's left hand and then bounced off Dean's left foot—and right to Foster, the Huskies' standout linebacker. Foster turned and ran 37 yards untouched the other way for the game-winning touchdown. "I don't know if [I've ever seen a game] that crazy," UW coach Steve Sarkisian said. "I mean, an interception off a guy's foot returned for a touchdown? I don't think so."

Arizona had effectively run a screen play to its receivers much of the game, and Foster, sensing the play was coming again, jumped the route. He trailed Dean by a few steps on the play, but Foster's presence seemed to throw Foles' timing off on the pass. "They were doing it all game long," Foster said. "I thought [the ball] bounced off his knee. I didn't know it was that close. I just play until the whistle blows, and they didn't blow the whistle."

Pandemonium followed on the Huskies sideline and in the Husky Stadium stands. "I was going as crazy as probably anybody did," Sarkisian said. "And I was thinking to myself, *Don't get a penalty for being on the field.* So I had to make a left-hand turn and get back on the sidelines."

Foster's touchdown came on Arizona's first play after the Huskies had scored on Jake Locker's 25-yard touchdown pass to Kavario Middleton. Arizona had scored 17 straight points in the second half and appeared to have put the game out of reach at 33–21 with 4:22 remaining.

"I'm sure a lot of people had counted us out," Locker said. "We knew as long as there was time on the clock that we had a chance to win the game. It's great to be able to be rewarded for that kind of effort."

45 A Season to Forget

The final insult in the most insulting season in the 120-year history of University of Washington football came against the worst opponent possible. The rival Cougars were just as bad, maybe even worse, than the winless Huskies when the 2008 Apple Cup kicked off in Pullman. There was talk about Washington State as one of the worst teams in college football history.

Then the Cougars went out and beat the Huskies 16–13 in double overtime. It was the lowest of the low for Washington, a gut-wrenching fall 17 years removed from a national championship season. "It just feels like a nightmare," UW defensive back Mesphin Forrester said.

Washington State fans rushed the field after their game-winning field goal in the second overtime, giving the Cougars their first conference victory of the season. "We just lost to the Cougars," linebacker Donald Butler said afterward. "I'm speechless."

For much of their 0–12 season of 2008, the Huskies were listless, punchless. "This one hurts real hard," UW running back Willie Griffin said. "No disrespect to them, but we went up against a team that everybody is saying is the worst in the nation, and you can't pull out a win. I mean, you've got to look at yourself and ask yourself, 'What are we?'"

Even after the Apple Cup, the Huskies had one more game to play, and they had to wait two more weeks before traveling to play the Cal Bears. The result was largely predictable. Cal won 48–7. "[Going] 0-12 is just horrible," Foster said. "It's appalling to go 0–12...[But] I think it's going to turn around real quick next season. Hopefully, guys will take this season and remember it so we never have this feeling again."

Tyrone Willingham's fate as UW's coach had been decided long before the Apple Cup. He was forced to resign in late October, two days after a 33–7 home loss to Notre Dame, the program that had fired him after the 2004 season. Willingham remained with the Huskies through the end of the winless season. "Obviously, if you're the head coach at this time, you take responsibility for what's going on," he said. "But it should also be noted the day that I arrived what the state of the program was. I take responsibility for where we're at, but there's also a process."

Willingham remained defiant to the end, speaking often about the 1–10 team he inherited when he took over the program four years earlier. His four-year UW record at was 11–37. "After a season of nothingness, the most thorough humiliation in 119 seasons of Huskies football, the man most responsible continued to act as if he were a bit player in the fiasco," *The Seattle Times* columnist Jerry Brewer wrote after the season-ending loss to Cal. "He grumbled when given opportunity to exit with grace. He expressed nothing more than disappointment he could not win more. For the last time Saturday, the Huskies played like, well, a Willingham team. Listless. Confused. Disjointed. The nothingness finally ended, spreading its misery as far as the schedule would allow."

The Huskies were outscored 463–159 in 12 games. The night before the season finale, news leaked that the Huskies had settled on USC offensive coordinator Steve Sarkisian as the team's new coach.

46 Lawyer Milloy

Before embarking on an All-American career at the University of Washington and before his All-Pro career in the NFL, Lawyer Milloy was just a kid from Tacoma. A kid who could do it all, it seemed.

Milloy starred in football, basketball, and baseball at Lincoln High School, and colleges wanted him for all three sports. Miami, Notre Dame, Washington State, and Colorado all wanted him. But he wanted to stay close to home and play for the Huskies.

He overcame a difficult upbringing to excel. When Milloy was 15, his parents were both arrested in a cocaine bust; his father went to prison, and his mother went through drug treatment. Milloy lived with a friend. "I look at everything I do as a challenge," a 17-year-old Milloy said. "It's the same in all sports. It's the same for any difficulties you have in life. I guess I've learned to handle pressure. I've been through a lot."

In 2012 Milloy had his No. 26 jersey retired at Lincoln High School. "Lawyer is the greatest athlete to ever come out of Tacoma," said quarterback Jon Kitna, a teammate of Milloy's at Lincoln who went on to have a long NFL career himself.

A talented pitcher, Milloy wound up getting drafted twice in the Major League Baseball draft—first out of high school and then after lettering for three seasons in baseball at UW. (In 1994 he was part of the Washington baseball team that lost to a Georgia Tech team that featured future major leaguers Jason Varitek and Nomar Garciaparra in a regional semifinal.)

But his future was football.

That was clear when the 6'0", 200-pound safety led the Huskies with 106 tackles as a sophomore in 1994 and was a consensus All-American as a junior in 1995. He won the Jim Thorpe Award as the nation's best defensive back.

After his junior season, Milloy declared for the NFL draft. "Through the [program's] probation, I had doubts in my mind about staying at Washington," he said. "But I felt loyal to my teammates and the program. I knew it was a good program and I wanted to do anything possible to get that tarnished image off the program. We went in as champions and went out as champions. I think I had a role in that. We kick-started the team."

He was a second-round pick by the New England Patriots and was a rookie on the Patriots' team that lost to the Green Bay Packers in Super Bowl XXXI. Five years later, when Milloy and the Patriots got back to the Super Bowl, they pulled off one of the great upsets in NFL history, beating the St. Louis Rams 20–17. By then Milloy was a team captain and the highest paid safety in the NFL. "I had a voice," Milloy said. "I told everybody: 'Nobody remembers who finished second.' I told them 'We can party now because we made it to the Super Bowl, or we can party forever because we won it.'"

Milloy played 15 seasons in the NFL, earning All-Pro recognition in 1998 and was named to four Pro Bowl teams. His final two years represented homecoming with the Seattle Seahawks in 2009 and '10. "He's very physical, very tough. He's living up to the billing of what he's always been," said Seahawks coach Pete Carroll, who was also Milloy's coach for three years in New England. "He's a real tough guy. We love that about him."

Milloy started more than 200 games in the NFL, missing only six out of a possible 226 games, and finishing with 1,033 career tackles and 25 interceptions. "This is what I do," he said. "It's what I love."

47 Do the Wave

It was an impromptu creation. Robb Weller, who as a University of Washington student in the 1970s was described by *The Seattle Times*' Bill Kossen as "one of the most popular yell leaders in the land, combining standup comedy with counterculture cool," was back at Husky Stadium for the Huskies' homecoming game against Stanford on October 30, 1981. Weller was up to old tricks, getting the student section riled up to cheer on the Huskies, when a new routine came to be. It quickly caught on, and the Wave has been rolling along all around the globe ever since.

At first, Weller had been prodding students to do a sort of vertical wave, which quickly faded. Seeing what was transpiring, UW Marching Band director Bill Bissell approached Weller and suggested he try the routine again—but this time laterally. "Like a gathering tidal movement, it began rolling slowly through the student section, then swept into the adjoining crowd sections," *The Seattle Times* described later. "As Bissell's band pounded out a beat, the tide continued lapping spontaneously around the stadium."

It had no name at the time—a reporter the next day wrote about the excited crowd doing "The Rose Bowl Sway"—but another name would eventually catch on. "Nobody thought, *Thank God, they invented the Wave*," Weller said.

Over the years there has been much debate about who—and where—the Wave actually began. "Crazy" George Henderson, a sports fan in the San Francisco Bay Area, claimed he invented the Wave at an Oakland Athletics baseball game two weeks before Weller and Bissell did so at Husky Stadium. "No way, no way those guys own something that belongs to me," he insisted. "I started it two weeks before they did. It's on film…I'm like the Wright Brothers."

As the 10th anniversary of the Wave's creation approached in 1991, Rick Anderson, a reporter for *The Seattle Times*, watched the film Henderson had. "The film shows a smattering of fans alternately standing and sitting, mostly in a vertical pattern. The motion then fizzles out," Anderson wrote. "It could have been a wave—or just a beer vendor passing through the crowd."

After graduating from UW, Weller went on to be a host of syndicated TV shows, including *Entertainment Tonight* and *Win, Lose or Draw.*

48 The Hitman: Dave Hoffmann

"Real Dogs Wear Purple" read the poster promoting the Huskies' 1992 season. On that poster Dave Hoffmann is completing a tackle of a flattened Kansas State player, and a pack of Washington defenders surround them.

As much as anyone, Hoffmann depicted the menacing nature of the Huskies' iconic defenses of the early 1990s. He was the middle linebacker, starting every game for the Huskies' three consecutive Pac-10 championship teams from 1990 to 1992, and he led the team in tackles during the 1991 national championship season. Hoffmann started 42 consecutive games for the Huskies and was an All-American and the Pac-10's Defensive Player of the Year as a senior in 1992. "I always thrilled at expending every ounce of energy I had on the field," Hoffmann wrote in his 2012 book, *The Husky Hitman.* "Going into battle and winning championships, hitting guys so hard that my helmet would dig into my forehead, causing rivulets of blood to trickle down my face, that was a special feeling for me—tangible evidence that I was doing a good job out there...that I was bringing intensity and violence to the opponent and they were feeling it."

Football was in Hoffmann's blood, but as a child he had to patiently wait for the chance to play. While growing up in the Dallas area, his parents made him wait until junior high to play tackle football for the first time. "I begged my mom and dad to let me play," he said. "I remember my dad would just kind of sit there, and my mom would shake her head, 'No, no.'"

Finally, in eighth grade he got the okay to play. "I remember just letting loose," he said. "Just letting it go. It was such a good feeling. It was like *finally*. I'll never forget it. I knew then that this game was for me. I found out you could run around and hit and do the stuff that I would get into trouble for doing to my little brothers. And people would pat me on the back for it."

After his family's moved to California, Hoffmann attended Pioneer High in San Jose, where his football coach was former UW linebacker Dan Loyd. In the 1970s Loyd had played for defensive coordinator Jim Lambright, and Loyd enthusiastically endorsed Hoffmann to Lambright during the recruiting process years later. "Jim Lambright believed in me," Loyd said.

Hoffmann was a throwback, sporting a 1950s-era flattop. He was tough—winning the Earle T. Glant "Tough Husky" award as a junior—and fundamentally sound. Playing behind star defensive lineman Steve Emtman, it was Hoffmann's job to clean up on plays when Emtman was the focus of double teams, which was often. He also orchestrated the defense. "He's got his mistakes down to almost zero," UW coach Don James said in 1991. "There are so many mental things—calls and shifts and judgments. He's done a good job with that."

Hoffmann played in the NFL for one season with the Pittsburgh Steelers and then transitioned into a career in the Secret

Service. "When I finished playing ball, I wasn't sure exactly what I wanted to do," he said. "I knew I wanted to do something where I could be physically active and think on your feet. I started looking into law enforcement. And I'm also a pretty patriotic guy. I wanted to do something that made a difference."

Among his assignments: protecting President George W. Bush and former president Bill Clinton. "To be on the president's detail, that's something I've wanted to do since I came on the job," he said. "It's a goal of mine. I'm working hard, keeping my nose down, getting after it."

Indeed, Hoffmann's defense never rests.

49 2003 Apple Cup Upset

There is perhaps no greater feeling for the Huskies and their fans than dashing the dreams of the Cougars. In 2003 the eighth-ranked Washington State came to Husky Stadium with an outside shot at a Rose Bowl bid. It was the rare occasion that WSU came to Seattle as the Apple Cup favorite, but the Huskies sent the Cougars back to the Palouse with a stunning 27–19 victory, UW's sixth consecutive win against its cross-state rival.

The Huskies scored twice in the final 70 seconds to pull off the upset, and elated Husky fans stormed the field and climbed the goal posts to celebrate. "Everybody thought it would be a landslide," said UW receiver Reggie Williams. "But we showed everybody we are still the Huskies, and they are still the Cougars."

Washington State tied or led for 58 minutes, 50 seconds in a sloppy game that featured 12 combined turnovers—seven by

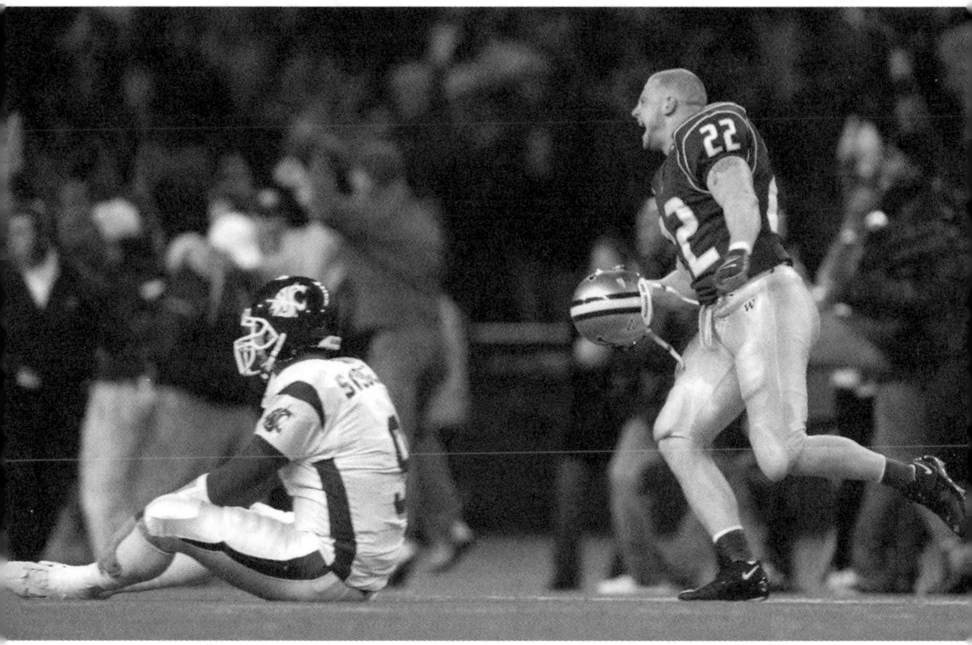

After Washington stunned No. 8 Washington State in the 2003 Apple Cup, Washington State quarterback Josh Swogger wallows in defeat while Washington's Ty Eriks celebrates. (AP Images)

WSU—and 18 penalties, including 10 by the Cougars, who set an NCAA season record with 144 penalties.

Senior quarterback Cody Pickett, in the final pass of his record-breaking UW career, gave the Huskies their first lead with 1:10 left in the game when he threw a 21-yard touchdown to Corey Williams, who made a diving grab in the end zone just beyond the outstretched hands of WSU safety Erik Coleman. Corey Williams, a freshman receiver, became an unlikely Apple Cup hero; he came into the game with just five catches on the season. "I just wanted to make an impression," Corey Williams said. "I've been waiting all season to make big plays…I knew I could catch the ball."

Linebacker Marquis Cooper returned an interception 38 yards for a touchdown with 14 seconds left to secure the victory for the Huskies, who had five interceptions in the game. It was quite the turnaround for UW's defense, which a week earlier allowed a school-record 729 yards in a 54–7 loss at California. "We challenged them," UW coach Keith Gilbertson said. "We told them, 'We believe in you and know that you've got another great game in you.'"

The Apple Cup victory salvaged a 6–6 season for the Huskies, who avoided their first losing regular season since 1976. "That's huge," UW linebacker Greg Carothers said. "That's a lot of teams that played before us that we would have let down."

UW seniors presented the game ball to Gilbertson, who guided the team through a tumultuous season following the abrupt firing of Rick Neuheisel that summer. "I don't know if this saves our season, but it's a marvelous moment," Gilbertson said. "If you are coaching at Washington, your first job is to beat Washington State. For the next 24 hours, I get to be the happiest guy on the planet."

50 Don McKeta

Described in one newspaper account as "a thinking man's halfback," Don McKeta didn't have long to think before the most memorable play of his Washington career. With the Huskies trailing rival Oregon 6–0 late on October 29, 1960, McKeta took a pass from quarterback Bob Hivner and appeared to be heading out of bounds to stop the clock. Instead, as Oregon defender Dave Grayson hesitated, McKeta spun upfield and sprinted for a 37-yard touchdown at Husky Stadium.

On the front page of the next day's paper, *The Seattle Times* ran a five-picture sequence of McKeta's touchdown. "I was going to go out of bounds. Whatever made me do it, I don't know," McKeta recalled. "[Grayson] started swearing and was just madder than hell. I thought, *Well, jeez I must have him beat pretty bad, so I'll turn the corner and go*. He could run a 100 faster than I could run a 50, but he just pulled up."

George Fleming then kicked the winning extra point, and Hiver intercepted a pass near the goal line to secure the ninth-ranked Huskies' 7–6 victory.

The week before, McKeta had intercepted Terry Baker—Oregon State's Heisman Trophy-winning quarterback—to help spark the Huskies' comeback from a 15-point deficit to beat the No. 18 Beavers 30–29. Against another UW rival, Washington State, McKeta had to have 13 stitches at halftime to shore up a laceration and then returned to catch the game-winning two-point conversion in the Huskies' 8–7 victory. "That speaks a lot about his mental toughness," teammate Chuck Allen said. "It epitomizes what we were all about—mental toughness. Most teams were bigger than us, stronger than us, yet we had that inner thing."

McKeta was the *Seattle Post-Intelligencer*'s Man of the Year in 1961 and was a team captain for UW's back-to-back Rose Bowl victories. Against No. 1 Minnesota in the 1961 Rose Bowl, McKeta knocked down Minnesota quarterback Sandy Stephens for a 13-yard loss during one key stretch and then intercepted a pass on the next play near the UW end zone. "He's the toughest player I've ever come up against," Minnesota fullback Roger Hagberg said after the game. "He knocked me down at least five times."

At least four times during his playing days, McKeta broke his nose, and his sideways beak became a bit of a running joke. He finally had his nose surgically repaired in 1964 after he had returned to Seattle to be an assistant coach on Jim Owens' staff. "I don't think my new face hurts at all when I'm out recruiting," he said. "You go into a high school athlete's home with that old hook-nose of mine, and the mother shrinks back in horror."

Growing up in coal mining country in rural Pennsylvania, McKeta had no electricity as a child and if he couldn't catch a ride he walked eight miles into the hills to get home after football practices. In part to escape life in the coal mines, he left home at 16 and joined the Navy. He spent four years in service during the Korean War and was 27 years old as a senior for the Huskies in 1960.

He was selected by the New York Giants in the 1961 NFL Draft, but the Saskatchewan Roughriders had a more lucrative offer so he went to the Canadian Football League. Just six games into his rookie season, he suffered a serious neck injury that ended his playing days.

51 Man of Steele

It's remembered as one of the greatest high school football games ever played in Seattle, and at the center of it all was one of the greatest football players Seattle has ever produced. In the end it was a fairly typical performance for Joe Steele, who rushed for 140 yards and two touchdown on 36 carries, caught a touchdown pass, and even threw the winning touchdown in the fourth overtime as his Blanchet High School team survived a 42–35 thriller to defeat Garfield for the Metro League championship in 1975. It was Blanchet's 23rd consecutive victory.

Some 25 years later, reporters and editors at *The Seattle Times* voted Steele the best prep running back in state history. "I don't have one bad memory of those days," said Steele, who had 3,814 yards rushing and 44 touchdowns at Blanchet.

At 6'4", 195 pounds, Steele had size and speed (a 4.5-second 40-yard dash), and his running style was once compared to a 737 coming in for a landing. The first major local recruit to commit to Don James at Washington, Steele was a sophomore on the 1977 UW team that upset Michigan in the Rose Bowl. In 1978 he set a single-season record with 1,111 yards rushing and in 1979 he became the Huskies' all-time leading rusher, breaking Hugh McElhenny's 28-year-old record.

McElhenny was in attendance at Husky Stadium when Steele broke the record in the 1979 season opener against Wyoming. His record-breaking run came early in the fourth quarter on a pitch sweep that gained eight yards. Many in the crowd gave a loud cheer, and Steele was pulled from the game a play later to a warm ovation. He finished the game with 106 yards rushing and three touchdowns in the Huskies' 38–2 romp. "I really don't try and concentrate on yardage," he said. "I really don't believe in it. If I go out and play as well as I can, the yardage will come. If I get 500 [in a season] and we're winning games, that's great."

Steele's career-record 3,091 yards stood until Napoleon Kaufman broke it in 1994. James later named Steele and Greg Lewis as the two best backs he coached at UW. "Steele did everything anyone could ever ask of a player," James said.

52 Cody Pickett

That Cody Pickett was playing through an injury shouldn't have come as a surprise. That the injury was a separation to his right (throwing) shoulder should have raised some eyebrows. That Pickett played with a separated throwing shoulder *and* threw for a school-record 455 yards was downright stunning.

And that wasn't all. Pickett dove into the end zone to score on a three-yard touchdown run with 13 seconds left, lifting the Huskies to a wild 31–28 victory against Arizona in 2001, surely one of the grittiest performances in UW history. "It would have hurt a lot more if I didn't get in [to the end zone]," said Pickett, who completed 29-of-49 passes with three touchdowns and four interceptions.

That sort of gutsy display typified Pickett. He was a quarterback in name, a cowboy by birth. Pickett's father, Dee, was a world rodeo champion, and Pickett himself was an accomplished roper as a teenager. "Cody is a tough son-of-a-gun," UW receiver Pat Reddick said. "I don't know if it is genetic or not, but for a guy to ride cows and mess around with animals that size, you've got to be tough. Man, he is."

And, boy, could he throw the football. In three years as the Huskies' starting quarterback, Pickett broke 21 different major records at UW. Most of those records still stand:

- 9,916 career passing yards
- 53 touchdown passes
- 792 pass completions
- 4,458 yards passing in 2002 (most in conference history)

Pickett grew up on his family's 20-acre spread just off Chicken Dinner Road in Caldwell, Idaho. His father, who played quarterback at Boise State and was later inducted into the Rodeo Hall of Fame, once held the world record for roping (3.9 seconds). Pickett followed in his father's footsteps, qualifying for the high school team roping National Finals Rodeo in 1997, 1998, and 1999. (And because the NCAA has no jurisdiction over the sport, Pickett was able to keep the cash prizes, some $30,000, for his success on the rodeo circuit.)

As a kid Pickett would spend his summer vacations with his dad on the rodeo circuit, riding the bus from one event to the next. "Sometimes I would go to sleep in Utah and wake up in Wyoming," he said. "It was fun for a kid, but it was a hard life for them. In rodeo they say, 'If you ain't winning, you ain't eating,' so guys practiced their skills all the time. I really got to see that there are no shortcuts."

At UW Pickett considered entering the NFL draft after his record-setting junior season in 2002. Coach Rick Neuheisel ultimately convinced Pickett to return for his senior season, and 2003 ended up being one of the most turbulent in program history. The revelation of Neuheisel's involvement in a college basketball pool prompted his firing just a couple months before the season, and Pickett suffered a torn pectoral muscle against Indiana in the second game of the year. At the time the quarterback didn't say much about the injury. "I was always raised that if you are playing, you are playing," he said. "So I played through a lot of things like that, that some people didn't really know about. Against Indiana I got hit by the safety, and my left pec swelled up and was black and blue all through my arm pit. I could barely throw all week in practice. But it was my team. I wasn't about to not play."

A knee injury against Oregon State and a head injury against Oregon further derailed Pickett's senior season. But he was able to help the Huskies salvage a 6–6 finish with a dramatic touchdown pass with 70 seconds left in the Apple Cup to beat No. 8 Washington State 27–19.

"It's been a long five years," Pickett said after the game. "I wouldn't trade it for anything. We've had a lot of ups and downs. We've had a great time here, a great experience for our senior class. This is a great way to go out on a winning note."

53 Who's the Best QB?

Given the Huskies' history at quarterback, selecting one as the best of all time seemed like an impossible task. But that was the goal in a 2015 survey by *The Seattle Times* of 40 former UW players, coaches, fans, and local media members. As many pollsters noted, it was not an easy chore, particularly when taking into account the varying styles of the many notable quarterbacks and the shifting landscape of college football over the decades. "This was really tough for me—lots of great choices," former UW linebacker Pete Tormey said.

It was a subjective project, of course, no doubt based largely on one's own nostalgic experiences watching, coaching, and/or playing alongside the quarterbacks. If the Huskies played in the Rose Bowl tomorrow, who would you want to start at quarterback? The most popular answer: Marques Tuiasosopo (eight votes). Warren Moon (four votes) and Billy Joe Hobert (three votes, plus a shared vote with Mark Brunell) were also popular.

Lincoln Kennedy, UW's Hall of Fame left tackle, pondered the Rose Bowl question for a few moments and shook his head. No, he couldn't choose only one of the two star quarterbacks he protected in the early 1990s to start in a Rose Bowl for UW. "I remember that spring practice when Mark [Brunell] tore up his knee [in 1991]. I was like, 'Oh my gosh, where do we go from here?'" Kennedy said. "But Billy Joe Hobert came in…and we really had a system with two quarterbacks. So I'm partial to them."

One former quarterback picked Hobert as his Rose Bowl starter, noting simply that Hobert was UW's most successful quarterback ever based on one important category. "He never lost," the other quarterback said.

Roland Lund was in junior high when he attended his first Huskies game in 1952. All-American Don Heinrich, a future College Football Hall of Famer, was UW's quarterback that year. Seven years later, as the sports editor of *The UW Daily*, Lund covered another Hall of Famer, Bob Schloredt, who led UW to

Survey Results

(Note that a first-place vote was worth five points, a second-place vote was worth four points, and so on.)

Best passer

1. Cody Pickett, 38 points
2. Brock Huard, 30
3. Sonny Sixkiller, 29
4. Warren Moon, 26
5. Keith Price, 23

Best dual threat

1. Marques Tuiasosopo, 68
2. Jake Locker, 61
3. Mark Brunell, 31
4. Bob Schloredt, 25
5. Warren Moon, 14

Most clutch performer

1. Marques Tuiasosopo, 66
2. Billy Joe Hobert, 46
3. Warren Moon, 34
4. Bob Schloredt, 18
5. Mark Brunell, 17

Best pro career

1. Warren Moon, 80
2. Mark Brunell, 55
3. Chris Chandler, 48
4. Damon Huard, 20
5. Don Heinrich, 12

back-to-back Rose Bowl victories (becoming the first player named Rose Bowl MVP twice). "I may show a bias toward the old guys," Lund said.

In a separate poll, *The Seattle Times*' online poll, 1,180 readers responded to the question: who is the best UW quarterback of all time? The most popular answer with 654 votes (34.8 percent) was Tuiasosopo. Next was Moon with 520 votes (27.7 percent) and then Brunell (13.5 percent) in third.

The lists are littered more with modern-era quarterbacks. Tuiasosopo, who quarterbacked UW to a victory against Purdue in the 2001 Rose Bowl, was the consensus choice to start any Rose Bowl game for the Huskies. Moon, a Pro Football Hall of Famer, was a unanimous selection as the Huskies quarterback who went on to have the best pro career. In all, 22 different quarterbacks received votes in at least one category, a sure sign of the strength and depth of UW's history at the game's most important position.

54 Browning's Breakthrough

The meticulous manner in which Jake Browning prepares to play each week quickly took on legendary status around the University Washington football offices. Teammates are often in awe with how much their quarterback dedicates himself to his craft. Coaches talk about how in sync Browning is with their vision for the offense.

Browning estimates he watches a couple hours of film study each day, every day. He's been that way since his days at Folsom (California) High School, when he would spend lunch periods watching film and talking ball with coaches. He is a football junkie, yes. But Browning wants to make clear, too, that he's not a mechanical, dispassionate quarterback. He enjoyed the Huskies' ride back to national relevance in 2016—even if his stoic shell sometimes suggested otherwise. "I'm not a robot," Browning said in late November. "Yeah, after a game I'll go hang out with friends and stuff like that. But we're playing for some pretty cool things right now, and it's pretty easy to be motivated when—I think we're 10–1 now—and you're going to play for the Pac-12 championship. That's something no one on this team has ever done."

The label of reluctant star has stuck, and Browning doesn't much mind. It fits. He certainly didn't embrace the spotlight as he led the Huskies to their first conference championship in 16 years. And en route to the program's first College Football Playoff berth, Browning placed sixth in the Heisman Trophy voting—the second best finish in UW history. (Steve Emtman was fourth in 1991.)

As his profile rose with his record-setting passing numbers and as national media outlets arrived in Seattle to try to tell his story, Browning typically offered little in the way of personality. During interviews he's not difficult…but he's not easy either. He answers the questions asked and seems eager to move on. "After a big win, I'm still thinking about some things I did wrong," said Browning, the 2016 Pac-12 Offensive Player of the Year. "But also, I'm happy in the locker room after a win. When we go talk to the media, it's a little different because there's all these cameras in your face, and you don't want to say anything wrong. I mean, like I said, I'm not a robot. I have fun. I like playing the game. But I'm kind of a perfectionist. That's how I've always been. I enjoy the locker room more than I enjoy any interview and I enjoy playing more than any interview. It's nothing personal."

That approach falls right in line with Chris Petersen's. Coach and quarterback are two perfectly matched perfectionists. "I probably appreciate him more because he's got a calmer demeanor than I do," Petersen said. "And I think it's easier when you're a player. You can just let [mistakes] go out there. As a coach on the sideline,

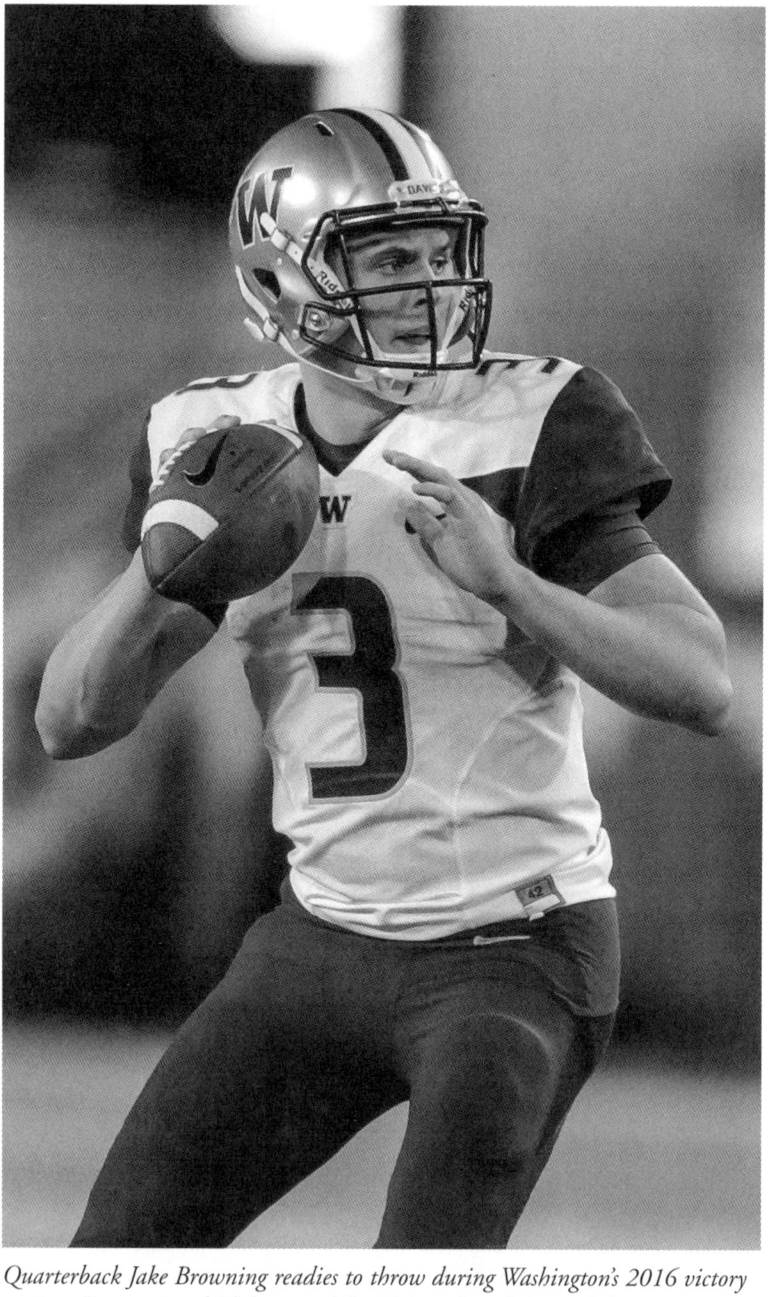

Quarterback Jake Browning readies to throw during Washington's 2016 victory against Oregon, in which he passed for 304 yards and six touchdowns.
(AP Images)

it just gets bottled up, and you try to bite your tongue as best you can. But I think the thing is we're both really competitive, and he's awesome. I try to do the best I can to not be too competitive and over-coach him because he gets it."

In 2015 Browning became the first true freshman in UW history to open the season as the starting quarterback. He's not an overly vocal leader, but early on he earned the respect of teammates and coaches. "Jake's definitely one of the most competitive guys I've ever met in my life," UW offensive lineman Jake Eldrenkamp said. "He hates to lose. Even in practice losing a rep pisses him off."

His is a quiet intensity few see. Browning will show it when challenged, as UW defenders try to do at times in practice. "If you talk mess to Jake during practice, he'll come right back at you," defensive tackle Elijah Qualls said. "He's competitive, man. He'll talk back. But the whole hype man, yelling at people, that's just not him. But don't get [confused]. He's one of the most fierce competitors I've ever met."

Browning's not shy about pointing out teammates' mistakes; that works because of how demanding he is of himself. "I'm hard on myself. I'm harder than anybody is on me," he said. "And I'm kind of the point guy for the offense, so I just kind of do my deal. If I think someone messed up something and I think I can say something to help, then I'll say something. I'm not afraid to talk to people by any means."

As a leader Browning says he'll never be the sort to stand up in the middle of the locker room and give a fiery pregame speech. That's not who he is. "It's about having character, it's about having connection to the guys, and it's about having competence," Petersen said of the leadership qualities he values. "All three of those things take time, and he has all three of those things. So you don't have to be a rah-rah guy. You just have to be yourself, which he always is. And when you have those three things, guys are going to trust him."

Browning had one of the best seasons by a quarterback in Huskies history in 2016, breaking the school record with 43 touchdown passes, which tied the Pac-12 single-season record. His 3,430 passing yards were second most in a season in program history, and his passer rating of 167.52 was a school record.

Not that Browning is bothered much by statistics or by the spotlight. He's off studying film somewhere, dissecting a defense, perfecting a craft, and trying to enjoy a few small moments along the way.

55 2011 Alamo Bowl

Never before had a college football bowl game produced such offensive wizardry. Or, viewed through another prism, never before had defensive ineptitude reached such depths.

If nothing else, at least the Huskies' 67–56 loss to Baylor in the 2011 Alamo Bowl provided plenty of excitement for viewers. As the final score would indicate, neither defense offered much resistance.

The total points set a record for any bowl game (in regulation), and the 1,397 combined yards of offense was also the most in a bowl game. The 123 combined points were also the most ever scored in a UW game (passing the Huskies' 120–0 victory against Whitman in 1919).

"What a great game to be part of," UW coach Steve Sarkisian said. "Our kids battled and competed, and it was just a back-and-forth game, one of those crazy games that these guys will remember for a lifetime."

Led by Heisman Trophy winner Robert Griffin III, Baylor finished with 777 yards total offense, the most the Huskies have ever allowed in a game (surpassing the 729 by California in 2003). Baylor's eight rushing touchdowns also set a UW opponent record. "That was crazy," Baylor coach Art Briles said. "It really was."

Sophomore quarterback Keith Price had one of the single greatest performances in UW history, completing 23-of-27 passes for 438 yards and four touchdowns. He also ran for another three touchdowns, ultimately outplaying Griffin. The Huskies finished with 620 yards of total offense, the fourth best total in school history at the time. "We'll have a hard time this bowl season to see a quarterback play as well as [Price] did," Sarkisian said.

On the second play of the third quarter, Price found a wide open Jermaine Kearse for an 80-yard touchdown to give the Huskies a 42–24 lead. That capped a 35–3 run for the Huskies, who had trailed 21–7 at the end of the first quarter. But Baylor's Terrance Ganaway wore down UW's defense in the second half, finishing with 200 yards rushing and five touchdowns.

UW players blamed poor tackling on the defense's shortcomings. The defense finished as the worst in school history, and defensive coordinator Nick Holt was fired two days after the Alamo Bowl. "There's a style of play in which I think we need to pride ourselves on playing, and that didn't happen tonight," Sarkisian said. "That is the frustrating part."

56 The Helmet Car

One old Husky Stadium tradition was a ton of fun. For more than 30 years, the Husky helmet car was a fixture at home games, circling the salmon-colored track, which surrounded the field, to celebrate a Huskies score. Standing about 10 feet tall and weighing a ton (about 2,000 pounds), the oversized gold fiberglass helmet was mounted on top of a 1960s Volkswagen chassis. *See, it was literally a ton of fun.*

The car could fit about eight cheerleaders and/or band members (not necessarily comfortably) as it circled the field. According to UW, the origin of the helmet car is believed to be traced back to the 1977 season, when the Huskies won the Pac-8 championship and earned a trip to the Rose Bowl. Several supporters had apparently hoped to drive the helmet car from Seattle to Pasadena, California, and into the Rose Bowl parade, but the car never made the trip that year. It is believed that in the following season, the helmet car started circling the track after every UW score with members of the UW band and cheer squad riding in celebration. The car was financed by the UW athletic department and maintained and operated by the Husky Marching Band.

Because the track was removed from Husky Stadium as part of the $280 million reconstruction completed in 2013, the helmet car was retired because there was simply no room at the new stadium. It was then donated to Seattle's Museum of History and Industry.

57 2012 Upset of Stanford

A year earlier Stanford humiliated the Huskies in Palo Alto, California, rushing for a school-record 446 yards in a 65–21 blowout of Washington. Going into their 2012 game for a Thursday night affair in Seattle, Stanford had won four in a row against the Huskies, the previous three by a combined margin of 140–35.

So there was obvious excitement when UW cornerback Desmond Trufant intercepted Stanford's Josh Nunes to preserve the Huskies' 17–13 upset of the No. 8 Cardinal, sending thousands of ecstatic Huskies fans onto the middle of CenturyLink Field in celebration. "I wanted to beat them more than anyone else," UW senior safety Justin Glenn said. "Just the fact that they have physically been beating us. The last couple of years it's just been beatdowns, especially on the defensive side of the ball. And I feel like they didn't really respect us. But they have to after tonight."

In a remarkable turnaround under new defensive coordinator Justin Wilcox, the Huskies held Stanford to just 68 yards rushing—378 fewer than Stanford had against UW the year before. The Huskies' defensive plan was to stack the box against the run and force Nunes, a first-year starting quarterback, to beat them through the air. It was vintage Huskies defense at its best. "From where we were a year ago, it was something for our defense to come over and show that kind of leadership," Washington coach Steve Sarkisian said.

A rowdy crowd of 55,941 certainly helped the Huskies' cause, too. "I love our fans. They bring it, man," Sarkisian said. "They were patient with me on offense. I think they knew what kind of game we were in. Part of me thinks that our fans probably appreciate these types of games more so than 48–45. There is something gritty about our mentality here. This was a black-and-blue type of game, and I think our fans appreciated that."

It appeared Stanford would have the Huskies' number again when it took a 13–3 lead in the third quarter. But UW junior quarterback Keith Price wasn't ready to give up. "We are going to win this game," he hollered at teammates on the sideline.

He was right, thanks in part to a gutsy decision from Sarkisian. Facing a fourth and one at UW's own 39-yard line, Sarkisian went for it. Bishop Sankey, UW's sophomore running back, burst through a hole on the right, sidestepped a would-be tackle, and raced 61 yards for a touchdown on the final snap of the third quarter. That cut the Huskies' deficit to 13–10 and firmly shifted momentum. "My first thought was just to get the first down and get positive yards," Sankey said. "And then the hole opened up so fast. Before I knew it, I stepped out of a tackle, and it was off to the races."

Running behind a depleted offensive line, Sankey finished with 144 yards on 20 carries, one of the first big steps in his breakout season. Price then delivered late when he threw to star receiver Kasen Williams, who broke a tackle and went streaking down the sidelines for a 35-yard touchdown, giving the Huskies a 17–13 lead with 4:53 remaining in the game. Williams had 10 catches for 129 yards. Trufant then sealed it late with his interception, a fitting finish for a much-beleaguered UW defense.

58 Greg Lewis

His record-breaking numbers still resonate more than 25 years later. What was less obvious then and now was the behind-the-scenes leadership Greg Lewis provided during Washington's breakthrough in 1990. In their second game of the season, the No. 22 Huskies trailed at halftime 14–10 in a road game at Purdue. For Lewis, UW's star senior running back, this was unacceptable. "Greg Lewis talked to us for 10 minutes," UW center Ed Cunningham recalled a few weeks later. "He told us what we needed to do to win, and I don't think the season has been the same since."

It was a defining moment for the team, which rode Lewis' legs to a 20–14 win against the Boilermakers. Lewis, who had 32 yards on 10 carries in the first half, added 70 yards on 18 second-half carries in the comeback victory. By the end of the season, Lewis had led the Huskies to the Pac-10 championship, their first Rose Bowl berth in nine years, and there was much debate about his place in the great lineage of UW running backs. Lewis, after all, was the first running back in UW history to post back-to-back 1,000-yard rushing seasons. In 1990 he set a school single-season record with 1,407 yards, which followed his 1,197 yards from 1989.

Was Lewis the best UW running back ever? Lewis himself deferred. "Hugh McElhenny was the greatest. They called him the king," he said late in the 1990 season. "He could play today, and if he were on this Washington team, I'd be second string."

Lewis had his best game late in the 1990 season, rushing for 205 yards on 29 carries in the Huskies' 46–7 victory against Cal. "It feels good to get 200 yards," Lewis said, "but it's more fun to win. That's all I really care about." Said Cunningham: "He's special."

And tough, too. A week after the Cal win, Lewis injured his left knee in a loss to UCLA on November 10. He had arthroscopic surgery three days later but returned in six weeks to help the Huskies beat Iowa in the Rose Bowl. "I've seen a lot of running backs around here who wear red [because they're injured] and don't practice a couple of days," offensive lineman Dean Kirkland said. "Greg not only plays hurt, but practices hurt. He's a team guy, a great personality."

Lewis, a graduate of Seattle's Ingraham High School, was named the Pac-10's Offensive Player of the Year, a first-team All-American by *The Sporting News,* and UW's only recipient of the Doak Walker Award, presented to the nation's top running back. He was also seventh in the 1990 Heisman Trophy voting, which at the time was the highest finish ever by a Husky. "The things you like about Greg is that he's bright, he's a team player, and he's got a great attitude," UW coach Don James said. "He's as complete a player as we've had back there. He can catch. He can block. And he can run."

Over the years Lewis has remained close to the Huskies, working in various roles in the athletic department and on local radio broadcasts. He is currently co-host of the UW football pregame show on KOMO-AM Radio 1000.

59 Ross' Speedy Return

John Ross III had been counting down the minutes for his chance to return to action for the Huskies. "It's hard to sleep. I'm just really excited," the junior wide receiver said three days before Washington's 2016 season opener against Rutgers.

It had been 20 months since Ross last played in a game. As a sophomore in 2014, he enjoyed a breakout season when he starred on offense, defense, and special teams. He scored seven touchdowns (four receiving, two kickoff returns, and one rushing) on plays of 100, 96, 91, 86, 75, 55, and 20 yards—an average of 75 yards per scoring play—and did it while playing most of the season with a torn meniscus in his right knee. He had that surgically repaired that offseason.

Then, a few months later, he tore the anterior cruciate ligament in his left knee during a spring practice. He had surgery in April 2015, effectively ending his 2015 season. So in the buildup to the much-anticipated 2016 season—and with the Huskies ranked in the top 15 and expected to challenge for a conference championship—Ross was eager to do his part. He did that and then some, hauling in touchdown receptions of 50 and 38 yards from Jake Browning in the first quarter in the Huskies' 48–13 dismantling of Rutgers. And on his first kickoff return of the season, Ross returned it 92 yards for a touchdown—the fourth kick-return touchdown of his career, a new UW record.

Recruited by Steve Sarkisian, Ross had come to Seattle from Long Beach, California, with high expectations. He was fast, and everyone knew it. Even before Ross played his first game for the Huskies as a 17-year-old true freshman, Sarkisian compared Ross' speed to that of Reggie Bush, the Heisman Trophy winner Sarkisian had coached at USC. "Every time [Ross] has the ball in his hands," UW quarterback Keith Price said, "you kind of hold your breath because you don't know what's going to happen."

The two knee surgeries didn't slow him down either. In early 2016 Ross signaled he was back to full speed—and then some—by

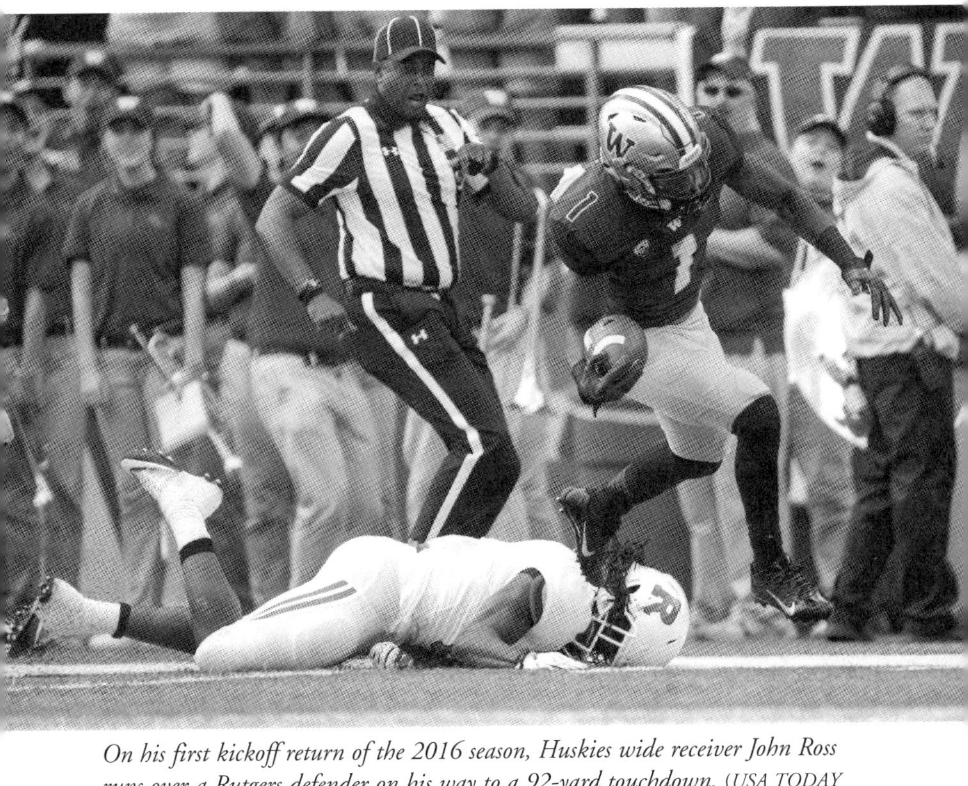

On his first kickoff return of the 2016 season, Huskies wide receiver John Ross runs over a Rutgers defender on his way to a 92-yard touchdown. (USA TODAY Sports Images)

running a hand-timed 4.25-second 40-yard dash during winter conditioning testing in March 2016. That is believed to be the fastest time by any player in UW history. At the NFL Scouting Combine in 2017, he ran a 4.22, the fastest time ever recorded at the event.

Ross, 5'11" and 190 pounds, had spent his first two seasons with the Huskies yo-yoing back and forth between offense and defense. A dearth of depth at defensive back meant Ross was asked to help out on defense. Entering 2016 he was firmly entrenched back on offense, and his goal going into the season was to refine the technical aspects of the wide receiver position.

To that end he sought out NFL All-Pro receiver DeSean Jackson, a fellow Los Angeles native, during the offseason. Jackson's message: slow down. "I learned things from him, and it's taken my game to a new level," Ross said. "He told me things like 'Understand that you're the fastest player on the field, but you don't have to use that speed all the time...Sometimes you have to slow down and run routes.'"

Ross was at the heart of the Huskies' 2016 resurgence, putting together one of the best—and most exciting—seasons by a UW receiver ever. He was named a first-team All-American by ESPN after posting 81 catches for 1,150 yards and 17 touchdowns, second most in conference history behind UW's Mario Bailey's 18 touchdown catches from 1991.

After the season Ross opted to forgo his senior season and enter the 2017 NFL Draft, where he was drafted ninth overall by the Cincinnati Bengals. That represented quite a comeback from two knee surgeries. "I'm just blessed to be here," Ross said after the Huskies' loss to No. 1 Alabama in the College Football Playoff national semifinal. "Just going back to last year, I wasn't even walking. So I'm thankful for anything."

60 Jacque Robinson

In Washington's biggest games, no one was better than Jacque Robinson. On New Year's Day 1982, the Huskies' 6'0", 212-pound running back from Oakland, California, became the first freshman named the Most Valuable Player of a Rose Bowl, earning that nod when he rushed for 142 yards and two touchdowns in a victory against Iowa. "My mom had a tape of the game, and I got a chance to look at it afterward," Robinson said. "I thought I did pretty good. But some of those runs…I don't remember making them. I'd look at myself and say, 'Did I do that?'"

Three years later he did it again.

In his final game in a Huskies uniform, Robinson rushed for 135 yards in the Huskies' upset of Oklahoma in the Orange Bowl, again earning MVP recognition in one of the most notable games in UW history. "Jacque Robinson is a nice, quiet guy that likes to go out and get things done," Robinson said, speaking in the third person. "He's always smiling, has a great personality. He just loves the game of football and really loves the Husky team. I was raised on smiling. My family was real close, and it seemed like we were always having fun. I guess the credit belongs to the personality of my mother. She was always smiling, and that told us that no matter what was going on in the world, the world was all right."

As a sophomore Robinson led the Pac-12 in rushing with 926 yards, earning all-Pac-10 recognition. But much of Robinson's career was scattered with unfulfilled promise—he himself had said after the Rose Bowl that he wanted to win the Heisman Trophy. He showed up to fall camp overweight in 1983—much to the frustration of UW coaches—and shared carries in a crowded backfield and finished with just 296 yards on 48 carries as a junior.

He turned things around as a senior in 1984, rushing for 152 yards against California and a career-high 160 in his final Apple Cup against Washington State. He finished his career fourth on the Huskies' all-time rushing list.

And two decades later, he was also responsible for sending one of the all-time great athletes to UW—his son, Nate. "I'm going to remember that I had a great career here," Jacque said before the Orange Bowl. "I'm going to remember all the good things about it. And I'm going to look back at the bad things but not for long. I'm going to look back at all the great people I've met and been associated with the last four years. And all the fans. And just all the great things about the University of Washington."

61 Nate Robinson

There was nothing, it seemed, that Nate Robinson couldn't do. One of the best all-around athletes in Washington state history, Robinson was a football star, a basketball marvel, and a record-breaking sprinter and jumper at Seattle's Rainer Beach High. "People come up to me and tell me how much they enjoy watching me play, and it makes me feel like I've made a difference. I like that," said Robinson, who as a Rainer Beach senior was the state Player of the Year in basketball and broke the state record in the 110-meter hurdles.

At the University of Washington, the 5'9" Robinson didn't want to limit himself. As a true freshman, he started the final six games of the 2002 football season at cornerback, coming up with a key fourth-quarter interception in the Huskies' Apple Cup upset of No. 3 Washington State. Just a few weeks later, he turned out for the UW basketball team—and wound up leading the team in scoring while being named to the All-Pac-12 freshman team as a guard. "I know I'm going to play in the NBA; that's a given," he said in 2003. "If that doesn't happen, I'll do football. If that doesn't happen, I'll learn to play baseball. I could do that. And I can fall back on my degree. I love to work with kids."

Robinson played with a childlike joy, and basketball coach Lorenzo Romar learned quickly that to get the best of Robinson, you have to let him play to the brink of recklessness.

"When Nate is almost completely out of control, he's at his best," Romar said. "When he's at his highest level of risk, he's at his best. That's when the highlights come. That's when he fills the arena with his energy."

Of course, there was much debate about Robinson's size. In UW's football program, he was listed at 5'9", but he once conceded he was actually 5'7.5". "I don't care what height you put me at. Put me at five feet, doesn't matter to me. I just play," he said.

Robinson played just the one season of football for the Huskies, choosing after that to focus on basketball. As a junior in 2004–05, he helped the Huskies advance to the Sweet 16 of the NCAA Tournament. "It's something I've never had a chance to do in my life, and I didn't want to die without finding out. It's not like I've given up football. It's just that I want to play basketball," he said. "I want to work on my game when all the other guards in the country are working on theirs. I want to get into basketball shape."

That he did. Robinson played 10 years in the NBA and remains the only player to win three Slam Dunk titles. Robinson, ever the showman, wore neon "Kryptonite" shoes and famously jumped over the 6'11" Dwight Howard, who was wearing a Superman cape, to win the 2009 Slam Dunk. "The kid in Nate will always be there," Romar said. "He'll be 90 years old and he'll still be a kid. But you see much more purpose in him now. He has a vision."

Few figured Robinson, at his size, could have the success he enjoyed for so long in the NBA. "It's incredible," Romar said. "There were a small, select few who thought he would be where he is now. The criticism for him leaving football was heavy. It was, 'You're crazy. You're not going to have a life after college in basketball.' Very few thought he would make it. He's had a phenomenal career. And he would tell you, 'I'm not done yet.'"

62 1981 Win Against USC

It was the sort of performance that typified the Don James era. The unranked Huskies—10-point underdogs—upset No. 3 USC 13–3 on November 14, 1981, doing so on the strength of their defense and special teams, as they always seemed to do during the James Gang reign.

USC star running back Marcus Allen, who would go on to win the Heisman Trophy a few weeks later, rushed for 155 yards on 38 carries against the Huskies (giving him more than 2,000 yards, the first college running back ever to do that in a season). But UW's defense otherwise shut down the Trojans in a game played in some of the most severe weather conditions ever seen at Husky Stadium. "It was a lot of fun," James said. "We were fortunate to beat an outstanding football team."

Throwing the ball in the monsoon-like conditions was nearly impossible. The two quarterbacks, UW's Steve Pelluer and USC's John Mazur, combined to complete just 8-of-24 passing attempts. "We knew it was going to be a defensive game because of the wind, and it was," USC coach John Robinson said. "We knew it was going to be a 3–3 or a 6–3 ballgame. We could not find any offensive momentum."

The score was indeed tied 3–3 late. That's when Pelluer engineered the game-winning drive, completing an 11-yard pass to Paul Skansi and a 15-yarder to Chris James, helping the Huskies move to the USC 30. That's when Chuck Nelson stepped in for one of the biggest kicks of his All-American UW career. "The wind was swirling so hard I just tried to kick it hard and straight," Nelson said. "I knew SC was not going to be able to score again."

His 46-yard field goal with 2:19 left was good, giving the Huskies a 6–3 lead. On Nelson's ensuing kickoff, USC fumbled the ball in the end zone, and UW freshman Fred Small recovered for a touchdown. "There was a big pile," Small said. "Everybody converged on the pile, and it just popped out."

With the win UW kept alive its Rose Bowl hopes while eliminating USC from the Rose Bowl race. Allen called the loss "by far" the most disappointing of his career. "This is my last season. I wanted to go to the Rose Bowl," he said.

A week later, in one of the biggest Apple Cups ever played, the Huskies knocked off No. 14 Washington State 23–10, to earn their second straight Pac-10 championship. The Huskies went on to beat Iowa in the Rose Bowl 28–0 and finished 10–2 and ranked 10th in the final AP poll.

63 The Dawgmother

On a warm summer morning, the views from this second-floor condominium in Kirkland are some of the grandest the region has to offer. One can see for miles around Lake Washington all the way to downtown Seattle—with the Space Needle peeking out in the distance. On fall Saturdays, though, the best views tend to be isolated indoors. Here, in one corner of Carol James' convivial home, college football still carries special significance.

There are two lounging chairs and a small sofa facing two television sets. If the action is good enough, Carol will roll in a third TV set from a bedroom. Each is tuned to a different game.

Some middle-aged men escape to their mancaves. This 83-year-old great-grandmother has Saturdays in her college-football nook.

In the fall of 2016, the action was especially good for her beloved Washington Huskies, and Don James' widow certainly liked what she was seeing. "I am so, so happy for them. I can't even tell you," Carol said. "We have everybody in place that we need right now. I've never seen it really [like this] since we left. There's this family feeling again. It's wonderful."

Carol and her family were there at Husky Stadium on September 30, 2016, when the Huskies beat up on Stanford. During its 25-year anniversary celebration, UW's 1991 national championship team got a standing ovation from the sold-out crowd at halftime. Players from the '91 team had insisted that the James family be involved, and there was Carol, the Dawgmother, standing front and center with the national championship trophy. Carol and her kids got another standing ovation before the fourth quarter when they were introduced during the traditional Husky Legend salute, a fitting tribute on a night that brought back all the nostalgic feelings of all those great Don James teams.

* * *

When she's not driving her red Corvette, Carol is usually walking barefoot around the condo. When she's not exchanging a Facebook messages with one former UW player, she's often on a phone call with another former UW player.

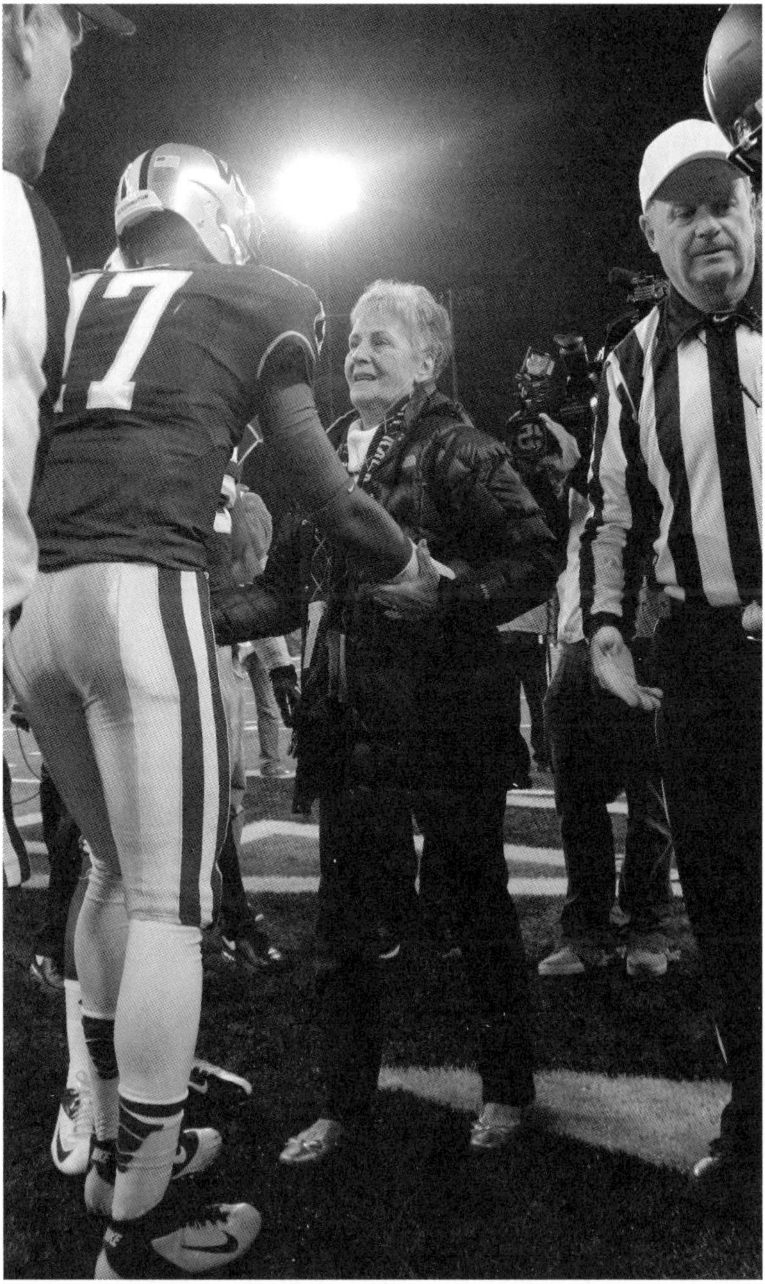

Quarterback Keith Price embraces Carol James during a ceremonial coin flip in 2013 to honor her recently deceased husband, Don James. (AP Images)

Don was 80 years old when he passed away from pancreatic cancer in October 2013. Don and Carol, married 61 years, usually rode the bus from Kirkland to attend UW games and they certainly weren't going to miss the grand reopening of Husky Stadium on August 31, 2013—a victory against Boise State. "He had a great time," she said.

The next morning, Don couldn't get out of bed. The day after that, on Monday morning, Carol called for an ambulance. That afternoon Don was diagnosed with cancer. He passed away seven weeks later on October 20, 2013.

Carol has remained humbled by the outpouring of affection, receiving dozens of letters from admirers and supporters offering their condolences. And on average she says she hears from upwards of a dozen former players each day. "For us, it was always such a family thing. And I think that's why all the kids—I call them kids, but some of them are grandfathers now—but that's why I think they still feel close," she said. "They keep in touch with me, and I really feel blessed. How many people have that many kids looking after them?"

* * *

The 1977 season was one of Carol's favorites despite the Huskies' dreadful start that year.

"We lost three out of the first four games, and, of course, people were pretty upset," she recalled. "It was our third year, and you're supposed to start doing well. Don one night said, 'Carol, you know, we might be moving. My contract is low; anybody out there can pay it.'"

Don's first contract paid him $28,000 annually. Adjusted for inflation that's the equivalent of about $111,000 today—or about $\frac{1}{32}^{nd}$ of the $3.6 million salary Chris Petersen earned in his third season as UW's coach. "I didn't know what he was making until

I started going through papers after he died and I was shocked at what his first salary was here. I thought, *What?*" She said, laughing. "But we were happy. We're not people that have to live fast lives."

It was a fast turnaround for Warren Moon and that '77 team, which won 54–0 at Oregon to start its run to the Pac-8 championship and the first of Don's six Rose Bowl berths.

* * *

There's a video out there somewhere on the web that has Carol on stage, ballcap tilted backward, her own rap lyrics spitting out of her mouth. After Don's retirement the couple spent its winters in Palm Desert, California. Carol continues that tradition and last year she agreed to participate in a talent show with friends, in which they rapped. Carol's always enjoyed writing poems, so she wrote the lyrics and served as the group's front woman. "It was fun. It was crazy," she said. She'll probably do it again this winter.

Most winters Don and Carol would head down to the desert around the first of November. For now she plans to stay until after Thanksgiving. She wants to see how this promising Huskies season plays out. "She kind of was and always will be a team mom," said UW athletic director Jennifer Cohen, who has been close to the James family since she was young. "She was as much an invested person in what Coach James built as anybody."

Sunday mornings were the busiest around the James' Bellevue home. "When we recruited them, I had every recruit in my home for breakfast," Carol said. "And sometimes I'd have 60 to 80 people. If the parents were there, they came. We usually had a professor from the schools that [the recruits] were interested in. And of course the key recruiters [came, too]. I had it down to a system."

It was catered? "No, no. I did it," she said. "My kids would come and help. I did all the prep so I could circulate, then they would take over and make sure the dishes were filled and everything.

I always served the same thing, and the butchers knew: I had ham that was pre-sliced and tied back together. I have a special recipe of eggs you can let set in a buffet dish for two or three hours, and they still are good. I had doughnuts—a lot of doughnuts. Orange juice, coffee, tea. What else? Oh, I have a hash brown recipe; you could bake 'em up and just keep 'em warm."

Carol would then write letters to recruits' mothers, often spurring a correspondence that spanned the player's UW career. "I was doing it because I love this," she said.

* * *

Introduced by a mutual friend, they had met when they were 14 years old at the Massillon (Ohio) Fireman's Festival. They were both born in December 1932; she is 26 days older—"and he never let me forget it." They were practically inseparable from then on, attending the University of Miami (Florida) together and then moving all around the country together during his 36-year coaching career. Correction: *their* coaching career.

Of course, she misses him. "Oh my gosh, every day I cuss at him for not being here," she said.

She has barely touched his office den in their Kirkland condo. It has many of his notable trophies, rings, pictures, and newspaper clippings—all fond memories.

A few months before Don passed, during their last summer together, the topic of their bucket list was broached. "We were sitting and talking, and he wasn't feeling well by then, and we were asking, 'Is there anything else we want to do before one of us kicks the bucket?'" she said. "And there wasn't anything we had left."

She pauses, then smiles. "Isn't that unbelievable?"

64 The Thursday Speeches

On October 1, 1977, the Huskies hardly looked the part of a Rose Bowl champion. That day the Huskies dropped a tight game at Minnesota 19–17 for their third loss in four games to start the season. Huskies fans began to grumble about Don James, then in his third season as the UW coach, who was sporting a 12–14 record.

What followed was a pivotal week for James and the future of the program. Following the loss at Minnesota, James had players rewrite the personal goals he had asked them to jot down before this season. He asked them to write new goals with one question in mind: "What can I do to help the team *today*?"

Then on October 6, two days before the Huskies were to travel to rival Oregon, James delivered one of his many famous speeches to the team. In his book *The Thursday Speeches: Lessons in Life, Leadership, and Football from Coach Don James*, Peter Tormey detailed many of those speeches from the coach. "By the time you were done with a lot of those speeches, you were jumping out of your chair and out on the field," said Joe Steele, UW's record-setting running back from 1976 to 1979.

For James the 48 hours before a game were the most crucial time—a time for visualization and mental preparation. "This is our Rose Bowl right here and now!" James told his players that Thursday. "We must perform NOW!...Think about how you would perform in the Rose Bowl. Hell men, this is our Rose Bowl right here and now. We must perform now...We haven't scratched the surface of our potential. Football is, or was supposed to be, important. Let's act like it. Let's play like it."

And they did. They most certainly did, dismantling the Ducks 54–0 in Eugene, Oregon, to begin their march to James' first conference championship and first Rose Bowl championship.

A linebacker from Spokane, Tormey had been part of James' second recruiting class for the Huskies in 1976, and he witnessed firsthand the growing pains in those early years. Four decades later James gave Tormey more than 100 of his speeches—handwritten on yellow legal paper—which Tormey transcribed and interpreted. About 55 of the best ones are included in his book, which Tormey published independently. "It's amazing to think about how fired up he would get and how much he inspired us," Tormey said. "My inspiration was to share some of his wisdom as a man and as a person—really on how to get through life. So many of his speeches had nothing to do with X's and O's. They were just tips to dealing with problems and the importance of attitude and why that's so critical."

65 Jim Lambright

A job Jim Lambright had yearned for and seemed destined to attain for so long—head coach of the University of Washington football program—was finally his. He hardly had the time or the inkling to celebrate his promotion in August 1993. It was a tumultuous time for the program. Less than two weeks before the start of the season, Don James resigned in protest of sanctions imposed by the Pac-10 conference. Lambright was named the new head coach two days later. "You would love to be happy, but you can't," Lambright said. "The term 'bittersweet' could not have been used more appropriately."

Lambright had tried to talk James out of resigning. When he couldn't he promised to carry on James' legacy. "I can't coach exactly the same way he did," Lambright said, "but all of his beliefs and all of the beautiful details that he put to work here will be carried on."

A graduate of Everett High School, Lambright has been described as "a Husky's Husky," who was born bleeding purple. Lambright joined the UW football team in 1961 as an offensive end and outside linebacker and was named All-Coast in 1964, the same year he received the team's Most Inspirational Player award. Jim Owens hired him to his coaching staff in 1969, and he was one of three assistant coaches retained when James took the reins in 1975.

Lambright spent 16 years as UW's defensive coordinator before succeeding James as head coach at age 51. "The one thing we can do is bind together and produce a product that will make everybody proud and commit the season to Don James," Lambright said.

In Lambright's head coaching debut, the Huskies defeated Stanford 31–14 at home to open the 1993 season. "This win really ties the kids and the coaches together," an emotional Lambright said after the game. "The tingles up your spine, tears welling in your eyes, it was a lot like it was as a player...I loved it. I loved being on the field. It was exciting seeing the players' faces, being involved with them at that level."

James cast a large shadow. The bar had been set high for the Huskies, and the sanctions leveled against the program proved a difficult hurdle for the program during Lambright's six-year run as head coach. There were notable achievements: back-to-back victories against Ohio State and Miami in 1994, a shared conference championship in 1995, and a 51–23 blowout of Nick Saban's Michigan State team in the 1997 Aloha Bowl.

But Lambright and athletic director Barbara Hedges were often at odds, and after the 1998 season, Lambright was dismissed. He had an overall record of 44–25–1 as head coach.

"You're very human, and it happens and it hurts so deeply and it's unbelievable," Lambright said in an interview years later. "You go through an adjustment period, and that, like anything else, is a shock. You have a choice of getting better or feeling sorry for yourself. I went through extreme pain. The really weird thing about it is Don James ended up stepping down because of the actions that were taken against us, and I was fired. There was nothing as far as a connection goes. I had to call to see if I had to buy tickets for the coming season."

Lambright could take solace that the Huskies won the Rose Bowl two years after his dismissal with a roster largely filled with players he helped recruit to UW, including star quarterback Marques Tuiasosopo. "I hope that in the final analysis," Lambright said, "you can look back on everything I did and say that I was extremely fair, that I worked well on a one-on-one basis in all phases of life."

66 Bark for Sark

Steve Sarkisian was the standout quarterback of an undefeated Brigham Young team that came to Husky Stadium in 1996. BYU left Seattle with what would be its only defeat in a 14–1 season, and the mayhem Sarkisian experienced against Washington's defense that day endured for years. "I got sacked eight times," Sarkisian said. "We had eight false start penalties. I got off the plane, went straight to the hospital for an MRI on my left knee."

Sarkisian was back in Husky Stadium 12 years later for his introductory press conference as Washington's new head coach in December 2008. He told a packed room of media members, staffers, and supporters that he knew what it was like to come into this raucous stadium as an opponent and knew the program's potential. "It's the year 2008," Sarkisian told the audience. "It's time to get back to the Rose Bowl, to Pac-10 championships, competing for a national championship. That's our goal, no question. I can't wait to get this thing going."

Two days after the Huskies concluded their most dreadful season in program history—going 0–12 in Tyrone Willingham's last year—Sarkisian officially took charge, bringing in an unbridled energy to a program in desperate need of just that. "It's a game of emotion, a game of passion, and that's been lacking out here," legendary UW quarterback Sonny Sixkiller said. "I've observed him on the sidelines at USC, and you see that true love between he and his players and that excitability, and I'm just excited to see some of that around here."

At 34, Sarkisian was the youngest coach at UW since Jim Owens was hired at age 27 in 1957 and the third youngest coach in major college football. "Two words just stuck out: winner and passion," athletic director Scott Woodward said. "Those were the ones that were just overarching in my mind. I just kept coming back to it. He's been a winner everywhere he's been every step of his life and he's done it with hard work and by being tough. And I think that's what Husky football is all about, and it just kept coming back to that."

Sarkisian had spent seven years at USC on Pete Carroll's staff during the Trojans' dynasty in the 2000s. He wasn't shy about bringing those same kind of great expectations to the Huskies, making lofty promises from the get-go. Sarkisian reenergized the fanbase—"Bark for Sark" T-shirts could be seen all around town—and reinvigorated recruiting. He got the program back on its feet, leading the Huskies to an upset of Nebraska in the 2010 Holiday Bowl, UW's first postseason appearance in eight years.

Ultimately, Sarkisian's tenure at Washington is notable for its extreme highs (including two thrilling upsets of USC in 2009 and 2010) but also extreme lows (five straight blowout losses to Oregon and a collapse in the 2012 Apple Cup). He stunned many when he abruptly left Washington for the head coaching job at USC three days after a victory in the 2013 Apple Cup. He called USC his "dream job."

In five years at UW, Sarkisian had a 34–29 record—and no regrets. "No, not at all," he said. "When you think about what we were able to accomplish when we got there—a program that essentially hadn't won a game in almost two years, hadn't been to a bowl game in nearly 10 years. To think that we went to four consecutive bowl games. Did I want to win more games? Yeah, of course. Are there games that I would love to have back? Of course. But I'm proud of the work...It's not always perfect, it's never going to be perfect, but I am proud of the fact that the program was in a better position the day we left than the day we got there."

Sarkisian had led UW to seven victories against ranked opponents from 2009 to 2013, but he was on the other end of it when the unranked Huskies, as 17-point underdogs, upset Sarkisian's 17th-ranked Trojans 17–12 in Los Angeles on October 8, 2015. It was a big moment for a young Huskies team in rebuilding mode in 2015. "This is one they can feel good about," said UW coach Chris Petersen, who succeeded Sarkisian. "This will give them a little juice."

Sarkisian was fired by USC the next week. In an odd twist, Sarkisian was working as an offensive analyst for Alabama when the Huskies were matched up against the top-ranked Crimson Tide in the 2016 College Football Playoff. Sarkisian was promoted to offensive coordinator a few days after Alabama's victory against the Huskies—and then left Alabama shortly after that to join the Atlanta Falcons.

67 Keith Price

As a sophomore in 2011, Keith Price took the reins as Washington's starting quarterback with the unenviable task of replacing UW legend Jake Locker. All Price did in his first full season was throw a school-record 33 touchdown passes, which was capped by his dynamic, seven-touchdown performance in a classic Alamo Bowl against Baylor.

Expectations then were understandably high for Price and the Huskies entering 2012. They failed to meet them. The Huskies had another up-and-down season, and Price's statistics plummeted (19 touchdown passes and 13 interceptions) as he played through a knee injury.

Price's last pass of 2012 was intercepted in the final seconds of the Las Vegas Bowl, ending the Huskies' comeback bid in a 28–26 loss to Boise State. That left UW with a 7–6 record for a third consecutive season and left the typically easygoing Price humbled and frustrated.

Playing behind an injury-riddled offensive line that allowed 38 sacks the previous season—more than all but 10 teams in the country—Price appeared to be in a constant state of scramble. A "dual-threat" quarterback, Price finished the season with a net gain of minus-34 yards rushing.

It was, however, a deeper duality that emerged within Price: as a leader he felt it was his responsibility to take the blame after tough losses—"That's just me, man," he said—and yet, when it mattered most, the veteran quarterback was often hesitant to put his faith in those teammates he was supposed to be leading. He eventually came to that honest realization. "I didn't trust the guys around me," he acknowledged later. "I didn't trust the calls. I didn't trust myself and my preparation."

He said it took an offseason of "soul searching" to clear his mind entering his senior season in 2013. Running the Huskies' new, hurry-up offense, Price was then terrific in the 2013 opener, the first game at the new $280 million Husky Stadium. He threw for 324 yards and two touchdowns—overcoming an interception on his very first throw—to lead the Huskies to a rousing 38–6 victory against No. 23 Boise State before a sold-out crowd of 71,963. Husky Stadium was back, and so too was Price. "It was good running around and just getting back to the old me," Price said.

In the win Price also broke Cody Pickett's school record for touchdown passes (with 56 and counting). And he regained his 2011 form. "I saw that same look in his eye," UW receiver Kasen Williams said.

Price, one could argue, was one of the most underappreciated quarterbacks in school history. He often took the brunt of fan criticism but wound up finishing his career as UW's all-time leader in touchdown passes (75), completion percentage (.640), and passing efficiency rating (143.2). He also got the Huskies over the seven-win hump in 2013, leading the Huskies to a blowout of Washington State in the Apple Cup and then a win against BYU in the Fight Hunger Bowl. "I love the kid," said UW quarterback great Marques Tuiasosopo, Price's position coach in 2012–13. "Coming back after [2012], with all the negative feedback from outside the program, that was impressive. He's tough. He's resilient. He keeps coming back."

68 Shaq: A Do-It-All Star

In his three seasons with the Huskies, Shaq Thompson did a little bit of everything on the football field. A three-sport star at Sacramento's Grant Union High School, the Californian came to Washington as the most heralded recruit in a decade—a can't-miss, five-star prospect who surprised many when he announced his commitment to UW on January 30, 2012.

A couple of months before formally joining the UW football team and several years before he would become a first-round NFL draft pick, Thompson first tried his luck as an experimental center fielder with the Boston Red Sox. Thompson hadn't played baseball since sixth grade, but the Red Sox were so intrigued by his athleticism that they drafted him in the 18th round of the 2012 MLB Draft. He reported to Florida to play in a rookie ball league, and the experience there quickly reaffirmed that his future was in football. Thompson famously went 0-for-39 with 37 strikeouts (for the record, he also drew eight walks) in what many have described as the worst pro baseball career ever. National websites poked fun at his baseball futility, but the difficult lessons learned were important. "I learned how to accept failure," Thompson said later. "I learned not to be afraid of it, to embrace it, that it's okay."

The youngest of four boys raised by a single mother, Thompson had grown up in Del Paso Heights, a hardscrabble neighborhood in Sacramento. His mom, Patty, was strict, setting the alarm for 5:30 AM each morning—enough time for her to get the boys up, ready for school, and herself to her job at the California Franchise Tax Board. She required her boys to have good grades before they could play Pop Warner football and on occasion she would sit in classes with Syd'Quan, her oldest, to make sure he was paying appropriate attention. "It was kind of like being on a roller coaster and being on top, but it won't come down," Patty said. "You're just dangling, and it's very scary at times…It was very difficult for us. The kids didn't have the best of things, but I tried to provide what I could. Shaq had a lot of hand-me-downs from his brothers."

Shaq looked up to his three older brothers as father figures. "I was grateful for that," he said during his final season at UW in 2014, "and now it's my turn to give them all the love back. That's my motivation."

He was an immediate star as a freshman at UW and he wound up doing just about everything for the Huskies. As a true freshman in 2012, he started every game as a hybrid safety/outside linebacker. In 2013 he earned honorable-mention All-Pac-12 honors as a strong-side linebacker. In his final season, as a junior in 2014, he shifted to weak-side linebacker, scoring four defensive touchdowns and becoming the Huskies' most potent offensive threat.

When injuries hit UW's backfield, coach Chris Petersen turned to the 6'1", 228-pound Thompson as the featured running back for a three-game stretch. Thompson rushed for 98, 174, and 100 yards in those three games and wound up leading the Pac-12 conference with an average of 7.48 yards per carry. "He's fun to watch," Petersen said.

The Huskies have never had a more versatile player, and Thompson was recognized as such at the end of the year when he received the Paul Hornung Award, annually presented to the nation's most versatile player. He was also named to the Associated Press All-American first team as an all-purpose player. The Carolina Panthers then selected him with the 25th overall pick in the first round of the 2015 NFL Draft.

69 Budda Baker

It's difficult to imagine Chris Petersen ever landing a more important recruit than Budda Baker. Petersen and his staff didn't have much time to persuade Baker, then a two-way star at Bellevue High School, which is located just across Lake Washington from the UW campus, to stay home. Petersen had been introduced as UW's new head coach on December9, 2013. Just 11 days later, Baker, the state's top recruit, announced his verbal commitment...to rival Oregon.

Once defensive backs coach Jimmy Lake and the rest of UW's new coaching staff arrived in Seattle in early January, they set in motion their plan to keep Baker home. They had but a month to pull it off. "Even to this day, the urgency that we had to get Budda Baker, we call it 'The Budda Effect,'" Lake said.

Baker had his heart set on playing in the Pac-12, but he had enjoyed earlier conversations with Petersen when the head coach was at Boise State. So when Petersen came to UW, Baker wanted to give the new coaches "a chance" to make their pitch. "There's no question, we were very intense on him because we really felt—after talking to his coaches and getting to know him a little bit—we felt passionately that this is where he should be," Petersen said. "From his family situation, to growing up in Bellevue...when you feel like a guy really fits you, that's when we were all in."

A couple weeks later, Baker announced he was de-committing from Oregon. Then, in a major coup for Petersen and the UW coaches, Baker announced his commitment to the Huskies during a live local newscast the day before National Signing Day in February 2014. "I'm a big family person. Family comes first," Baker said. "I'll be close to my family, they'll get to come see me play, so it's just a true blessing."

Family is important to Baker. His mom is a cancer survivor who has battled Crohn's disease most of her life. His need to remain close to her is part of the reason he backed out of his commitment to Oregon. "I've never quit on anything and I always try my best," he said, "and I owe that all to her."

In 2014 Budda Baker had his locker situated right next to Shaq Thompson's. Like Thompson, Baker became a starter immediately for the UW defense, taking over as the free safety as a true freshman. And like Thompson, Baker was soon a star. As a sophomore

One of Chris Petersen's first and most important recruits, Budda Baker patrols the field in 2015. (AP Images)

the 5'9", 175-pound Baker was named to the All-Pac-12 first team (along with fellow UW sophomore defensive back Sidney Jones).

In 2016 Baker was one of the catalysts on a team that won the Pac-12 championship and earned the program's first College Football Playoff berth. Baker earned consensus All-American honors, just the second Husky so honored in the previous 19 years. After the season Baker was one of four UW underclassmen to declare for the NFL draft, joining Jones, wide receiver John Ross, and defensive lineman Elijah Qualls. Baker (Arizona Cardinals), Jones (Philadelphia Eagles), and cornerback Kevin King (Green Bay Packers) all were selected in the second round of the 2017 NFL Draft.

70 Three Dawg Night

It was quite a sight—and quite a night for three Washington Huskies at the 2015 NFL Draft.

Wearing a formal Samoan wrap, Danny Shelton took the stage at Chicago's Auditorium Theatre and rejoiced as only the 340-pound nose tackle would—by lifting and bear-hugging Roger Goodell. Shelton then posed for cameras with the NFL commissioner and his Cleveland Browns jersey after being selected with the 12th overall pick. Shelton was the first of three Huskies selected in the first round that night, the most ever for the Washington football program.

Mercurial cornerback Marcus Peters was selected by the Kansas City Chiefs with the 18th overall draft pick. Seven picks later the Carolina Panthers drafted linebacker Shaq Thompson.

Shelton was the highest drafted defensive player from UW since Steve Emtman went first overall in the 1992 NFL Draft. "It means everything to the people who are here with me right now, to the people who are watching back home in Washington, Samoa, Australia, California…It's crazy to think that I finally made it," Shelton said.

It was an emotional night for Shelton and his family. Shelton's selection came one day before the four-year anniversary of the death of his older brother Shennon in a shooting in a Seattle suburb. Shelton wore a button featuring a picture of Shennon on his left chest at the draft.

"I know my brother's watching from up above," he said.

In his final season at Washington, Shelton had blossomed into one of the most decorated defensive linemen in school history. He earned first-team academic All-American honors, the first Husky to do since 1991 and the only player in the nation in 2014 to earn first-team All-American honors on the field and in the classroom.

The last time UW had multiple first-round picks was 1995 (Napoleon Kaufman and Mark Bruener). There were also two Huskies selected in the first round in 1992 (Emtman and Dana Hall) and in 1941 (Rudy Mucha and Dean McAdams). The program never had three first-rounders before. "I'm still speechless right now," Thompson said after his selection.

Peters, meanwhile, had done enough damage control to earn the trust of the Chiefs. In November, Peters was dismissed from the UW program by first-year coach Chris Petersen after a series of discipline issues. Multiple NFL teams were reportedly concerned enough about Peters' troubles that they dropped him entirely from the draft board, even though some scouts considered him the most talented cornerback in the draft.

Peters had 11 interceptions in 34 games over three seasons for UW. "How would I describe my style of play? Aggressive," Peters said. "I'm going to do whatever it takes to protect my island and protect my team." Peters went on to become the NFL Defensive Rookie of the Year in 2015 and was named a first-team All-Pro in 2016.

71 Happy Sack King

He was known as Hau'oli Jamora when he first burst onto the scene for the Huskies as a true freshman defensive end in 2010. He started the final seven games that season, recording one sack and 3.5 tackles for loss in UW's Holiday Bowl victory against Nebraska. The future was bright. Then, in UW's Pac-12 opener against California in late September 2011, he tore the anterior cruciate ligament in his left knee.

Eager to get back on the field, he rushed his rehabilitation, then tore the same ligament while covering Austin Seferian-Jenkins on a wheel route during the first week of training camp in August 2012. He lay on the practice field turf and prayed. If nothing else, the prayers brought him patience and a new perspective—plus a new name—for his third shot on the field in 2013.

The two major knee injuries Hau'oli Kikaha (pronounced KEY-kah-HA) sustained made him realize football wouldn't be around forever. His mother, Dawn Cockett, said her son first stated his dream of playing professional football when he was three years old, and his goals outside football are no less ambitious.

Kikaha's academic work in anthropology and ethnic studies became a passion, too. He even dreamed of becoming a professor one day. He's proud of his heritage—"He Hawai'i Au: I am Hawaiian," he said—and dreams of creating a program that will help reunite the people of the Pacific Islands.

Dr. Holly Barker doesn't doubt he can do it. Barker, a lecturer in UW's anthropology department, helped lead a group of students—including Kikaha and two of his closest friends on the football team, John Timu and Danny Shelton, among others—on a 10-day trip to Tahiti in June 2013 and she was a proud mentor for them during their college careers. "Hau'oli is one of the very smartest students I have ever had in all my years here," she said. "And I'm not putting him in the category 'as a football player.' I mean everybody. The guy is brilliant. His academic potential is whatever he wants it to be."

"Hau'oli" means "happy" in Hawaiian, his mother explained. If her happy son is being honest, though, he was angry. He changed his last name because Hau'oli never knew his father.

They didn't meet until Hau'oli was 16, when he and his teammates on Kahuki High School's judo team were competing in a tournament. Just before going to the tournament, an uncle told Hau'oli that the sensei for another team was also named Jamora—his father. "Kind of shocking," Kikaha said, looking back.

He said that his cultural passion now comes from a personal place of not knowing much about his own family's history growing up. "I didn't have that access to it," he said. "It angered me that I didn't have that access to it."

Dawn had raised Hau'oli and her two oldest sons, Kahiapo and Kila—Hau'oli's half-brothers, five and four years older, respectively—on her own. As Hau'oli put it, "The struggle was real." He believes his brothers made great sacrifices for him, and they are close—so close that Hau'oli has adopted their last name, Kaniaupio, as his middle name. He wanted to make them—and the name—proud. "Those three are really the reason I'm here," he said. "All I want to be here for is to take care of them one day. If I was [in Hawaii], I would be able to do something as a higher member in my household or family to help support everyone under us or close to us. So being here is a sacrifice, and I gotta make the best of it. And if I don't, I'm failing them."

Hau'oli and his father have built a friendly relationship off that first meeting. Still, Hau'oli had toyed with the idea of changing his last name for awhile before doing so as his 21st birthday approached in the summer of 2013. Dawn and her mother helped research their genealogy and came up with two suggestions. "He chose Kikaha—'to soar, to fly,'" she said. "And he is soaring in his life."

He was certainly soaring in his return to the Huskies. Teammates voted him a captain in 2013 despite the fact that he hadn't played in almost two years. In an early-season shutout of Idaho State, Kikaha was credited with three of UW's seven sacks in the game. "To finally have that rewarding moment was a good feeling—and short-lived because we have to get on with our lives and the next play," he said.

In 2014 Kikaha led the nation with 19 sacks, a school single-season record, en route to becoming a unanimous All-American—just the fifth player in UW history to earn the unanimous distinction. He holds UW records for career sacks (36) and single-season tackles for loss (25) and he was twice named to the Pac-12's academic first team. Kikaha was a second-round draft pick by the New Orleans Saints in 2015.

72 Huskies Shut Down Desmond Howard

Washington's 1991 defense typically played with an aggression and anger that made many an opponent crumble. The Huskies were particularly fired up to play Michigan in the Rose Bowl. Sure, cementing their national championship resume was motivation enough, but UW's defenders were irked that Heisman Trophy winner Desmond Howard, Michigan's star receiver, was getting much of the fanfare in the buildup to the Rose Bowl—and felt UW's star receiver, Mario Bailey, was getting short-changed. "The defense said they were going to stop Desmond Howard," Bailey said. "They said they were going to do it for me."

The Huskies shut down Howard—whose nickname was "Magic"—like no one had, holding him to one reception in a 34–14 victory. "Was he even out there today?" UW center Ed Cunningham said.

The defensive performance was the perfect bookend to a perfect season for Washington.

"We've known the key since November 23, when we learned we'd play Michigan," UW standout cornerback Dana Hall said. "If you shut down Desmond Howard, they become one-dimensional."

The gameplan designed by UW defensive coordinator Jim Lambright called for in-your-face man-on-man coverage from Hall and Walter Bailey. Safety Shane Pahukoa offered support over the top when necessary, and UW's outside linebackers often faked as if they were going to shadow Howard on shorter routes. The coverage seemed to confuse Michigan quarterback Elvis Grbac, who was intercepted by Walter Bailey on a long pass intended for Howard (and tipped by Pahukoa).

No one in the Big Ten had been so aggressive in defense of Howard, and Michigan was held to season lows for points and net yards (205) and made just 2-of-15 third-down conversions. "It wasn't like they just shut Desmond Howard down," Howard said. "They shut the whole offense down."

UW's defenders could sense Howard's frustration on the field. "He was going through the motions, just running his routes," Pahukoa said. Added Hall: "He got frustrated. When he wasn't getting the ball anymore, he stopped running his routes so fast."

73 Huskies in the Hall

Washington is well represented in the College Football Hall of Fame. Sixteen Huskies have been inducted. Coach Gil Dobie and halfback George Wilson were the first after getting inducted in the inaugural Hall of Fame class in 1951. A look at the 15 Huskies in the Hall:

Gil Dobie, coach, 1908–16
Inducted: 1951
Record at UW: 59–0–3
Career record: 182–45–15
Born: January 21, 1879, Hastings, Minnesota
Death: December 23, 1948, Hartford, Connecticut

George Wilson, halfback, 1923–25
Inducted: 1951
Height: 5'11"
Weight: 185
Jersey number: 33
Born: September 6, 1901, Everett, Washington
Death: December 27, 1963, San Francisco

Chuck Carroll, halfback, 1926–28
Inducted: 1964
Height: 6'0"
Weight: 190
Jersey number: 2
Born: August 13, 1906, Seattle
Death: June 23, 2003, Seattle

Paul Schwegler, tackle, 1929–31
Inducted: 1967
Height: 6'4"
Weight: 205
Jersey number: 66
Born: May 22, 1907, Raymond, Washington
Death: December 7, 1980, Newport Beach, California

Jim Phelan, coach, 1930–41
Inducted: 1973
UW record: 65–37–8
Career record: 137–87–14
Born: December 5, 1892, Sacramento, California
Death: November 14, 1974, Honolulu, Hawaii

Vic Markov, tackle, 1935–37
Inducted: 1976
Height: 6'1"
Weight: 220
Jersey number: 65
Born: December 28, 1915, Chicago
Death: December 7, 1998, Seattle

Hugh McElhenny, halfback, 1949–51
Inducted: 1981
Height: 6'1"
Weight: 197
Jersey number: 32
Born: December 31, 1928, Los Angeles

Darrell Royal, coach, 1956
Inducted: 1983
UW record: 5–5–0
Career record: 184–60–5
Born: July 6, 1924, Hollis, Oklahoma
Death: November 7, 2012, Austin, Texas

Bob Schloredt, quarterback, 1958–60
Inducted: 1989
Height: 6'0"
Weight: 190
Jersey number: 15
Born: October 2, 1939, Deadwood, South Dakota

Don Heinrich, quarterback, 1949–52
Inducted: 1987
Height: 6'0"
Weight: 180
Jersey number: 22
Born: September 19, 1930, Chicago
Death: February 29, 1992, Saratoga, California

Max Starcevich, guard, 1934–36
Inducted: 1990
Height: 5'11"
Weight: 198
Jersey number: 66
Born: October 19, 1911, Centerville, Iowa
Death: August 9, 1990, Silverdale, Washington

Rick Redman, guard/linebacker, 1962–64
Inducted: 1995
Height: 5'11"
Weight: 215
Jersey number: 66
Born: March 7, 1943, Portland, Oregon

Don James, coach, 1975–92
Inducted: 1997
Record at UW: 153–57–2
Career record: 178–76–3
Born: December 31, 1932, Massillon, Ohio
Death: October 20, 2013, Kirkland, Washington

Don Coryell, coach, 1950
Inducted: 1999
Record: 126–24–3 (college); 111–83–1 (NFL)
Born: October 17, 1924, Seattle
Death: July 1, 2010, La Mesa, California

Steve Emtman, defensive tackle, 1989–91
Inducted: 2006
Height: 6'4"
Weight: 280
Jersey number: 90
Born: April 16, 1970, Spokane, Washington

Lincoln Kennedy, offensive tackle, 1989–92
Inducted: 2015
Height: 6'4"
Weight: 325
Jersey number: 75
Born: February 12, 1971, York, Pennsylvania

Oregon attempts to block Steve Emtman, who was inducted into the College Football Hall of Fame in 2006, in 1991. (*USA TODAY* Sports Images)

74 Randy Hart

When Ikaika Malloe returned to Washington as the Huskies' new defensive line coach in December 2015, one of the first people to call and congratulate him was Randy Hart. Malloe, like so many Huskies before and after him, considered Hart a mentor, a friend, and a pillar of Washington football for more than two decades.

For 50 years Hart was a part of college football. He played for legendary coach Woody Hayes at Ohio State and then coached for 46 seasons under four Hall of Fame coaches. Hart took part in 10 Rose Bowls—one as a player, nine as an assistant coach—the second most in the history of the famed New Year's Day bowl.

At age 68 Hart retired back in Seattle to live with his wife, Linda, in 2016. "The nation won't understand just how many lives that guy has touched," said Malloe, a UW defensive back in the mid-1990s. "He really changed our lives. There were things that were way more important than football for him."

For 21 seasons, one of the longest coaching stints in UW history, Hart was a defensive assistant for the Huskies. It was Hart who helped recruit Steve Emtman, a two-star recruit defensive lineman from Eastern Washington, and molded him into the best player on the Huskies' 1991 national championship team and the No. 1 pick in the NFL draft.

In September of 2016, Hart was back in Husky Stadium for the 25-year reunion with the '91 team. The team was honored at halftime during the Huskies' game against Stanford. "Like any championship team, they just loved to play football, they respected each other, and they played for each other," Hart said of the '91 squad. "It was like a forest fire: there's a spark and then a fire and then a raging inferno."

Hart was demanding of his players. "Randy forced you to reach a limit that sometimes you didn't even understand," Malloe said. "But as a coach, he thought he was cheating us out of life [by not pushing us]. For him, the answer was always 'Yes.' It was never 'No.'…It's something I hope to accomplish. Not to be him—there's only one Coach Hart—but to make a difference in someone's life like he did for us."

Hart's coaching philosophy was simple. "They play good, I'm going to rip their ass," he said. "They don't play good, I'm going to try to pump them up…My style is not good for the NFL. I'd be locked in a locker. They'd kill me."

Hart was a standout high school player in suburban Cleveland in 1965 when Hayes called to set up an impromptu recruiting visit in the Harts' home—with only 45 minutes' notice. This was no ordinary visit. It was Thanksgiving day, and the Harts had 28 guests at their house. "That place was cleaned up," Hart recalled. "Twenty-eight people were grabbing their stuff and running out the door eating turkey wings. Woody Hayes is coming!"

An offensive guard, Hart was a member of Ohio State's 1968 national championship team and then got his first coaching job on Hayes' staff in Columbus, Ohio. He landed on Don James' staff at Washington in 1988 and then helped Stanford to three more Rose Bowls between 2010 and 2015. "I always say, 'My life has been better than most people's vacation,'" he said. "I really am a lucky guy. I know it."

75 Marshawn's Joy Ride

Regulation ended with one of the wildest plays of the Tyrone Willingham era at Washington. Leave it to Marshawn Lynch to steal the show from there. The scene: Memorial Stadium in Berkeley, California. The date: October 21, 2006. The final score: Cal Bears 31, Huskies 24 in overtime. The game is barely a footnote for the Huskies. It was the third consecutive loss in what would be a six-game losing skid in Willingham's second season at UW.

What made the game memorable was Lynch—specifically the joy ride he took on an injury cart in celebration of the Bears' victory. It's the sort of antics Seattle fans would come to know and love during "Beast Mode's" stellar run with the Seahawks from 2010 to 2015.

Late in the fourth quarter, Lynch scored the go-ahead touchdown to give Cal a 24–17 lead against the Huskies. Washington got the ball back with 1:43 left in regulation and drove to the Cal 40-yard line with six seconds left. From there, UW quarterback Carl Bonnell—who replaced injured starter Isaiah Stanback earlier in the game—heaved a Hail Mary pass that was deflected by several Cal defenders near the goal and caught by UW junior receiver Marlon Wood, who dove into the end zone for the tying touchdown as time expired.

It was an improbable play, and it was Wood's only career touchdown at UW. But it was a short-lived celebration for the Huskies, who didn't muster much of a fight in overtime. Cal had possession first in the overtime, and Lynch scored on a 22-yard touchdown run to give the Bears the lead. A Bonnell interception on UW's overtime possession ended the game.

From the sideline, a jubilant Lynch hopped in the cart and made several circles around the field as players and coaches from both teams exchanged handshakes. "I was excited, man," said Lynch, who rushed for 152 yards against UW. "In Oakland we like to express ourselves in a lot of different ways, and one way is driving."

A decade later, when the Huskies returned to Berkeley in November 2016, Cal had a Marshawn Lynch bobblehead promotion that featured the star running back riding in the cart.

"It's pretty funny that they're doing a bobblehead because I got in trouble for that, like I planned it or something," said Jeff Tedford, Cal's head coach from 2002 to 2012 who was an offensive analyst for UW during the 2016 season. "The next day I got a call from the [athletic director] saying, 'He can't be doing that.' Marshawn is so fun-loving and he was excited after a big win, had a great game, and all that. When you looked over there and saw it, it was funny. But after you sit back and look, all the fans are coming on the field. It could have been dangerous. So I get it, but he was having fun. I had to tell him, 'No more.' Keep the keys away from Marshawn. He can't take the golf cart."

As part of the bobblehead promotion, Lynch himself was on hand for the game. Just before the Bears took the field, he emerged from Cal's tunnel driving a cart—with his mom in the passenger seat—to the middle of the field as the crowd stood in applause.

76 Reggie Williams

Before arriving on campus in 2001, Reggie Williams had made it clear that he expected to start—and star—immediately for the Huskies as a true freshman. Bold and brash, Williams did start the very first game of his Washington career in a top 15 game against Michigan at Husky Stadium. But it wasn't immediately clear that Williams would be the star many others expected him to be. The first two passes Cody Pickett threw to Williams were…dropped.

Even so, Williams' confidence grew even after the missed opportunities. "I'd heard about how fast and physical the college game was," the 6'4", 215-pound Williams said. "On the first play, I got open, which is the tough part, and dropped the ball, which is the easy part. After that, I knew I could play."

He rebounded quickly, finishing with four catches for 134 yards against Michigan—the most receiving yards by a Husky in three years. A star was indeed emerging. Williams always believed he would be one. "I work harder than a lot of people," he said his senior year of high school. "Inside, you have to know you're the best. I'll really try to embarrass the DB."

Coming out of Lakes High School near Tacoma, Williams was regarded as the No. 1 wide receiver prospect in the country. "I called him every day last year it was legal to do so," UW coach Rick Neuheisel said of recruiting Williams, "and the neat thing was he never seemed tired of talking to me. There is a kid who can be as good at that position as anyone who has ever played the game."

Statistically, he's unquestionably the best receiver to don a Huskies uniform. In Neuheisel's passing offense, Pickett and Williams seemed the perfect pairing. Williams remains the most prolific receiver in program history with school records of 238 receptions and 3,536 yards in three seasons (plus 22 touchdowns), which ranked second in Pac-10 history. His 94 receptions in 2002 and 89 receptions in 2003 rank No. 1 and 2 on UW's single-season list. He was a consensus first-team All-American in 2002. Williams was especially great against rival Washington State, hauling in 11 passes for 203 yards in one Apple Cup and 12 passes for 169 yards in another. "He's been very special for this university," UW coach Keith Gilbertson said in 2003.

Williams declared for the NFL draft after his junior season, and the Jacksonville Jaguars made him the No. 9 overall pick in the 2004 NFL Draft. "I've accomplished a lot of individual goals, but we didn't win the Rose Bowl or the national championship," Williams said. "But I'll always be proud to have attended the University of Washington."

77 Pettis' Historic Punt Return

Immediately, Dante Pettis knew he was in trouble. He fielded the punt at the Washington 42-yard line...and ran four yards in the wrong direction. That's a big no-no for Washington coach Chris Petersen, who personally instructs the Huskies' punt returners in practice each week.

"I knew Coach Pete would be mad if I got tackled right there," Pettis said. "I somehow slipped out of it. The blockers did a good job of opening up space, and I just ran. That was it."

Pettis' 58-yard punt-return touchdown late in the fourth quarter lifted the No. 4 Huskies to a 31–24 victory against No. 17 Utah in Salt Lake City on October 29, 2016. That gave Pettis, UW's junior wide receiver, a new school record with five career punt-return touchdowns. After the game Petersen found Pettis on the field and gave him an emphatic high-five and a hug.

That Pettis did it against Utah was especially impressive. The Utes are known for their special teams and hadn't allowed a punt-return touchdown in seven years.

This was the most special return for Pettis—not only because it ended up being the game-winning score and not only because it came against the best punter (Utah's Mitch Wishnowsky) he'd ever faced, but also because he promised his older brother he would do it for him. "My brother had been going through a lot of stuff and I was like, 'I'm going to score a touchdown for you this game,'" said Pettis, whose brother, Kyler, is an actor on the NBC soap opera *Days of Our Lives*. "So when I got back there, I was like, 'I told him I'm going to score. This might be my last chance to do it.' And it was the perfect time to score that touchdown."

As a freshman in 2014, Pettis had his first punt-return touchdown at Colorado. Before that Washington had gone 11 years without one. It was the longest stretch without one for any Power 5 program. "What I think is really amazing about that," Petersen said of Pettis' record, "is it is much harder to return punts nowadays than it was back in the day."

Pettis says his No. 1 priority on a return is to get the ball back to the offense, first and foremost—i.e., don't fumble. The No. 2 priority is to not let the ball hit the ground. Pettis and Petersen worked together on returns daily, usually for two or three practice periods a day, and Pettis often watched film of the opposing punter each week to get a feel for what kind of kick to expect.

They're together so often that Pettis hears Petersen's voice in his head as he's fielding punts. "I've heard everything he has to say about it," Pettis said. "Any time he says something to the younger guys, I'm like, 'Yep, I could finish that sentence for you.' I've spent so much time with him back there, so definitely a lot has rubbed off. You want to have everything perfect in front of him. That's really what he expects. He expects every single rep we have to be perfect. And if not, he's on us: 'Do that rep over.'"

78 Simply Marv-elous

Marv Harshman was an icon throughout Washington state and an irritant in Oregon.

In the mid-1970s, Oregon Ducks coach Dick Harter would have a handful of his players stand at midcourt, arms folded, quietly staring down the opponents during pregame warmups. One night in Eugene, several UW players brought out Groucho Marx masks and wore them in a mock staredown before the game. Harter was furious. Harshman's Huskies won that night, and afterward the coach wore one of the masks in a celebratory UW locker room, an image captured in the Eugene newspaper the next day.

One of the most respected sports figures in state history, Harshman spent 40 years as the coach at Pacific Lutheran University (1945–57), Washington State (1958–71), and Washington (1972–85). He won 637 games as a college basketball coach and was voted into the Naismith Basketball Hall of Fame in 1985.

His legacy extends far beyond his records. He was warm and honest and he cared. "The thing I'll always remember is that Marv always treated you like you were his second family," said Chuck Curtis, who played for Harshman at Pacific Lutheran.

In the late '70s, Lorenzo Romar was a junior college guard looking to transfer to a major college school when he crossed paths with John Wooden, the famed UCLA coach. Romar asked him for advice. "I'm thinking, *Who would know better than the Wizard of*

Westwood?" Romar said. "He didn't hesitate. He said: 'If you have a chance to play for Marv Harshman, I don't think you should pass that up. He's one of the finest men and one of the finest coaches in the country.'"

Romar played two years for Harshman and then got the job as the Huskies' head coach in 2002 in part because of Harshman's recommendation. "It appealed to me, the way he taught basketball," said Detlef Schrempf, the Huskies' star forward in the early 1980s. "It was all about fundamentals. All the players took the same steps. It was based on team basketball. He didn't care about showing other people up or how many times you can dribble between your legs. He taught me how to play basketball the right way, and that had a lasting impact on me and many people."

At heart, Harshman was a teacher. "Harshman's genius," wrote *The Seattle Times*' Bud Withers, "was in squeezing every last drop from modest talent. Spare parts to somebody else were linchpins to him. Marv wasn't much for cooing in the ears of recruits. He did his best work after the kids got to campus, not before. The great John Wooden used to say that the coach whose work he admired as much as anybody's was Marv Harshman."

A graduate of Lake Stevens High School, Harshman went on to win 13 letters in four sports at Pacific Lutheran. He was twice named an All-American in football and he was selected by the Chicago Cardinals in the 1942 NFL Draft. He was also an All-Conference basketball player at PLU and then served three years in the Navy during World War II.

Jack Sullivan, a longtime television critic for the *Seattle Post-Intelligencer*, served with Harshman in the Navy. "Most competitive guy I've ever met," Sullivan once said. "One time, while we were in the Navy, he challenged me to a game of one-on-one basketball. Being taller, I beat him, barely, and it made him mad. So he challenged me to a wrestling match. He couldn't beat me because I was too big. That made him madder. So he challenged me to a boxing match. Son-of-a-bitch broke my nose."

After the Navy, Harshman played a couple seasons of semi-pro football and basketball. He then settled in as the basketball coach at PLU, leading the Lutes to four NAIA District I championships and four national tournament appearances. At Washington State, Harshman's Cougars finished second in the Pac-8 three times behind Wooden's UCLA dynasty. He moved to Seattle in 1972 and led the Huskies to four 20-win seasons, three NCAA tournament berths, and two NIT appearances. He retired with 246 victories at UW, second most in program history behind Hec Edmundson (and since passed by Romar).

In 1985 Harshman, then 68, was quietly forced into retirement by UW president William Gerberding, who wanted a younger coach. That was a mistake: Harshman had a 46–17 record—28–8 in conference—and back-to-back NCAA Tournament appearances in his final two seasons.

The program slid into mediocrity after that. It took three coaches and 13 years before the Huskies made consecutive NCAA Tournament appearances again.

In his final game against Washington State, in his penultimate game coaching at Hec Edmundson Pavilion, Harshman was surprised at halftime with a tribute from some 200 of his former players at PLU, WSU, and UW. As part of the Marv Harshman Appreciation Night, those players all chipped in to buy their coach a new $17,000 pickup truck. Harshman's eyes welled as he talked about the gesture after the Huskies' 68–55 victory against the Cougars. "That was something that made the 40 years worthwhile," Harshman said. "I was completely flabbergasted."

79 Bicentennial Breakthrough

They won their first 14 games, rose to No. 6 in the Associated Press poll, and became the first Huskies team to reach the NCAA Tournament in 23 years. For all that and more, the Huskies' 1975–76 squad ranks among the program's greatest teams. And if you ask the players from that team, they will tell you they were the greatest in program history. "I'd feel pretty good about our chances," forward Ken Lombard, the Huskies' sixth man on that team, said in 2005.

By the end of the season, the 1975–76 Huskies were the most prolific offense the program had ever produced, averaging 80.2 points per game (in an era before the three-point shot was introduced to college basketball). That scoring record stood at UW until 1984.

The Huskies had an intimidating frontcourt led by seven-footer James Edwards (17.6 points, 7.1 rebounds), one of the most accomplished centers in program history. There was also the 6'10" Lars Hansen (14.2 points, 7.5 rebounds) and 6'7" forward Kim Stewart (9.1 points, 6.3 rebounds, 4.2 assists). Clarence Ramsey (15.7 points) was an electric shooting guard, and point guard Chester "Chet the Jet" Dorsey was the catalyst. "I could get the ball wherever I wanted," said Dorsey, who graduated in 1977 as the Huskies' all-time leader in assists. "I felt there was nobody on Earth who could stop me."

The Huskies had an invincible feeling early that season. Road wins at Wyoming and Nebraska on back-to-back nights in December set the tone. The Huskies then beat Florida State, Northwestern, and Texas Tech at the Far West Classic in Portland and climbed to No. 8 in the AP poll early in January 1976. It was just the second top 10 ranking for the program since the 1953 season. (The 1970 team reached the No. 6 ranking.) "What I remember most that year is that we just didn't believe we could lose," Hansen said. "We just had an enormous amount of confidence."

The Huskies wound up staggering to a 5–5 finish to close out the season, including a disappointing first-round loss to Missouri in the NCAA Tournament. UW had clinched an NCAA berth a week before the regular season wrapped up, thus giving the team little incentive for its final two games (losses at Oregon State and at Washington State). "We got a little cocky and lost our focus," Lombard said.

With a 21–5 record, the Huskies were sent to Lawrence, Kansas, for the matchup against Missouri. UW led by 11 points in the first half and by eight points midway through the second. But Missouri rallied for a controversial 69–67 victory. Four Huskies wound up fouling out of the game—Edwards, Hansen, Dorsey, and Lombard—and Missouri attempted 31 free throws to the Huskies' 13. "It was a very strange game," UW coach Marv Harshman said.

80 Washington's Wunderkinds: Schrempf and Welp

Christian Welp didn't give any other school a chance. He wanted to play at Washington and he wanted to play alongside Detlef Schrempf. Like Schrempf, Welp grew up in West Germany and moved to Washington state for his final year of high school. During his one season at Centralia High in 1980–81, Schrempf led the Tigers to the Class AA championship and was named the tournament's MVP. Two years later Welp did the same, winning tournament MVP honors while leading Silverdale's Olympic High to a state title.

Naturally, Welp followed Schrempf to the University of Washington, too. He had signed financial aid papers with UW so early on—before his senior season at Olympic—that no other major colleges even had a chance to recruit him. And that's just how Welp wanted it. "I didn't want the phone calls," he said. "Some players on our team have been recruited. One went to parties at Pepperdine. I don't like that. I don't want to be interviewed. I want to play at the U-Dub."

In their two seasons together on Montlake—the final two seasons of Marv Harshman's coaching career—Schrempf and Welp led the Huskies to back-to-back Pac-10 championships and NCAA Tournament appearances. The seven-foot Welp looked up to Schrempf, the Huskies' 6'9" star. "I give him lots of advice," Schrempf said, "but always in English."

Harshman had a history of importing overseas talent, and Schrempf and Welp were his two best, two of the best—period—to ever play for the Huskies. Schrempf and Welp were trailblazers for German basketball players and European players in general looking to play in the U.S. "Normally, I feel that with the foreign players who have been coached overseas, it is a handicap because their team understanding is less than American kids,'" Harshman said. "But I think what was a great advantage to Detlef and Christian is that they were playing from a fairly young life for coaches who were American, mostly ex-UCLA guys. They learned more as an American would learn it. That's why I think they are a kind of breed apart."

Schrempf could do it all on the court and he often did. In his final two seasons, he led the Huskies in scoring, rebounding, *and* assists (16.8 points. 7.4 rebounds, 3.0 assists in 1983–84 and 15.8 points, 8.0 rebounds, and 4.2 assists in 1984–85). He was twice named to the All-Pac-12 first team. Oregon coach Don Monson, who helped recruit Magic Johnson to Michigan State, once called Schrempf "the white Magic."

Schrempf was flattered. "Magic Johnson's style gets me every time he plays," Schrempf said. "It's not just his skills; it's his enthusiasm. I like Dr. J because he's so controlled. He's a leader on the court. But if I could choose, I'd like to play more like Magic. I get satisfaction passing the ball—maybe too much, the coaches say."

In their first season together, Schrempf and Welp helped the Huskies to a school-record 15 conference victories in 1983–84. In the final regular-season game of the season, a 67–51 rout of Washington State in Pullman, the Huskies clinched their first conference championship in 31 years with Schrempf pouring in a team-high 27 points and Welp adding 19 points and 13 rebounds.

The Huskies' triple-overtime victory against UCLA that season is one of the program's more memorable games. Welp had 17 points and 17 rebounds in the game. That night, the UW victory led ESPN's *SportsCenter* with a dunk by Schrempf, who played all 55 minutes in the 89–81 victory, scoring 27 points in UW's longest game ever played at Hec Ed. "That's like playing four hours out on the blacktop," Harshman said. "Some guys get tired after three games and quit. Detlef is looking for somebody else to play."

In 1984 Welp was the Pac-10 Freshman of the Year and two years later the Pac-10 Player of the Year as a junior. He broke UW's all-time scoring record with 2,073 points—a record that still stands 30 years later. He also holds UW career records for made field goals (820), field-goal attempts (1,460), blocked shots (186), and 20-point games (43), and is third all time with a 56.2 career field-goal percentage.

In 2015 Welp died of an apparent heart attack at age 51, a sudden and shocking loss for the UW basketball community.

When Welp came to UW as a freshman, Harshman said that the seven-footer wasn't "as competitive as Detlef was, coming in. Detlef would fight you right away. I don't think Christian backs off, but his nature is probably a little softer. Welp is a happy player. I like that. He smiles a lot, even when you yell at him. He has great hands, a pretty good sense for the game. That's what Detlef had that captured my imagination. He has some things you don't coach—that you try to coach but never get across to the guys."

Schrempf was the eighth overall pick in the 1985 NBA Draft by the Dallas Mavericks. He played 16 seasons in the NBA, including seven back in Seattle when the SuperSonics were the toast of the town. He made three NBA All-Star teams and finished his career with averages of 13.9 points, 6.2 rebounds, and 3.4 assists.

Alongside Paul Fortier, Shag Williams, and Greg Hill, Welp led the Huskies to a third consecutive NCAA Tournament appearance in 1986. Welp was a first-round pick by the Philadelphia 76ers in 1987 and played four seasons in the NBA. He returned to Europe to play in Greece, Germany, and Italy, winning nine consecutive championships. Perhaps Welp's greatest achievement was when he scored the last three points for the German national team in its 71–70 triumph against Russia in the 1993 European Championship Game. He was named the tournament's MVP.

81 Todd MacCulloch

His NBA career prematurely cut short, Todd MacCulloch turned to the one hobby befitting a seven-foot center with soft hands and a delicate touch: pinball. *Yes, pinball.*

A decade after battling Shaquille O'Neal in back-to-back NBA Finals, MacCulloch was the host for the International Flipper Pinball Association World Championships in June 2012. Yes, he hosted the event—at his house on Bainbridge Island, a 30-minute ferry ride from downtown Seattle. MacCulloch and his family opened their doors for 64 players from 12 countries, and most of the machines used were his. At one point he owned about 80 machines. "It's a very addictive hobby and really wonderful people. I was excited to have them come and hang out here," he said. "My wife said this is like planning a wedding. But I think it's a wedding with Porta Potties. It's more of a trashy wedding. But we all love this game so much, and that's why I was willing to open my home up for these players."

Growing up in Winnipeg, Manitoba, MacCulloch didn't dream of NBA stardom. He lived mostly for the pinball machine located in one corner of his neighborhood 7-Eleven. "I grew up in Winnipeg, Manitoba, smack dab in the middle of Canada. It's very isolated and very cold for a good chunk of the year, but for some reason, the 7-Eleven Slurpee is a cultural icon beverage there," MacCulloch said. "Ever since 7-Eleven has kept records, Winnipeg has won the Slurpee Cup for per capita sales of any metro city in the world, and we're very proud of that. So I would go to 7-Eleven for my Slurpee, and most of them would have a pinball machine, and I would play pinball while drinking my Slurpee."

When he arrived at the University of Washington in 1994, MacCulloch was a seven-foot mystery, a project of massive proportions. He sat out that first season, redshirting and watching Huskies games from the end of the bench as the Huskies struggled to a 10–17 finish during the 1994–95 season. Few could have guessed then that MacCulloch would blossom into one of the premier centers the Huskies have had. "That was a difficult year—to redshirt because you weren't ready to play," MacCulloch said a few years later. "I hated it at the time, but what a blessing it has become for me. It gave me a chance to develop skills, fitness, and confidence."

MacCulloch is easygoing and humble with a dry sense of humor, and opposing post players would often try to take advantage of his friendly nature in the paint. They'd try and bully him. Early in his UW career, that often got MacCulloch in foul trouble. "There've been some guys who have wanted to prove something against me. They play me a little more physical, not really dirty," Todd said. "I just get back at them my own way by scoring and winning the game."

Coaches often tried to coax out of him a more fiery, aggressive temperament. "Other players are more confident in attacking Todd than other players, who they know when they push too hard, there might be some type of retaliation," UW coach Bob Bender said during MacCulloch's senior season in 1999. "But Todd's way is usually to punish people by getting them in foul trouble, or when he does catch it inside, to make him pay with the basket."

MacCulloch's way did wonders at UW. As a sophomore he hit the go-ahead shot against a ranked Oregon team, then raced to the other end of the court to block the Ducks' final shot, securing the UW victory. A week later he hit another game-winning shot to beat Washington State. As a junior MacCulloch helped lead the Huskies back into the NCAA Tournament for the first time in 12 years. As a No. 11 seed in the tournament, the Huskies upset Xavier and knocked out Richmond to advance to the Sweet 16, where they lost to UConn on Richard Hamilton's heartbreaking, last-second shot. MacCulloch and standout guard Donald Watts led the Huskies back to the NCAA Tournament a year later, but they lost in the first round in another tight game to Miami of Ohio (which got 43 points from All-American Wally Szczerbiak).

MacCulloch was twice named to the All-Pac-12 first team and graduated with 1,743 points, which at the time ranked third on UW's all-time scoring list (it currently ranks seventh), and his 142 blocked shots ranked No. 1 in program history (currently No. 3). For three consecutive seasons, he led the NCAA in field goal percentage—only one other player in NCAA history has done that—and MacCulloch ranks as UW's all-time leader in field goal percentage at 66.4 percent, a record that may never be broken.

As he grew at UW, an NBA career became more and more of a reality for MacCulloch, though it wasn't his life mission. "Everyone wants financial security to do what they want, be what they want, and provide for their families," MacCulloch said during his senior season. "But, at the same time, I don't want it to be my goal and whole reason for doing it. Growing up, I never expected to be playing in the NBA and I never thought I'd be a failure if I didn't play in NBA. I have a combined $6 in my two bank accounts right now, but I'm quite happy with my life."

Drafted by the Philadelphia 76ers, MacCulloch was a backup center when Allen Iverson and the 76ers advanced to the 2001 NBA Finals against O'Neal and the Lakers. A year later, after signing a $34 million free-agent contract with the New Jersey Nets, MacCulloch was back in the NBA Finals against the Lakers again. "By far, he's the best center I've ever played with," Nets star Jason Kidd once said.

During his lone season with the Nets, a painful genetic neuromuscular disorder was discovered in his feet. At times MacCulloch could hardly walk and he was forced to retire after the 2002–03 season. Pinball became his competitive outlet. At one point he was ranked among the top 125 players in the world pinball standings.

82 1953 Final Four

They were two of Seattle's brightest stars in the early 1950s—and two of the most celebrated college basketball players to ever play in the Emerald City. And for three years, there was much clamoring for a showdown between Bob Houbregs' Washington Huskies and Johnny O'Brien's Seattle University Chieftains.

They would never play against each other in Seattle, but the matchup finally came to be a few hundred miles south during the opening round of the 1953 NCAA Tournament. The game was in Corvallis, Oregon, but was the first sporting event broadcast live in Seattle. "Almost overshadowing the game itself will be the battle between Bob Houbregs of the Huskies and Johnny O'Brien of the Chieftains. The duel between those two All-American players—and there are no better anywhere in the nation—should provide tremendous thrills for the 11,000 spectators crowded into Gill Coliseum tomorrow night and the countless thousands who will view the great contest by television," *The Seattle Times* wrote in advance of the game. "The stage is set for the clash of two mighty teams. The game has been a long time in the making. It will be a topic of discussion and argument for many months after it is over."

Turns out, it wasn't much of a contest. The Huskies, with an all-senior lineup, cruised to a 92–70 victory, and the 6'7" Houbregs had his way with Seattle U, scoring 45 points and making 20 field goals—both NCAA Tournament records. Washington jumped out to a 24–11 lead at the end of the first quarter and cruised from there. UW's 92 points were also a tournament record. O'Brien had 25 points but had just six field goals (and 13 made free throws) against "a net woven around him" by UW's trio of Joe Cipriano, Mike McCutchen, and Doug McClary. (O'Brien's twin brother, Eddie, chipped in nine points.)

A day later, the Huskies were to play Santa Clara, which a year earlier had advanced to the national semifinals played at UW's Hec Edmundson Pavilion. UW and Santa Clara would play in the Corvallis regional championship game. "Stopping Bob Houbregs alone is a terrifying thought," Santa Clara coach Bob Feedrick said. "And after him you have to consider Joe Cipriano. And Charlie Koon and Mike McCutchen gave a demonstration that they can shoot as well as put up a really tight defense. McClary surely goes after those rebounds, doesn't he? Washington is truly a great team."

1953 Starting Lineup

The 1953 UW men's basketball team won the Pacific Coast Conference title with a 15–1 record and finished 28–3 overall after advancing to the NCAA Final Four. Here was UW's lineup that year:

F—Mike McCutchen, 9.8 points, 6.2 rebounds
F—Doug McClary, 6.9 points, 10.6 rebounds
C—Bob Houbregs, 25.6 points, 11.5 rebounds
G—Joe Cipriano, 12.8 points, 3.0 rebounds
G—Charlie Koon, 7.8 points, 3.7 rebounds
Sixth Man—Dean Parsons, 4.7 points, 5.0 rebounds

Under third-year coach Tippy Dye, the Huskies had won their third consecutive North division championship and then swept two games against rival California in the Pacific Coast Conference playoffs to win the conference championship for the second time in three years. A win over Santa Clara would deliver UW's first Final Four berth.

Santa Clara, led by future NBA star Kenny Sears, took a 30–22 lead in the first half before the Huskies hit their stride in the second half and won 74–62, giving them the Western regional championship. From Corvallis the Huskies bused to Portland and flew from there to Kansas City on a Sunday, where the Kansas Jayhawks awaited for a Tuesday night showdown in the national semifinals. "That game against Seattle U had been building up for four years to a crescendo," Houbregs said years later. "We were awfully high after that one. We beat them pretty bad. We were fortunate to get past Santa Clara. Then we went right to Kansas City. We practiced Monday, the semifinal was Tuesday, and the final was Wednesday. I just think we didn't have the time to regroup our emotions."

With a 26–2 record, Washington was considered the favorite over Kansas (18–5), which had won the national championship a year earlier when the Final Four was played at UW's Hec Edmundson Pavilion. Only one regular, Dean Kelley, from that championship team was back for Kansas in 1953. But Houbregs had one of the most frustrating games of his UW career, scoring only 18 points—all in the first half—and fouling out with two minutes left in the third quarter. Kansas upset the Huskies 79–53. "We picked a bad night to play our worst game in three years," Houbregs said years later. "I had four fouls in the first half and I hadn't fouled out in a game that year."

Kansas had used a punishing full-court press to throw the Huskies off their game. "We were scared going into the game, but the players were set," Kansas coach Phog Allen said. "I'll admit we played our best game of the year. Our defense worried Washington, and our fellows shot like sharpshooters. Luck was with us all the way."

Despite the disappointing finish, the 1953 team goes down as one of the greatest the Huskies have ever had.

83 Bob Rondeau

For many Washington fans, the experience of fall Saturdays is incomplete without the accompanying narration of Bob Rondeau, whose "Touchdown, Washington!" calls are a fabric of Huskies football. Rondeau began broadcasting Washington football games for KOMO radio in 1978 and has called many of the biggest games in program history. "Bob's as much a part of the Husky tradition as anyone else," said Jim Lambright, UW's head coach from 1993 to 1998. "You can listen to his broadcasts and actually see the game. He just has a marvelous voice and paints such a good picture."

In the 1978 season opener, the Huskies hosted UCLA, which represented a matchup of top 15 teams and Rondeau's first game

Craig Heyamoto

Behind the scenes Craig Heyamoto is a Seattle sports legend. He has been the stats crew chief for UW football and basketball since the 1970s and for the Seattle Seahawks since 1982.

Huskies voice Bob Rondeau called his close friend "my security blanket" for UW broadcasts. "He's a computer, an absolute computer," Rondeau said.

In 2016 Rondeau was induced into the Husky Hall of Fame. At the same ceremony, Heyamoto was fittingly presented the Don H. Palmer Award, which recognizes those who have "exemplified a special commitment to the UW Athletic Department." "It's just a small repayment for what the university has done for me," Heyamoto said.

as the color analyst, and he was alongside KOMO's Bruce King. It remains one of Rondeau's favorite memories in four decades at UW. "I remember like it has just gone by," he said. "We lost [10–7], but I remember sitting back in my chair and saying, 'We did this. We can do this.' I was wound up for days."

Two years later Rondeau took over as the play-by-play voice. He started calling UW men's basketball games in 1985. Initially, Rondeau didn't set out to be a football broadcaster. He was a young news director at a Phoenix radio station that unexpectedly folded. "When that happened," Rondeau said, "I started thinking about getting out of the business for good. But I did some nosing around and found that KOMO radio in Seattle was looking for a sports director. Until my job interview, I'd never even been to the Northwest, but I was very impressed with what I saw, to say the least."

The calling, if you will, seemed to find him. He's now one of the most revered broadcasting personalities in Seattle sports. "Some of the best things are what you didn't plan on," he said. "Sometimes you can make your own breaks and sometimes you get very lucky. I've sure had my fair share of both. It's been a fabulous ride, and I wouldn't change a thing."

In 2016 the National Football Foundation awarded Rondeau its highest honor for a broadcaster, presenting him with the Chris Schenkel Award during the NFF's annual College Football Hall of Fame induction ceremony at the Waldorf Astoria Hotel in New York. The award recognizes individuals who have had distinguished careers broadcasting college football with direct ties to a specific university. "From Day One I've always enjoyed radio," he says. "I really like the intimacy and immediacy of it all and I certainly can't imagine a better situation to be in with a college program. The UW is first class in terms of its national exposure and the way it's embraced by the community."

Another favorite memory for Rondeau occurred on July 26, 1997. It was his wedding day and it was celebrated at Husky Stadium. "The day I married Molly," he said, "has to be my perfect day and my everlasting memory. There were 300 of our friends there. Molly and I stood at the 50-yard line. Full disclosure: it was actually Molly's idea and not mine. From a personal standpoint, it was 'Touchdown, Washington!' for sure." In April of 2017, Rondeau announced he would retire following the 2017 football season.

84 Messin' with Texas

The seeds of Washington's dominance in the 1980s were planted on one windy afternoon in El Paso, Texas, in December 1979. It was there that the Huskies finished a 10–2 season with a 14–7 victory against the storied Texas Longhorns—doing so on Texas' turf—and further augmented Don James' reputation as something of a giant slayer. The Sun Bowl win came two years after James' Huskies knocked off heavily favored Michigan in the Rose Bowl. "James,"

The Seattle Times columnist Georg N. Meyers wrote, "is the copper-topped rascal with the quiet voice and deceptive smile who takes on the nation's giants with his University of Washington football teams and makes them wonder where they went wrong...What the Huskies did here in the Sun Bowl to faintly arrogant, overwhelmingly confident Longhorns of Texas was a masterpiece of treachery."

The Huskies' two touchdowns in the Sun Bowl both came in a four-minute stretch in the second quarter after Texas fumbles, and both were scored by freshmen—wide receiver Paul Skansi and running back Willis Ray Mackey. Skansi hauled in an 18-yard touchdown reception at the side of the end zone from junior quarterback Tom Flick in the second quarter. Flick's pass, Skansi said, was "thrown perfectly" in the strong windy conditions.

Mackey scored the game-winning touchdown later in the second quarter on a four-yard run up the middle, carrying a Texas linebacker on his back across the goal line. It was an especially gratifying victory for Mackey, who was the lone Texan on the Huskies' roster. Mackey, in fact, had initially committed to play for the Longhorns out of high school before changing his mind and signing with Washington. Mackey was one of the most touted recruits to ever sign with James, but the homesick running back wouldn't play another game for UW after the Sun Bowl. After winning the job as the Huskies' featured back in the spring of 1980, he went home to Texas that summer and never returned to Seattle. He didn't play another down of college football but did go on to earn his doctorate degree from Texas A&M two decades later.

Doug Martin, Stafford Mays, and Greg Grimes led UW's inspired defense, which set the tone on Texas' opening drive with a goalline stand at the UW 2-yard-line. The Huskies forced four turnovers and held Texas to 236 yards of total offense on 75 plays (3.1 yards per play).

"We capitalized on their errors," UW linebacker Antowaine Richardson said. "When you have two great teams playing against each other, the winner is going to be the one who capitalizes on errors."

The Huskies were ranked 11th in the final AP poll, and the momentum from the Sun Bowl victory helped propel them to back-to-back Pac-10 championships in 1980 and 1981. "When you start the season, you hope to win the national championship," James said. "But we had some midseason adversity and the fact that we overcame that and didn't give up pleases me."

85 Chris Polk

Before his career at Washington had really even started, Chris Polk was ready for it to end. Even as a true freshman, the 220-pound running back was expected to be one of the key contributors for the Huskies in 2008. Instead, a separated shoulder in the second game of the year wiped out Polk's season. The Huskies wound up going 0–12, and Polk began giving serious consideration to transferring to another program—or giving up football altogether. "I wish that pain upon nobody," Polk said a year later. "It was nagging and burning. I couldn't raise my arm. It was just terrible. I'd never had a serious injury like that in my life, so I really took it to heart. I blamed me for not working hard enough in the offseason, so at first I kind of gave up on myself. It got so bad, it was like I was second-guessing myself for coming here. I didn't believe in myself anymore. I didn't think football was something I wanted to do anymore."

Steve Sarkisian's arrival at UW before the 2009 season helped change Polk's mind. Polk had a previous relationship with his new coach. When Sarkisian was the offensive coordinator at USC, he had tried to recruit Polk to the Trojans. Polk chose UW instead. "I loved his versatility," Sarkisian said. "And I loved the ability he had to play violent. He had a tendency to run people over. And that's what he's shown for us now. He's getting more confidence that his shoulder's fine. He's able to lower that shoulder. He's showing good speed, good elusiveness, and good hands."

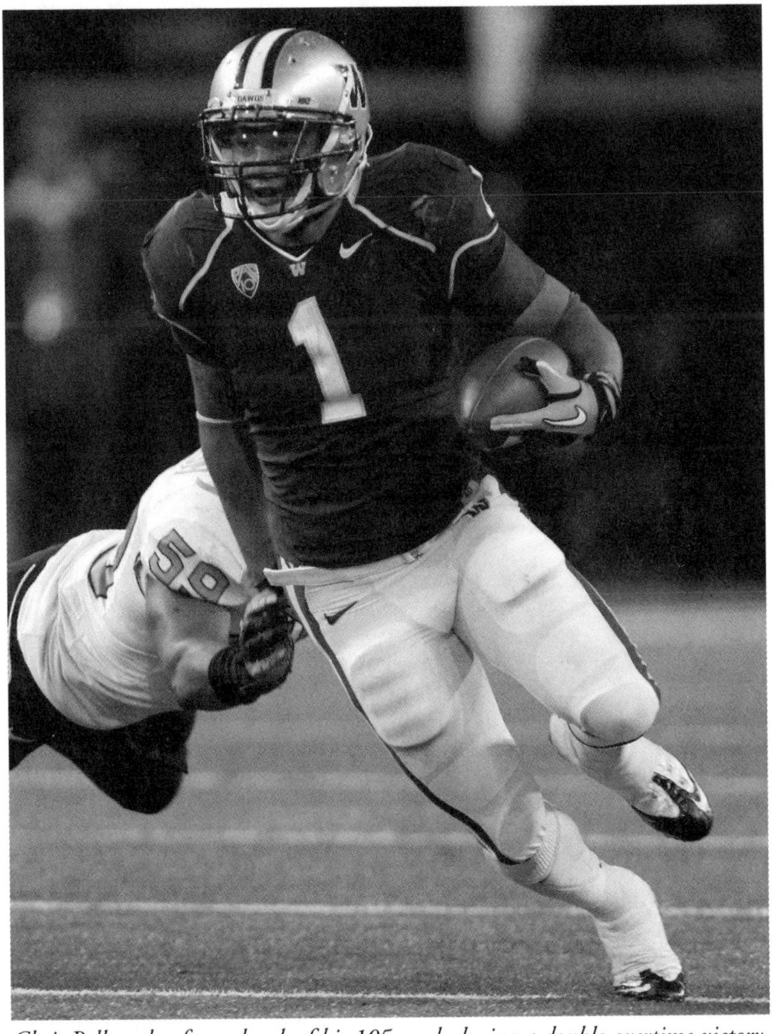

Chris Polk rushes for a chunk of his 105 yards during a double-overtime victory against Oregon State in 2010. (AP Images)

It was a rejuvenated Polk, paired with star quarterback Jake Locker, who helped lead the Huskies' return to relevance following the 2008 debacle. "I told myself that in the offseason I was really going to work hard, so that when the new coaches got here I would have something to show them," Polk said entering the 2009 season. "And thank God it was the coaches who recruited me. I knew them, and they knew me. It's way better now. I actually have a perspective on football again. I'm actually positive about football again. I can't wait to get out there now and show people what I can do."

He showed 'em, all right. In three seasons from 2009 to 2011, Polk established himself as one of the best backs in school history, finishing second on UW's all-time rushing list with 4,049 yards (trailing only the 4,106 yards of Napoleon Kaufman, who played four seasons). Polk's 799 career carries are a school record, and at the time so was his career average of 101.2 yards per game. (In his first two seasons, Myles Gaskin averaged 101.6 yards per game in 2015–16.)

The debate rages on about the best back in school history. Hugh McElhenny (1949–51) is generally seen as having the overall edge. Among modern backs, there seems to be no wrong choice between Polk, Kaufman, Greg Lewis, and Corey Dillon. "Napoleon was more of a speed, downhill back, which is nothing against Chris because he has the speed in the open field to run away from guys, too," said Damon Huard, who was Kaufman's quarterback. "I guess the biggest difference might be the size. Chris is more of a bruiser. Both get the job done. Both are exciting players. They're the two best backs to ever play at this school. Chris is more of a punishing back, the way guys bounce off him, the way he gets stronger as the game goes on. I think Chris is even more of a complete back because of his ability to catch the ball out of the backfield and to pass protect."

Polk's 21 career 100-yard games are the most in school history. He had his best game in the 2010 Apple Cup, when he rushed

29 times for 284 yards—the second best single-game total in UW history behind McElhenny's 296 yards against Washington State in the 1950 Apple Cup. Better yet, Polk's performance helped the Huskies finish the regular season with a 6–6 record, making them bowl eligible for the first time in eight years. "You know, it feels great," Polk said. "You're just going to have to treat it like any other game. Being that it was the Apple Cup and we're bowl-eligible, it's just that much sweeter."

Polk was a first-team All-Pac-12 pick in his final season in 2011, when he rushed for a career-high 1,488 yards and 12 touchdowns.

86 Get in Line

Greg Lewis knew whom to thank for much of his success as the Huskies' standout running back from 1987 to 1990. "People always ask me: 'What was your best asset as a running back? Was it your speed? Your strength? Your size?'" Lewis said. "I always tell them, 'No, it was my offensive line.' The offensive line that I ran behind put quite a few people in the NFL."

Indeed, five offensive linemen from UW's 1990 Pac-10 championship team went on to be drafted in the NFL—Dean Kirkland and Jeff Pahukoa in 1991, Ed Cunningham and Siupeli Malamala in '92, and Lincoln Kennedy in '93—continuing the Huskies' impressive lineage of offensive line stalwarts.

From 1937 to 2001—from Rudy Mucha to Curt Marsh to Bern Brostek to Olin Kreutz, and on and on—Washington produced 78 offensive linemen who were drafted in the NFL or about 1.2 per year. "Growing up around here, I knew about Blair Bush [the starting center on the 1977 Rose Bowl team] and Bern Brostek [an All-American in 1989]," said Kyle Benn, a Seattle-area native and the starting center on UW's 2000 Pac-10 championship team. "Everyone always looked at UW as 'Quarterback U' or 'Tight End U,' but it was 'Line U' in my mind. Those were the guys I was watching. I knew how dominant they were."

Of the 11 Washington players elected into the College Football Hall of Fame, five are offensive linemen: Paul Schwegler (1929–31), Vic Markov (1935–37), Max Starcevich (1934–36), Rick Redman (1962–64), and Kennedy (1989–92). The Huskies, however, went through a 15-year dry spell without a first-team All-Conference offensive lineman from 2001 to 2016, certainly a contributing factor to the program's struggles for much of that period. Similarly, since 2002 Washington has produced just three NFL draft picks on the offensive line.

Benn was a first-team all-Pac-10 selection as a senior in 2001. The Huskies didn't have another first-team pick until senior guard Jake Eldrenkamp and sophomore tackle Trey Adams were chosen from the 2016 Pac-12 championship team. (Eldrenkamp was also named the Pac-12's Scholar-Athlete of the Year.)

Under the tutelage of offensive line coach Chris Strausser, the line stayed healthy in 2016 and helped the Huskies set a school record in averaging 41.8 points per game. It's no coincidence that with that stability up front, the 2016 Huskies won the program's first conference title in 16 years. "Line U" is back. "With Strausser, I really like what he's doing with those guys. His philosophy is what we want and what we need," Benn said. "You're seeing it slowly materialize, and you want to build something that's going to last every year and have for that next generation. You want those ninth graders right now going, 'I want to play for them.'"

87 Skansi's Miracle Catch

Three days each week, Paul Skansi commuted from his home in Poulsbo and head back to the Washington football offices. There, using his 15 years' experience as an NFL scout, he volunteered his time to break down film of the Huskies' upcoming opponents. Thirty-five years after he made one of the most memorable plays in Apple Cup history, Skansi was still playing a part, however small, in helping the Huskies during their breakthrough 2016 season. "I hope it helps a little bit," said Skansi, who graduated in 1982 as the Huskies' all-time leading receiver.

Skansi was particularly eager for the 2016 Apple Cup. With the Pac-12 North title on the line, the 109th Apple Cup was one of the biggest ever. The stakes hadn't been so great for both sides since the 1981 game in which Washington won its second straight Pacific-10 conference championship—by stealing the crown away from the Cougars on a chilly November afternoon at Husky Stadium.

Skansi had the starring role for the Huskies in that game. It was his diving touchdown reception on a wayward Steve Pelluer pass that dramatically altered the teams' fortunes that day, a play that ranks as one of the three greatest Apple Cup catches right there with Spider Gaines' miracle reception from Warren Moon in 1975 and Philip Bobo's diving grab from Drew Bledsoe in the 1992 Snow Bowl.

Skansi took a most unusual route to finish the play. He had broken free in the far right corner of the end zone—only to turn back and see that Pelluer's wobbling pass was well underthrown and heading right into the arms of WSU cornerback Nate Bradley. But as the ball arrived, Bradley slipped just enough on the AstroTurf to give Skansi a chance to dive back toward the goal line and go over the top of Bradley to make the improbable catch. "The field was a little slick. It was wet," Skansi recalled. "I got to the back of the end zone, saw the ball coming up, fluttering and I think the DB slipped in front of me. I dove back over. The ball was just fluttering up in the air, and I dove on top of him."

From the Huskies' sideline on the far side of the field, UW kicker Chuck Nelson didn't have the best angle on Skansi's catch. It wasn't until later that he had "the sense of wonder I certainly had when I saw the replay. I thought, *How'd that happen?* It went from interception to touchdown in about five feet. It was obviously a nice turning point in the game for us."

The touchdown came with less than 10 seconds left in the second quarter and gave the Huskies a 10–7 halftime lead. The Cougars had lost Clete Casper to a hamstring injury in the first half and they couldn't overcome their six turnovers. The Huskies went on to win 23–10, sending them back to the Rose Bowl for the second straight year and spoiling the Cougars' hopes of their first Rose Bowl berth in 51 years.

The Cougars did finish the regular season 8–2–1, their best season since 1930. But after the game, WSU coach Jim Walden said it was the most disappointing defeat of his career. To win the conference title, however, the Huskies went into the game, knowing that USC had to beat UCLA. And when the Trojans did win—22–21 after blocking a late UCLA field-goal attempt—the USC victory was announced over the public address system midway through the Apple Cup, much to the delight of Husky fans. "We had been in the Rose Bowl the year before [losing to Michigan] and we were determined to go back and win," Nelson said. "That was a nice confluence of factors. It was effectively a playoff game. We had to win to advance. To get a win in a situation like that is kind of the ultimate of why you compete. We had great respect for [the Cougars]. They were good. We were good. The rivalry piece—with everything on the line—there was lot of reasons to feel good about winning."

Skansi, a Gig Harbor native who went on to play eight seasons for the Seahawks and spent the past 15 years as a scout for the San Diego Chargers, still ranks fifth all time at UW with 161 receptions. None was bigger than his catch in the 1981 Apple Cup. He proudly noted that the Huskies were 3–1 against the Cougars during his UW career, though the end of his senior season was spoiled when WSU upset the Huskies in Pullman in 1982, keeping UW out of a third straight Rose Bowl.

88 Jennifer Cohen

Inside the Washington football offices, the Husky Marching Band lined a hallway and played the school's fight song as Jennifer Cohen took center stage for her formal introduction as Washington's new athletic director in May 2016. The gathering featured many Huskies coaches, athletes, staffers, and supporters, and it felt like a celebration of Cohen's vision for a promising future for UW athletics as much as a rekindling of the past glory.

Infatuated with the Huskies, Cohen grew up during the heyday of the Don James era, relishing Saturdays at Husky Stadium with her family and her favorite team. "My favorite tradition on gameday was going down to the tunnel and barking at the opponent. I would legitimately bark," she said. "This place is woven into every fabric of my being of who I am."

When she was in the fifth grade in University Place, near Tacoma, Cohen penned a letter to James, whom she idolized. She wrote to James that she was hoping to succeed him one day as the Washington Huskies football coach. "That is a really great idea," James wrote back to her, as Cohen recalled. "But girls are not really getting that opportunity very often...but they are going into the business of sport." That was all the motivation she needed. "I had this crazy idea as a kid that I was going to work here," she said.

Cohen's correspondence with Coach James didn't stop with that one letter. The coach tried to respond to every fan letter, but he grew fond of the young fan from University Place who would always track him down for a photo op during UW's annual Picture Day event before each season. They kept in touch over the years and more so after Cohen began working in the UW athletic department as an assistant director of development in 1998.

She now keeps a framed picture of her and Coach James taken at Husky Stadium during her first week on the job on her office wall. "I still remember the first day I drove in [for work at UW in '98] and just the goose bumps of, gosh, this childhood dream came true. A naïve one, but it ended up being my life's passion," she said. "I feel really lucky."

As one of UW's senior associate athletic directors, Cohen helped lure Chris Petersen away from Boise State in December 2013. Three years later, in Cohen's first season as athletic director, Petersen and the Huskies won the program's first Pac-12 championship in 16 years.

"When I look at what this place stands for as a university and as an athletic department...and then I look at Chris Petersen, I just can't picture somebody that's a better match," she said. "He makes everybody around this place better. Personally, he has made me a lot better. He has high expectations every day of every person, starting with himself. And he is so consistent with that and he is so thorough with that and so thoughtful with that and he is so unselfish with it, and you can see that style and that approach already reaping benefits."

Cohen's promotion as new athletic director was lauded by many in and around the department, including Petersen. "I've been impressed with her since the day I got here—her day-to-day interactions, how she deals with people, how sharp she is, solves problems," he said. "She knows what this place is about and she knows where this place needs to go."

Cohen became the only female athletic director in the Pac-12 and one of just three among the 65 Power Five conference schools. UW president Ana Mari Cauce and Cohen are also the only female president/AD combination among those 65 schools. "My entire career, I really haven't thought a lot about my gender," Cohen said. "I really wanted to work hard and prove myself on my own merits, which I think I have. That being said, there's something really special about that. I want women on my staff and folks across the country, I want them to be able to see that women can do it, and if there aren't women doing it, they're not going to see that they can. So I take that role seriously and I'm honored to be able to do that for other women."

89 Sing "Bow Down"

The University of Washington's official fight song is called "Bow Down to Washington," which was written in October 1915 by Lester J. Wilson as part of a contest by the student newspaper, *The Daily*. Wilson couldn't read music but wrote the lyrics and entrusted a friend to put the music to paper. For writing the winning entry, Wilson was awarded a $25 prize.

The song debuted in a game at Denny Field, the football's team's home field at the time, against Whitman College on October 30, 1915. Washington won 27–0. A week later "Bow Down" debuted as Washington's official fight song for a game against rival California—a game Gil Dobie's UW team won 72–0.

Wilson copyrighted the song and turned proceeds over to the university. He later wrote "Bow Down to Uncle Sam" during the First World War, using the same melody as "Bow Down to Washington" but with different lyrics.

The lyrics have been altered on several occasions since 1915 (initially to take out a reference to Dobie, the legendary coach who left UW following the 1916 season). Here is the most recent rendition, which was last updated in 1997:

Bow Down to Washington,
Bow Down to Washington,
Mighty Are the Men
Who Wear the Purple and the Gold,
Joyfully We Welcome Them
Within the Victors Fold.
We Will Carve Their Names
In the Hall of Fame
To Preserve the Memory of Our Devotion.
Heaven Help the Foes of Washington;
They're Trembling at the Feet
Of Mighty Washington,
The Boys Are There With Bells,
Their Fighting Blood Excels,
It's Harder to Push Them Over the Line
Than Pass the Dardanelles.
Victory the Cry of Washington…
Leather Lungs Together
With a Rah! Rah! Rah!
And O'er the Land
Our Loyal Band
Will Sing the Glory
Of Washington Forever.

90 A Defensive Renaissance

After the 2014 season, the Huskies graduated seven starters off their defense, including three first-team All-Americans—Danny Shelton, Hau'oli Kikaha, and linebacker Shaq Thompson. Star cornerback Marcus Peters, who would join Shelton and Thompson as first-round NFL draft picks, was also gone. So the prospect of retooling the defense entering the 2015 season seemed especially daunting for UW defensive coordinator Pete Kwiatkowski. And yet here was Kwiatkowski's approach to that challenge: "This," he said, "is fun stuff. That's the beauty of college football…Every year, someone is leaving, and someone is coming in."

He was right.

Few outside the program could have reasonably projected what would happen next during the 2015 and '16 seasons—a defensive resurgence that would stir comparisons to the great UW defenses of the 1980s and '90s. In 2014 the UW defense ranked third in the Pac-12, allowing 24.8 points per game. Given the enormity of the personnel losses, the results in 2015 were stunning: the Huskies led the Pac-12 in scoring defense (18.8 points) and total defense (351.8 yards).

With its nucleus returning intact, the Huskies were even better on defense during the program's breakthrough 2016 season, allowing 17.7 points per game and 316.9 yards per game.

"This defense, we're stout and we're hungry," linebacker Keishawn Bierria said. "That's the best thing. We'll keep coming at you."

The Huskies began calling themselves the "Death Row" defense and they lived to punish.

"We don't want any points on the board," All-American safety Budda Baker said. "That's our goal. No first downs, all that type of stuff. Ultimately, we just want to help our offense get the ball, stop their offense."

UW's defense led the nation in takeaways in 2016 with 33 total turnovers forced—19 interceptions and 14 fumbles recovered. "We're always talking about creating turnovers, but we're not unique in that sense," Kwiatkowski said. "Every football team in America says they want to win the turnover battle, and we're no different. So you start with that. You create drills, teach good habits, diagram schemes, and stress the importance of getting the ball out...Then you kind of have to wait and see what happens."

The Huskies were especially dominant in their 2016 Pac-12 championship game victory against Colorado, holding the Buffaloes to 10 points, 163 yards of total offense, and forcing three turnovers.

A few weeks later in the buildup to their College Football Playoff semifinal matchup, Alabama coach Nick Saban had lofty praise for UW's defensive secondary, comparing it to the Seattle Seahawks' vaunted "Legion of Boom." Baker, cornerback Sidney Jones, defensive lineman Elijah Qualls, and linebacker Azeem Victor were all named to the all-Pac-12 first team in 2016 with Bierria and defensive lineman Vita Vea earning second-team recognition. Defensive tackle Greg Gaines, cornerback Kevin King, and linebacker Psalm Wooching were honorable mention selections.

Kwiatkowski, a longtime assistant under Chris Petersen, had shifted to a 3-4 defensive front before the 2015 season, and UW players have labeled him a defensive "genius" and "mastermind." "Any time we're having problems, the adjustments are there," Bierria said. "He always has the answer for something and he always plays on players' strengths. He wouldn't send a guy on the blitz if he hasn't been doing well that game. He always makes good adjustments, not only what we're seeing offensively, but what we're seeing defensively, too. That's just traits of a great coach."

"He knows how offenses are going to try to beat us and he can counteract that," King said. "Having a guy like that is game-changing."

91 UW's All-Time Team

The greatest players in Huskies history? It's a heck of a list to choose from—and a heck of a debate to select an all-time first team and an all-time second team. Here's my list:

First team

Offense

QB: Marques Tuiasosopo
RB: Hugh McElhenny
RB: Napoleon Kaufman
WR: Mario Bailey
WR: Reggie Williams
TE: Mark Bruener
OL: Lincoln Kennedy
OL: Max Starcevich
OL: Rudy Mucha
OL: Vic Markov
OL: Paul Schweger

Defense

DL: Steve Emtman
DL: Ron Holmes
DL: Tom Greenlee
DL: Hau'oli Kikaha
LB: Rick Redman
LB: Dave Hoffmann
LB: Michael Jackson
DB: Dana Hall
DB: Lawyer Milloy
DB: Budda Baker
DB: Al Worley
PK: Chuck Nelson
P: Skip Boyd

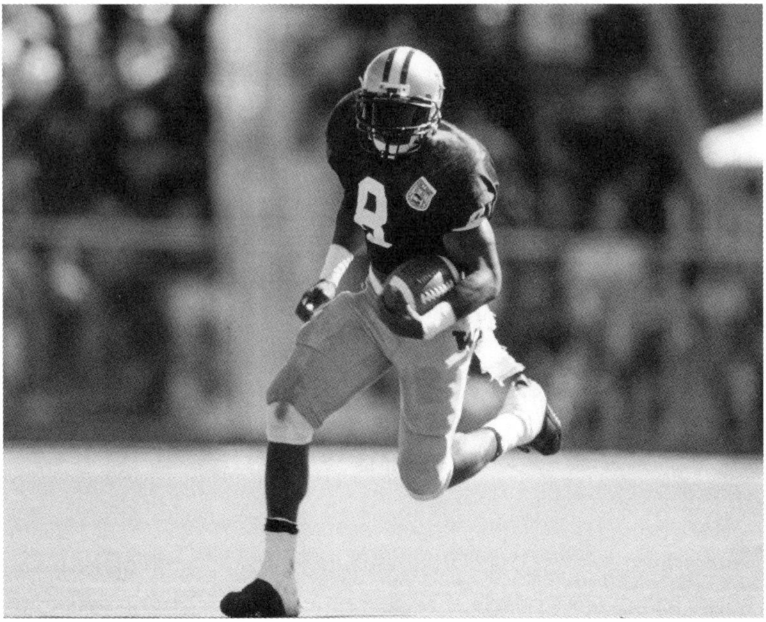

Napoleon Kaufman, who runs for yardage in 1994, deserves a spot on any all-time Washington team. (*USA TODAY* Sports Images)

Second team

Offense

QB: Warren Moon
RB: Chuck Carroll
RB: Greg Lewis
WR: John Ross III
WR: Paul Skansi
TE: Austin Seferian-Jenkins
OL: Benji Olson
OL: Olin Kreutz
OL: Blair Bush
OL: Bern Brostek
OL: Chad Ward

Defense

DL: Danny Shelton
DL: Larry Tripplett
DL: D'Marco Farr
DL: Reggie Rogers
LB: Donald Jones
LB: Mark Stewart
DB: Ray Horton
DB: Calvin Jones
DB: Sidney Jones
DB: Nesby Glasgow
PK: Jeff Jaeger
P: Rich Camarillo

92 Read *Boys in the Boat*

The Husky Clipper, the famous racing shell constructed by George Yeoman Pocock, still hangs in the University of Washington crew house more than 80 years after the Huskies' 1936 eight-oar varsity crew rowed onto the world stage with a gold medal performance in the Berlin Olympics. In his best-selling book published in 2013, *Boys in the Boat,* Daniel James Brown tells the remarkable story of the young men who rowed to Olympic glory in Nazi Germany in perhaps the greatest crew race of all.

Brown brilliantly crafts together the many layers of history to tell the complete tale of UW's rise as a rowing powerhouse—from the young rowers who endured many hardships growing up during the Great Depression; to their rugged coach, Al Ulbrickson, and his right-hand man, Pocock; to the political propaganda and growing unrest in Nazi Germany; to the thrilling races.

Initially, Brown was inspired after meeting Joe Rantz, one of UW's veteran rowers on the 1936 team. Rantz, who had been abandoned by his family as a teenager, was left to fend for himself and worked odd jobs and spent summers in brutal heat on the Grand Coulee dam to pay his way through school at UW. "I had that tingle the first day [after meeting Rantz]," Brown told *The Seattle Times* in a 2014 interview. "The big arc of the story—these rough-and-tumble kids rowing their boat against Hitler…as I dug into it, it got richer and richer, though you never know. Sometimes the story sounds good, then it fizzles out. It wasn't until six months or a year later that I started talking to the other families of the boys in the boat…I became more optimistic. They could have been jerks, but they turned out to have interesting back stories."

Hitler himself attended the Olympic championship race. Despite setting a world record in one of earlier heats, the UW crew was given poor starting position on the outside, and the crews from Germany and Italy were given preferential inside lanes. Still, the Huskies were able to pull together and rally from third to first over the final 200 meters to claim gold in a dramatic photo finish. For the Huskies "their grimaces of pain turned suddenly to broad white smiles, smiles that decades later would flicker across old newsreels, illuminating the greatest moment of their lives," Brown wrote.

"I make the case—at the end of every book talk—that these nine Americans, who climbed in the boat and learned to pull together, [are] almost the perfect metaphor for what that generation did," Brown says. "They endured the Depression and the war. Pull together, build great teams, get things done."

93 Kelsey Plum

As she broke record upon record, Kelsey Plum cemented her legacy in 2017 as the greatest women's basketball player ever at Washington—and one of the most decorated in NCAA history. It is a delicate, incongruent balance, but few have combined grace and tenacity as well as Plum.

Both qualities were on full display in the Huskies' upset of 11th-ranked Stanford, one of the more notable wins in program history, at the 2016 Pac-12 Conference tournament at Seattle's KeyArena. Plum, a 5'8" junior point guard from Poway, California, was as good as ever that night. She drove around double (and triple) teams, she swished pull-up three-pointers, she zipped cross-court passes to teammates forgotten in a far corner. She finished with 29 points that night, breaking the Huskies' all-time scoring record in the process. She was also hit with a technical foul after wrestling for loose ball, during which she flailed and blindly (and unintentionally, she said) hit a Stanford player in the mouth with the back of her hand, drawing blood.

Growing up in Poway as the youngest in a family of ultra-competitive athletes, Plum played football in the yard with her brother and cousins. Her intensity had long been nurtured.

"I'm just competitive and I want to win," Plum said. "Sometimes I get overly competitive. I think that would come from my family. I was the youngest girl [among four siblings]. I have a younger brother, but he's 6'3", 235, so he's not really the little brother, you know? I was the baby and I got hammered growing up in everything—physically, mentally. Now I'm not the baby anymore, but I still walk around like I've got to prove everything all the time."

As a senior in 2016–17, Plum became the first Pac-12 player—man or woman—to score 3,000 points. She averaged 26.2 points per game as a junior and led the Huskies to their first Final Four berth and was even better as a senior, leading the country with an average of 31.7 points per game en route to breaking Jackie Stiles' 20-year-old record (3,393 points) as the most prolific scorer in women's Division I history.

She broke the record with a remarkable 57-point outburst in her final regular-season home game, converting 19-of-28 field goals, including 6-of-11 three-pointers and 13-of-16 on free throws, in a victory against Utah. "It was pretty special," Plum said. "It was kind of icing on the cake. Getting the win on Senior Night with my family here and then that ceremony after just kind of put it into perspective. This was an amazing day."

Yet whenever she was asked about individual records, Plum offered little more than a shrug. Her desire to excel has been genuine but largely in the context of leading her team to something more, something better. "She chose to come to Washington during a time when we weren't making the NCAA Tournament," UW coach Mike Neighbors said. "She was one of the first McDonald's All-Americans in the country to choose a place that didn't have NCAA Tournament pedigree. She wanted to go someplace and be a part of something really special and building that."

Plum oozed confidence. As a touted freshman, she arrived at Washington and told veteran teammates she planned to break records. She put the Pac-12 on notice, too. "Kelsey's an enormously talented player and she's a fierce, fierce competitor," Washington State coach June Daugherty said. "She is so focused and has so much intensity about what she is [doing]. She is in the moment all 40 minutes."

Over her final three seasons, Plum led the league in minutes played. As a sophomore she did so while playing on a torn meniscus that required offseason surgery. As a junior she played 39 minutes a game and brought the ball up the court on virtually every possession. The focal point of every opponent's gameplan, she played her senior season with the added attention of chasing the all-time scoring record. "I think you can shut her down for maybe a quarter, but it's like the *Jaws* music. At some point the shark's going to come out. You'll be looking around wondering when it's going to happen," Pac-12 Networks analyst Mary Murphy said. "She's just fantastic. What can you say?" Plum went on to be the No. 1 overall pick in the 2017 WNBA Draft by the San Antonio Stars.

94 Women's Final Four

Late on a Sunday night in March 2016, after the Washington women's basketball team's chartered flight was delayed on its return from Kentucky to Seattle, the team bus finally rolled back onto the UW campus just before 10:00 PM. Just hours after pulling off yet another major upset in the NCAA Tournament, the Huskies expected maybe a few fans to show up and greet their arrival home. Instead, 100 supporters strong were there as the Huskies disembarked from the bus, joining in the celebration of the program's first berth to the Final Four. "When we got off that bus—honestly, I was like, 'It's cold, it's late, we're late. There might be a handful of [UW] staff,'" UW senior forward Talia Walton said. "No, the show-out was tremendous, and we really appreciate it."

There was much to celebrate. The most improbable postseason march in UW basketball history was also among the most unlikely tournament runs in its history. As a No. 7 seed, the Huskies were the lowest seed to advance to the women's Final Four in 12 years. They were also just the second team in history to reach the Final Four after finishing the regular season unranked (joining Arkansas, which reached the national semifinals as a 9 seed in 1998).

Led by Walton, Kelsey Plum, and Chantel Osahor, UW advanced to the Final Four while crisscrossing the country three times in two weeks, toppling giant after giant in a storybook postseason. "I think a lot of people are starting to fall in love with this team because they relate to somebody on the team," said Plum, the Huskies' All-American point guard. "Whether someone in their family had cancer—like Katie [Collier], or somebody walked on and didn't really get a shot at first and kept persevering—like 'Lex' [senior guard Alexus Atchley], or somebody went through some injuries and just kind of battled—like 'T' [Talia Walton], they've just kind of taken heart around the country, and people are starting to see, 'I don't have to be a 6'5", 200-pound athletic player that can dunk to succeed.' And I think people are starting to realize that and I think that's why we've been fun to watch."

Their postseason run got off to an inauspicious start. Playing their first-round game in College Park, Maryland, the Huskies actually trailed 10th-seed Pennsylvania 13–7 at the end of the first quarter. Plum (24 points, seven assists) then led the charge en route to a 65–53 victory—UW's first NCAA tournament victory in 10 years.

That set up a showdown with host Maryland. The second-seeded Terrapins finished the season ranked No. 5 in the AP poll. Plum's 32 points, six rebounds, and seven assists led the way as the Huskies notched their first upset of the tournament and advanced to the Sweet 16 for the first time since 2001. "It was a feeling that I can't really describe," Plum said. "I think it's just like all the doubters that have told our team that we're not good enough, or all the people that told me that Washington was the wrong school, or [Mike] Neighbors was the wrong coach. I just think in that moment, God said, 'You know what? Nope, you're right where you are and you're right where you're supposed to be.'"

The Huskies' Sweet 16 matchup looked just as daunting with another East Coast trip to face No. 3 seed Kentucky on its home court. No matter: Walton had a torrid shooting performance, hitting 14-of-25 shots for 30 points to lead the Huskies to an easy 85–72 upset of the Wildcats. Osahor had 19 points, 17 rebounds, and five assists, and Plum overcame a cold start to finish with 23 points, six rebounds, and seven assists. "Our group today was about as good as we've played," UW coach Mike Neighbors said, "and I think we're peaking at the right time."

Two days later on Kentucky's famed Rupp Arena court, the Huskies faced off against Pac-12 powerhouse Stanford, the region's

No. 4 seed. Under legendary coach Tara VanDerveer, Stanford was making its 16th appearance in the Elite Eight; the Huskies were there for the first time. In a wildly entertaining game, Osahor was the difference. The 6'2" forward hit two flat-footed three-pointers as the Huskies jumped out to a 12–0 lead and she finished with 24 points and 18 rebounds in an 85–76 victory, sending UW to Indianapolis for the national semifinals.

"I don't think it's really hit us. We're in the Final Four," Osahor said. "It's an opportunity that a lot of people never get."

As is custom, the Huskies cut down the nets in celebration of the Final Four berth. "I've heard people say a lot of times it's surreal and it's numbing, but it really is," said Neighbors, UW's third-year coach. "I thought they were full of it."

After a fun buildup at the Final Four, the Huskies came out flat in their national semifinal against Syracuse. The Orange employed a devastating full-court press, which took the ball out of Plum's hands and the wind out of the Huskies' sails. UW's magical march came to a halt with an 80–59 loss in Indianapolis. "I told them: this is the kind of thing where they bring you back when you're 60 and 70 years old and celebrate," Neighbors said after the game. "I'm sad right now, but inside I'm almost going to be jubilant in about 20 minutes because it's been so much fun watching these kids enjoy this ride."

Walton was a bright spot for the Huskies, hitting her first eight three-point attempts—a Final Four record—and finishing with 29 points on 10-of-15 shooting in her final game for the Huskies. "This is kind of a fairy tale, you know," Walton said. "You see those movies where the underdog wins and all that, and that's basically what this has been...This is definitely something that I will remember for the rest of my life."

95 Uncle Hec

He was a runner first, always a runner. Born and raised in Moscow, Idaho, Clarence Edmundson used a pair of his mother's cast-off rubber soles for his first track shoes and then he would time himself at frequent intervals while running around town. "Aw, heck!" the critical boy would say after checking his time. So his mom nicknamed him "Hec."

He became a track star for his hometown University of Idaho Vandals, winning the 800-meter race at the 1908 U.S. Olympic Trials. At the 1912 Olympic Games in Stockholm, he finished sixth in the 400-meter run and seventh in the 800.

From there, he naturally turned to coaching, getting his start back home at Idaho. By 1920, at the age of 33, Edmundson was hired as the Washington Huskies' track coach. Here's how he described his transition into coaching: "I ran against them in every event, outside the hurdles, and won them all that year. The next year I had my appendix out and had to start asking for handicaps. When you reach handicap stage, it's time to quit running."

The following year, in 1921, Edmundson started to make a new name for himself in another sport: basketball. He kept his track philosophies when he took over as the UW basketball coach and he's long been credited as "the father of the fast break." The faster you run, he believed, the more you'll score. And the more you score, the more you'll win. "He transformed the stodgy, dainty, low-scoring game of the past into the run-run-run, basket-a-minute game of the future," *The Seattle Times* wrote.

He never quit running. Teaching it to others was his gift. In 27 years as the Huskies' basketball coach, "Uncle Hec" won four Pacific Coast Conference championships and 10 Northern

Division titles. He's UW's all-time winningest coach with a record of 488–195, a remarkable 71 percent winning percentage. From 1921 to 1940, the Huskies had 19 consecutive winning seasons under Edmundson.

He coached six All-Americans in basketball, starting with guard Alfie James in 1928 and ending with guard "Battleship" Bill Morris in 1943. In 36 years as UW's track coach, his teams won eight Northern Division titles and three PCC crowns. Thirteen of his track and field athletes have been inducted into the Husky Hall of Fame, and three won medals in the Olympic Games: discus thrower Gus Pope (1920, bronze), hurdler Steve Anderson (1928 silver), and shot putter Herman Brix (1928, silver).

Edmundson is a Hall of Famer in both sports. He died in August 1964 at age 78 after a series of strokes.

On December 27, 1927, Edumndson helped dedicate the multi-purpose structure, then called Washington Pavilion, with a 34–23 win against Illinois. In 1948, a year after he stepped down as basketball coach, that pavilion was renamed in his honor. The iconic building next to Husky Stadium still bears his name.

Edmundson, along with UW's Tubby Graves, also co-founded the Washington state high school basketball tournament. Upon his retirement in 1954, more than 350 of his former athletes attended a ceremony to honor him. "I can't understand," an emotional Edmundson said that night, "why everyone is so thoughtful."

96 Down Goes Gonzaga

In their one-sided rivalry with Gonzaga, the bragging rights for Evergreen State supremacy were not going well for the Huskies. Entering their 2005 showdown at Hec Ed, the Zags had won the previous seven meetings against Washington, including a 99–87 victory in Spokane in 2004. "It will be like winning the national championship when we beat them guys," UW guard Nate Robinson said after the '04 loss.

A year later, Gonzaga looked even better. The Bulldogs were ranked No. 6 in the nation, and star forward Adam Morrison was on his way to being named national Player of the Year.

And yet the Huskies were in the early stages of one of their best seasons in program history, a season that really took off after No. 18 UW posted a thrilling 99–95 home victory against Gonzaga on December 4, 2005. It was the Huskies' first victory against the Bulldogs since 1998.

"It feels good to finally get that win," UW forward Jamaal Williams said. "There was a lot of talk, a lot of stuff going back and forth. You could tell it was a rivalry."

UW coach Lorenzo Romar compared the pregame atmosphere to that of a heavyweight title bout. A sold-out Hec Ed shook as much as it ever has. "That was about as high-level a basketball game as you are going to get in college," he said. "Both teams lifted their play to the nature of the environment."

The Huskies won despite a rare off night from star guard Brandon Roy—and despite a remarkable performance by Morrison, who matched his career high with 43 points, which came as a result of a 18-of-29 shooting display. Romar said it was the best performance he had witnessed as an opposing coach. "Crazy as it sounds,

I think our guys guarded him pretty good," Romar said. "The tougher the defense was, the higher level he played."

Roy, UW's leading scorer, fouled out with 2:20 remaining in the game, having scored a season-low 10 points in just 21 minutes. The game featured nine lead changes in the final 11 minutes, and the noise inside Hec Edmundson Pavilion was louder than in recent memory.

Williams had 22 points, and forward Bobby Jones added 15 points for the Huskies. Freshman point guard Justin Dentmon scored 13 of his career-high 17 points in the final 13 minutes. "He really stepped up," said Romar of Dentmon. "He kind of has a flair for the dramatic."

Trailing by 11, Gonzaga used a 21–6 run to take a four-point lead with just under 10 minutes remaining. But Dentmon was clutch down the stretch for the Huskies, and it was his three-point play that put UW ahead 97–93 with 1:09 left. In the closing moments, Morrison missed a tough three-point try over Jones, and the Huskies held on. "They let us know that breaking that streak was not going to be easy," Roy said. "It means a lot to just beat them."

The Huskies went on to finish second in the Pac-10 Conference and were awarded a No. 5 seed in the NCAA Tournament. They defeated Utah State and Illinois to advance to the Sweet 16 for the second year in a row before losing a heartbreaker to Connecticut 98–92 in overtime.

97 Washington Stuns UCLA

The 10,000 fans at Hec Ed refused to leave the court on Febuary 22, 1975. They stood and cheered after the Huskies' stunning 103–81 upset of second-ranked UCLA, hoisted Chester Dorsey on their shoulders, and then carried him to one of the baskets, where the UW guard cut down one of the nets. UW coach Marv Harshman brought the net with him into a celebratory locker room. "It is the most satisfying victory for me ever," Harshman said.

Larry Jackson had 27 points and 14 rebounds, and Dorsey added 15 assists for the Huskies, who had lost 25 straight to the Bruins, including a 100–48 drubbing the year before in Seattle. It was UW's first victory against UCLA in 12 years and the Bruins' worst defeat in a decade. "I am very happy for Marv—and very disappointed for my team," Wooden said outside the UCLA locker room. "I can't say we were jobbed. We weren't out-lucked. It was just a good beating."

The Huskies won despite two of their post players, James Edwards and Lars Hanse, being in foul trouble. Edwards, the former Roosevelt High School star who had picked UW over UCLA, fouled out with more than 10 minutes remaining. Helping to clinch the victory was the defensive effort of forward Larry Pounds, who held UCLA's All-American center, Dave Meyers, to 11 points. It would be the final loss in Wooden's illustrious career at UCLA. The Bruins won their next eight games, including the NCAA championship against Kentucky, sending Wooden into retirement with his 10th national championship.

Exactly four years to the day later, Harshman's Huskies did it again. Stan Walker's 17-footer from the side of the key with three seconds left gave Washington a 69–68 upset of No. 1 UCLA at

Hec Ed. It was the Huskies' first win against a No. 1 team in 21 attempts.

With 15 seconds left, the Bruins had taken their first lead of the game 68–67 on Brad Holland's two free throws. The Huskies' final play was an intended shot for Petur Gudmundsson, UW's 7'2" center from Iceland. But as had been the case most of the game, Gudmundsson attracted a double team from UCLA, which often left Walker alone for the open shot. "I was on balance, it felt good, it was on line, it went through," Walker said.

Gudmundsson had a team-high 17 points and Lorenzo Romar, in his first season at UW, had 10 points and six assists. "I'm just so happy for the guys," Harshman said. "I've maligned them. But I haven't given up on them, and they haven't given up on themselves. That is great for them...Even if we don't win another one, that is a pretty good climax."

Indeed, the victory was the highlight of a trying season for the Huskies, who would lose their next three games to close out the 1978–79 season with an 11–16 overall record. UCLA went on to win the conference championship and advanced to the Elite Eight of the NCAA tournament, where it lost to DePaul.

98 Lorenzo Romar

When Washington coach Marv Harshman was recruiting the star point guard from Cerritos (California) Junior College, part of the appeal for Harshman was the way the player's name rolled off the tongue of the public address announcer during games. *Lor-en-zo Ro-mar.*

The name rang nicely off the rafters at Hec Edmundson, too. For two years as a player from 1978 to 1980, Romar was the steady floor general for the Huskies. He was an overachiever, Harshman said, who went on to play five seasons in the NBA. More than 20 years later, in part because of Harshman's recommendation, Romar returned to his alma mater as Washington's head coach in 2002. "This is the best fit," Harshman said, "that I've seen for any college for a long time."

Romar was the Huskies' fourth choice at the time. Mark Few, Quin Snyder, and Dan Monson, coaches with glossier resumes, all turned down UW athletic director Barbara Hedges.

"Once I knew they wanted me," Romar said, "if I was the 10th choice or the 12th choice, didn't matter to me." He was UW's first African American head coach in basketball or football. "African Americans have struggled quite a bit in trying to get lead positions in athletics," he said. "To be in a position where I'm the first is pretty overwhelming to me."

Romar saw a "gold mine" in Seattle's high school talent, and perhaps his greatest asset as a coach was his ability to recruit that talent to UW. It didn't take him long to get the Huskies rolling again. In his second season, Romar's Huskies reached the NCAA Tournament in 2004, their first postseason berth in five years. Led by Nate Robinson, Brandon Roy, Will Conroy, Tre Simmons, and Bobby Jones, the Huskies were even better in 2005, winning the Pac-10 Tournament, the program's first conference championship of any kind in 20 years. "This is the first time I've ever won a championship—high school or college," Roy said after the Huskies knocked off top-seeded Arizona 81–72 in the Pac-10 title game. "This is special, man. And to do it beating the No. 1 and No. 3 seeds back to back, we proved that we were really the Pac-10 champs. Three games in a row, we were the toughest team in the conference."

The Huskies' reward was a surprising No. 1 seed for the NCAA tournament, the first—and only—time that's happened at UW. "I didn't see this one coming," Romar said. "But I was hoping it would come because I felt we deserved it."

A crowd of about a thousand fans had joined the team inside Hec Ed for the tournament's Selection Show, and all erupted in cheer when the Huskies were announced as a top seed. "This is a great moment for Washington athletics," athletic director Todd Turner said. "This is what college is all about. We were all kind of hoping something good would happen, but we probably didn't really expect it. That was as emotional a reaction to a tournament seed as I've ever seen. It was really genuine, very collegiate. That's a lifetime memory right there."

Romar led the Huskies to the Sweet 16—where they were upset by No. 4 seed Louisville—and matched a school record with 29 victories that season. A year later, in their third straight NCAA Tournament, the Huskies reached the Sweet 16 again before falling to top-seeded Connecticut in overtime. In 2010 the Huskies won the conference tournament title and reached the Sweet 16 for the third time under Romar's watch. In all, Romar led the Huskies to six NCAA Tournament appearances, three Pac-10 Tournament championships, and two regular-season conference titles. And entering the 2016–17 season, his 289 victories were the second most in UW history behind Hec Edmundson's 488.

Entering the 2016–17 season, however, the pressure was on Romar. And when the Huskies stumbled to a 2–16 finish in conference play—the worst record of his 15-year run—the 58-year-old Romar was dismissed as the Huskies coach. Four days later, the Huskies hired Syracuse assistant Mike Hopkins as the program's new head coach.

99 Freshmen Phenoms Chriss and Murray

The young talent, like the team, was raw. Even Lorenzo Romar was surprised at how quickly things came together for Dejounte Murray, Marquese Chriss, and the Huskies in 2015–16. The Huskies were coming off a "very dismal"—Romar's words—season a year earlier, when they limped to a 5–13 finish in conference play and saw the departure of standout point guard Nigel Williams-Goss, who transferred to rival Gonzaga.

Enter Murray and Chriss, two freshmen who infused promise and energy into a program desperate for both. With steady leadership from senior guard Andrew Andrews—who would lead the Pac-12 in scoring—Murray and Chriss got the team in the NCAA Tournament discussion for the first time in a long time. "They helped create a buzz for our program again," Romar said.

The Huskies went 9–9 in Pac-12 play (19–15 overall) and reached the National Invitational Tournament, their first postseason appearance in three years. And then, almost as quickly as they emerged, Murray and Chriss were gone. Projected as first-round picks, both declared for the NBA draft after their lone season at UW. "I don't think Dejounte or Marquese thought they would have a chance to go in the first round after one year. I don't think anybody thought that," Romar said. "It's a credit to them and how hard they worked and how they developed so fast to get to that point."

Murray, a 6'5" guard from Seattle's Rainier Beach High, had one of the finest freshman seasons in UW history, averaging 16.1 points, 6.0 rebounds, and 4.4 assists. Over the previous 20 years, just three freshmen in college basketball posted similar numbers:

LSU's Ben Simmons (19.2, 11.8, and 4.8), also in 2015–16, and Iowa State's Curtis Stinson (16.2, 6.0, and 4.3) in 2003–04.

Chriss, a 6'10" forward from Sacramento, California, averaged 13.8 points, 5.4 rebounds, and 1.6 blocks and he tantalized with his incredible leaping ability and highlight-reel dunks. Chriss was especially raw, but "we thought it was just a matter of time before the NBA was going to recognize what he could do," Romar said.

Indeed, both wound up being selected in the first round of the 2016 NBA Draft. Chriss was drafted with the eighth overall pick by the Sacramento Kings (and traded immediately to the Phoenix Suns) to become the fourth Husky to play for Romar to be drafted in the top 10. "He's an absolute freak athlete," ESPN college basketball analyst Jay Bilas said. "He's 6'10" and he plays above the rim. He can rebound. He can block shots and he can step away and hit that three-point shot."

Murray, in attendance at the draft in New York, sat with family and friends for about three-and-a-half hours before his name was finally called with the 28th overall selection. But he did land with

NBA First-Round Picks

2016: Marquese Chriss (eighth overall, Sacramento Kings, traded to Phoenix Suns), Dejounte Murray (28th overall, San Antonio Spurs)
2014: C.J Wilcox (28th, Los Angeles Clippers)
2012: Terrence Ross (eighth, Toronto Raptors), Tony Wroten Jr. (25th, Memphis Grizzlies)
2010: Quincy Pondexter (26th, Oklahoma City Thunder)
2007: Spencer Hawes (10th, Sacramento Kings)
2006: Brandon Roy (sixth, Minnesota Timberwolves, traded to Portland Trailblazers)
2005: Nate Robinson (21st, Suns)
1987: Christian Welp (16th, Philadelphia 76ers)
1985: Detlef Schrempf (eighth, Dallas Mavericks)
1953: Bob Houbregs (third, Milwaukee Hawks)
1948: Jack Nichols (12th, Washington Capitols)

the San Antonio Spurs, one of the NBA's best franchises. "I had to sit a long time, but I didn't pout," Murray said. "I didn't try to show nothing negative, tried to stay positive and I feel like I'm going to the best organization in the NBA…a team that contends for a championship every year. I'm just blessed to be in a position and blessed to be a part of their organization."

Chriss and Murray became the second duo from UW to be drafted in the first round of the same draft, joining Terrence Ross and Tony Wroten Jr. from 2012. "Anyone that follows Husky basketball and pulls for us would have to say they wish they would have stayed another year because it would have been so exciting," Romar said. "But they went out for a reason. They didn't rent our program. They did it the right way, and I couldn't be happier for them."

100 Markelle Fultz

He could have gone just about anywhere. All the college basketball bluebloods—Kentucky, Kansas, Louisville, Arizona—recruited him. Instead, Markelle Fultz came across the country, all the way from Maryland, to play for Lorenzo Romar and the Washington Huskies.

Fultz was one of the nation's most hyped prospects in the Class of 2016, a 6'4" point guard many were projecting as the top pick of the 2017 NBA Draft even while he was still playing at DeMatha Catholic High School. So why Washington? Why move so far from home to play for a program that hadn't made the NCAA Tournament in five years?

For Fultz, the reasons went beyond basketball. It was UW associate head coach Raphael Chillious, who has strong ties to the

Maryland-Washington D.C. basketball community, who recognized Fultz's potential when the point guard was a 5'9" sophomore still playing on the JV team. And it was Romar who became like a father figure for a boy who grew up without one.

"Who cared about me more than basketball?" Fultz said. "Obviously, everyone can say something good, but Coach Romar was the first to actually tell me something that I needed to work on. I think that was big, and then him just building a relationship with my mom. It was hard to get her trust, so he did a good job of having her feel like I'm safe and that I'm going to be around people doing the right things."

Fultz was raised by a single mother, Ebony, who often worked two jobs to provide for him and his older sister, Shauntese. "She is almost like my heartbeat," he said of his mother. "Without her, I don't think I would have been able to do anything in my life."

Entering high school Fultz wasn't labeled a can't-miss star. He wasn't a coddled basketball prodigy you'd find on the cover of *Sports Illustrated.* Until his junior year of high school, he was largely unnoticed by the elite basketball community. "If he were in North Dakota, then it's understandable," Romar said. "For him to be where he was in that area and a guard, it's unheard of...He's not gone through that thing where everybody's putting you on this high pedestal and kissing your feet. He's had to work and he's been motivated for so long. Now, it's just ingrained in him to be that way."

Growing up, Fultz was just a kid—and a self-described crazy kid. He loved his BMX bikes and loved to attempt wild stunts on them. "I was a daredevil when I was younger," he said. "I used to do crazy things, try to do backflips off monkey bars and stuff like that."

Chillious had long had a close relationship with Fultz's personal trainer, Keith Williams. And when Chillious first saw Fultz play as a sophomore on JV, he quickly noticed the physical makeup—big hands, big feet, long arms—that would help the kid grow and blossom into something more and maybe even something

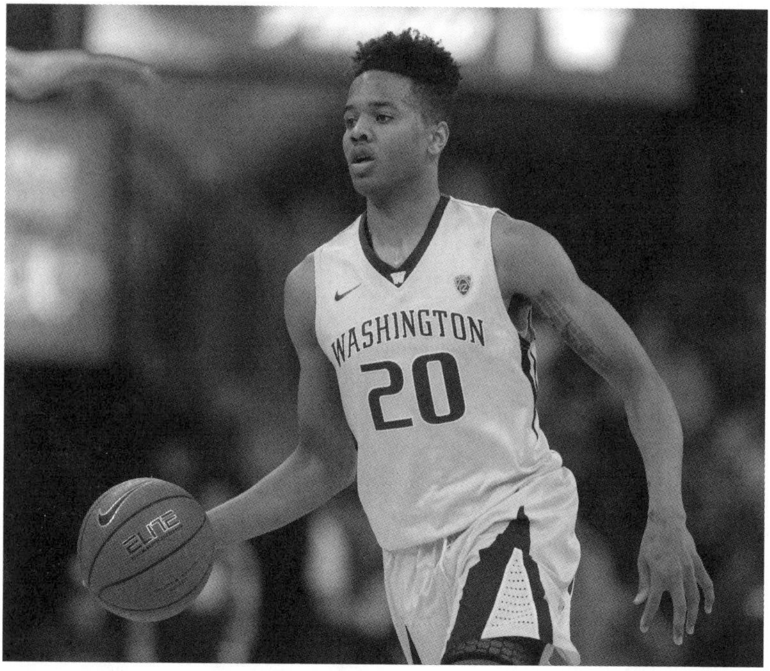

A one-and-done star, Markelle Fultz dribbles the ball during a victory against Western Michigan, in which he had 27 points and 10 assists. (AP Images)

great. "By halftime I was like, 'That kid right there, if he grows at all, he's not going to be just good, he's going to be an NBA All-Star,'" Chillious said.

First, Fultz would become the most coveted recruit ever to sign with the Huskies. He entered the 2016–17 season at UW with much fanfare and much promise to lift UW back into the NCAA Tournament picture. Fultz is "more talented than any player we've ever had walking through the door," Romar said before the season. "You watch him for two or three minutes, the way he moves on the floor with his size, you realize that one's pretty good. But what you don't see behind the scenes is what kind of teammate he is. Markelle doesn't play with the idea of trying to make the NBA. He plays to win."

Immediately, Fultz lived up to the hype. He had 30 points, seven rebounds, and six assists in his collegiate debut and then scored 35 points four days later. During a three-game stretch in conference play, he scored 34, 37, and 30 points. "He has a high basketball IQ," Romar said. "It's almost like he's computer-generated or something. And on top of that, he's a great teammate and he's extremely coachable. So he has the whole package."

Fultz made it look easy. He was the picture of cool, often appearing to be a step ahead of everyone else but never straining to get there. He wanted to be great, yearned to be the best, but didn't carry himself as if he deserved such status. "He's an unassuming potential superstar that will assume any role you tell him," Chillious said. "That's the best part about him. His teammates see that. If all of us walk out of the gym and come back five minutes later, he'll still be there, still goofing off, and shooting trick shots."

Romar rated Fultz among the best guards he's coached—right up there with Brandon Roy and Isaiah Thomas. What those two UW legends achieved in their long college careers was something Fultz couldn't: postseason success. The Huskies missed out on the NCAA Tournament berth for the sixth straight season in 2017. "Anything that has to do with us not winning enough has nothing to do with Markelle," Romar said early in 2017. "Markelle has been phenomenal."

On several occasions Fultz flirted with UW's first ever triple-double. And midway through the season, he led the Pac-12 in scoring and averaged 23.2 points, 6.0 assists, and 6.0 rebounds. "He understands and plays the point guard position better than anyone I've ever seen in this conference," said Pac-12 Network analyst Don MacLean, a former UCLA great. "Go back and tell me who's done it better? You can't. At least, I can't think of anyone. He's doing things as a freshman that most guys in the [NBA] don't learn until their second or third year. He's incredible."

Acknowledgments

This being my first book project, I had much to learn, and many people to thank along the way.

So thanks to the team at Triumph Books for the opportunity to dive deeper into University of Washington athletics, with a special shout out to Jeff Fedotin for his guidance, patience, and persistence.

Thanks to my editors at *The Seattle Times*, Paul Barrett, Scott Hanson, and Ed Guzman. And to Bob Condotta, the hardest-working sportswriter around and a one-man encyclopedia on Huskies history.

And most importantly, thanks to my wife, Ashley, and our three children, whose support and inspiration made this project worthwhile.

Sources

1. The Dawgfather

—Jude, Adam. "Legendary Washington football coach Don James dies at age 80." *The Seattle Times*, 20 October 2013.

—Newnham, Blaine. "James engineers split national title." *The Seattle Times*, 2 January 1992.

—Rockne, Dick. "James named Husky grid coach." *The Seattle Times*, 23 December 1974.

—Withers, Bud. "Huskies coach Don James was 'The Dawgfather' to the Northwest." *The Seattle Times*, 20 October 2013.

2. The Greatest Setting in College Football

—Condotta, Bob. "New Husky Stadium: on time, on budget." *The Seattle Times*, 24 August 2012.

—Jude, Adam. "New, improved Husky Stadium ready to shine." *The Seattle Times*, 24 August 2013.

—Reader, Bill. "A 91-year history: Farewell to old Husky Stadium."

3. The 1991 National Championship Team

—Condotta, Bob. "Second half against Huskers gave UW swagger in 1991 season." *The Seattle Times*, 15 September 2011.

—Newnham, Blaine. "Washington responds with confidence, true grit." *The Seattle Times*, 22 September 1991.

—Rockne, Dick. "UW sticks it in their ears: Huskies overpower Cornhuskers." *The Seattle Times*, 22 September 1991.

4. Purple Reign: 1985 Orange Bowl

—Condotta, Bob. "Sooners, 21 years later." *The Seattle Times*, 5 September 2006.

—Stone, Larry. "30 years ago, the Huskies won Orange Bowl but somehow missed national title." *The Seattle Times*, 31 December 2014.

5. Return to Glory: 2016 Pac-12 Champs

—Jude, Adam. "Huskies roll early, rout Cougars in Apple Cup." *The Seattle Times*, 25 November 2016.

—Jude, Adam. "Huskies stuff Colorado, win 41–10 in Pac-12 title game." *The Seattle Times*, 2 December 2016.

— Stone, Larry. "The Huskies have a lot to be proud of, but still are a ways off from becoming consistently elite." *The Seattle Times*, 31 December 2016.

6. 1960 Rose Bowl upset

—Donohoe, Mike. "Washington slaughters Wisconsin." *Seattle Post-Intelligencer*, 1 January 1960.

—Meyers, Georg N. "Huskies bend heads in prayer before giving captain a 'ride.'" *The Seattle Times*, 2 January 1960.

—Raley, Dan. "Where Are They Now? George Fleming, UW football legend." *Seattle Post-Intelligencer*, 14 August 2007.

7. Another Rose Bowl Stunner

—Condotta, Bob. "1960 Huskies recognized as champs, at last." *The Seattle Times*, 27 September 2007.

—Crowe, Jerry. "Fifty years ago, Caltech pulled off a prank for the memory banks at Rose Bowl." *Los Angeles Times*, 26 December 2010.

—Eskenazi, David. "Wayback machine: Jim Owens' Purple Gang." SportsPressNW.com, 4 November 2015.

8. Too Much Tui

—Condotta, Bob. "Huskies will face Stanford 11 years to the day after Marques Tuiasosopo's historic performance against Cardinal." *The Seattle Times*, 28 October 2010.

—Withers, Bud. "Too Much Tui—Huskies In Driver's Seat After QB's Historic Day." *The Seattle Times*, 31 October 1999.

9. Moon's Miracle: The 1975 Apple Cup

—Condotta, Bob. "Ex-UW WR Gaines makes up for lost time." *The Seattle Times*, 17 November 2005.

—Lyons, Gils. "James, 57,00 fans: 'I don't believe it!' *The Seattle Times*, 23 November 1975.

10. Chris Petersen Comes Aboard

—Jude, Adam. "For Huskies football, the 'Coach Pete' era begins." *The Seattle Times*, 7 December 2013.

—Jude, Adam. "Husky coach Chris Petersen is a perfectionist with a personal touch." *The Seattle Times*, 24 August 2014.

11. Steve Emtman

—Miller, Ted. "Q&A: Former Washington great Steve Emtman." *The Seattle Times*, 30 June 2011.

—Newnham, Blaine. "Emtman proves why defense makes the offense." *The Seattle Times*, 6 October 1991.

— Rockne, Dick. "Emtman exemplifies Husky DL tradition." 29 August 1991.

12. The Father of Husky Football

—Newnham, Blaine. "Statue of Owens at stadium would honor 'father of Husky football.'" *The Seattle Times*, 29 June 2003.

—Withers, Bud. "Jim Owens, coaching legend of UW football, dies at 82." *The Seattle Times*, 7 June 2009.

13. Dobie's Perfect Decade

—Borland, Lynn. "Legendary coach Gil Dobie's only loss at Washington: his legacy." *The Seattle Times*, 20 November 2010.

—Brown, Matt. "Top 100 CFB coaches ever." SportsOnEarth.com, 27 July 2016.

—Coyle, Wee. "The Spell of Gil Dobie." *The Seattle Times*, December 1948-January 1949.

—"Suzzallo silent on football strike." *The Seattle Times*, 30 November 1916.

—"Dobie and Suzzallo agree that coach is done at Washington." *The Seattle Times*, 9 December 2016.

14. The King: Hugh McElhenny

—Eskenazi, David. "Wayback Machine: McElhenny's 100-yard return." SportsPressNW.com, 4 October 2011.

—Newnham, Blaine. "McElhenny still reigns as top Husky back." *The Seattle Times*, 12 November 1996.

—Raley, Dan. "The untold story of Hugh McElhenny, the King of Montlake." *Seattle Post-Intelligencer*, 1 September 2004.

15. All I Saw Was Purple

—Crowe, Jerry. "In a Purple Haze: USC Hasn't Been the Same Since Its Last Trip to Seattle in 1990." *Los Angeles Times*, 25 September 1992.

—Newnham, Blaine. "Huskies make USC see purple." *The Seattle Times*, 23 September 1990.

—Rockne, Dick. "Huskies heat it up: Washington stuns USC 31-0 on 92-degree day." *The Seattle Times*, 23 September 1990.

16. Napoleon Kaufman

—Kugiya, Hugo. "Fast forward: Kaufman grows into a starring role." *The Seattle Times*, 1 September 1993.

—O'Neil, Danny. "A leap of faith." *The Seattle Times*, 17 July 2011.

17. Lincoln Kennedy

—Jude, Adam. "Lincoln Kennedy returns to Husky Stadium: 'It's like a proud papa coming home.'" *The Seattle Times*, 12 August 2015.

—Rockne, Dick. "He wasn't always Linc: Once troubled, UW lineman makes peace with himself." *The Seattle Times*, 12 November 1991.

18. Sonny Sixkiller

—Blount Jr., Roy. "The magic number is Sixkiller." *Sports Illustrated*, 4 October 1971.

—Schwarzmann, Bob. "Sixkiller, Huskies shoot down Alums, 43–7." *The Seattle Times*, 17 May 1970.

—Sixkiller, Sonny, and Bob Condotta. *Sonny Sixkiller's Tales from the Huskies Sideline*. Sports Publishing LLC, 2002.

—http://www.seattletimes.com/sports/uw-husky-football/sonny-sixkiller-talks-of-his-movie-role-his-song-and-his-life-after-uw/

19. Warren Moon

—Bishop, Greg. "The man that is Moon." *The Seattle Times*, 30 July 2006.

—Eskenazi, David, and Steve Rudman. "Wayback Machine: Moon, officially a legend." SportsPressNW.com, 10 February 2016.

—Powell, Michael. "Warren Moon, who helped clear way for black quarterbacks, recalls his struggles." *The New York Times*, 5 February 2016.

20. George "Wildcat" Wilson

—Caple, Christian. "On Washington's history with Alabama, and 'the game that changed the South.'" *The News Tribune*, 23 December 2016.

—Porter, W. Thomas. *Go Huskies! Celebrating the Washington Football Tradition*. Triumph Books (September 2013).

—Rockne, Dick. "Yeah, but if Wilson had played the whole game ..." *The Seattle Times*, 8 October 1975.

—Rudman, Steve. *Celebrating 100 Years of Husky Football*. Professional Sports Publications (1990).

21. Don Heinrich

—Rockne, Dick. "UW Great Heinrich Dies Of Cancer; Qb Synonymous With Husky Football." *The Seattle Times*, 2 March 1992.

—Eskenazi, David, and Steve Rudman. "Wayback Machine: 'The Deadeye' Don Heinrich." SportsPressNW.com, 9 October 2012.

22. Whammy in Miami

—Kugiya, Hugo. "Huskies bust Miami vice." *The Seattle Times*, 25 September 1994.

—"Miami's Streak Is Ended." The Associated Press, 25 September 1994.

23. 2001 Rose Bowl

—Newnham, Blaine. "Williams makes it a Dawg day for friends." *The Seattle Times*, 2 January 2001.

—Withers, Bud. "An amazing ride to last a lifetime for Huskies." *The Seattle Times*, 2 January 2001.

24. 2002 Apple Cup

—Condotta, Bob. "Sweet and sour: UW wins epic Apple Cup." *The Seattle Times*, 24 November 2002.

—Condotta, Bob. "Ten years ago, Huskies won a wild Apple Cup in Pullman." *The Seattle Times*, 21 November 2012.

25. Sailgating

—Culpepper, Chuck. "Long-dormant Washington throttled Stanford and put college football on notice." *The Washington Post*, 1 October 2016.

—"Husky Stadium Sailgating, Tailgating Gets Even Better." GoHuskies.com, August 2013.

26. Rick Neuheisel's Abrupt Exit

—Bruscas, Angelo. "Hedges: Lies cost Neuheisel his job." *Seattle Post-Intelligencer*, 2 February 2005.

—Condotta, Bob. "Rick Neuheisel's sorry, but says he would have kept UW football strong." *The Seattle Times*, 11 November 2008.

—Withers, Bud, and Bob Condotta. "Neuheisel could lose job over NCAA basketball bets." *The Seattle Times*, 5 June 2003.

27. Knocking Off USC

—Brewer, Jerry. "Huskies' win the start of something special." *The Seattle Times*, 20 September 2009.

—Condotta, Bob. "Game-winning kick? Just like practice for UW's Folk." *The Seattle Times*, 20 September 2009

—Kelley, Steve. "Locker drives into UW lore." *The Seattle Times*, 20 September 2009.

28. Montlake Jake

—Condotta, Bob. "Ferndale's finest: Huskies QB Jake Locker lives and plays by hometown rules." *The Seattle Times*, 29 August 2010.

—Condotta, Bob. "Revengeful Holiday for Huskies." *The Seattle Times*, 31 December 2010.

—Condotta, Bob. "Finding the meaning of Washington's Jake Locker." *The Seattle Times*, 1 January 2011.

—Trotter, Jim. "Jake Locker: Was it worth the wait?" *Sports Illustrated*, 25 April 2011.

29. Cold-Blooded Isaiah Thomas

—Allen, Percy. "Huskies' Isaiah Thomas says he will enter NBA draft." *The Seattle Times*, 31 March 2011.

—Allen, Percy. "Huskies win Pac-10 tournament title on Thomas' jumper at OT buzzer." *The Seattle Times*, 12 March 2011.

—Bolch, Ben. "Isaiah Thomas' shot lifts Washington over top-seeded Arizona in Pac-10 tournament final." *Los Angeles Times*, 12 March 2011.

—Jenks, Jayson. "Isaiah Thomas was unstoppable in his 51-point state-tournament game in 2006." *The Seattle Times*, 26 February 2016.

—O'Connor, Kevin. "Isaiah Thomas: 'I feel like I'm the best player in the world." The Ringer, 23 January 2017.

30. Brandon Roy

—Evans, Jayda. "UW retires former basketball star Brandon Roy's No. 3 jersey." *The Seattle Times*, 23 January 2009.

—Jenkins, Lee. "It's a Bumpy Ride, but Roy Gives the Huskies a Lift." *The New York Times*, 19 March 2006.

—Quick, Jason. "Blazers Top 40: No. 6 Brandon Roy." *The Oregonian*, 5 April 2010.

—Quick, Jason. "Brandon Roy: An unexpected end for one of the most popular Trail Blazers ever." *The Oregonian*, 9 December 2011.

—Tokito, Mike. "Brandon Roy's 'right way' lifts his No. 3 to Washington's rafters." *The Oregonian*, 22 January 2009.

31. "Hook" Houbregs

—Allen, Percy. "Bob Houbregs, Husky basketball icon, dies at 82." *The Seattle Times*, 29 May 2014.

—Sherwin, Bob. "Houbregs set records at UW for the century." *The Seattle Times*, 16 February 2002.

—Withers, Bud. "Remembering Bob Houbregs, one of basketball's giants." *The Seattle Times*, 29 May 2014.

32. Super Mario

—Rockne, Dick. "Mario Bailey: Overlooked Husky 'other receiver' no longer." *The Seattle Times*, 2 January 1992.

—Lyons, Gil. "Bailey: Too legit to quit: Small Husky receiver has defied skeptics." *The Seattle Times*, 23 December 1991.

33. Iron Man

—Withers, Bud and Jim Brunner. "Charles Carroll, 1906–2003: Legendary Husky, veteran prosecutor." *The Seattle Times*, 25 June 2003.

34. Oh, What a Night!

—Jude, Adam. "No. 10 Huskies rout Stanford, 44–6." *The Seattle Times*, 30 September 2016.

35. Huskies Make Their Point

—Jude, Adam. "Huskies end losing streak to Oregon in 70–21 rout." *The Seattle Times*, 8 October 2016.

—Jude, Adam. "Jake Browning's finger wag against Oregon earns him locker room cred." *The Seattle Times*, 12 October 2016.

36. Bob Schloredt

—Jude, Adam. "What makes a great UW quarterback? Chris Petersen hopes to find out." *The Seattle Times*, 30 August 2015.

—Raley, Dan. "Where are they now: Bob Schloredt, Huskies QB."

—Wright, Alfred. "One eye on the Rose Bowl." *Sports Illustrated*, 3 October 1960.

37. The Huards

—Allen, Percy. "Brock Huard to go from field to studio as talk-show host on new 710 ESPN Seattle." *The Seattle Times*, 1 April 2009.

—Allen, Percy. "Huard's hard lesson." *The Seattle Times*, 20 November 1998.

—Belt, Derek. "True Hued: The Huard Brothers." *Columns, the University of Washington Alumni Magazine*, June 2016.

—Perdue, Andy. "Dan Marino, Damon Huard team up to make wine in Woodinville." *The Seattle Times*, 8 April 2016.

38. The Billy Joe Hobert Scandal

—Carpenter, Les. "Billy Joe Hobert: Villain, hero? Debate rages." *The Seattle Times*, 20 June 2002.

—Rockne, Dick. "Billy Joe just a regular Joe." *The Seattle Times*, 29 December 1991.

39. Sound the Siren

—Stark, Chuck. "Huskies' siren has Bremerton roots." *Kitsap Sun*, 25 September 2013.

40. Dillon's Spartan Effort

—Allen, Percy. "Huskies keep it simple, dominate with Dillon." *The Seattle Times*, 17 November 1996.

41. 1990 Rebirth

—Newnham, Blaine. "Iowa sees purple." *The Seattle Times*, 2 January 1991.

—Rockne, Dick. "Triumph another validation." *The Seattle Times*, 2 January 1991.

—Rockne, Dick. "UW back can take the rap." *The Seattle Times*, 2 January 1991.

42. Back on Top: 1992 Rose Bowl

—Farrey, Tom. "Husky defense hounds Elvis." *The Seattle Times*, 2 January 1992.

—Newnham, Blaine. "James engineers split national title." *The Seattle Times*, 2 January 1992.

43. From Sundodgers to Dubs

—"Husky—That's the new U-W title." *The Seattle Times*, 4 February 1922.

—Mascot history, Washington Huskies. GoHuskies.com. Undated.

44. The Miraculous Interception

—Caple, Christian. "Foster, Huskies pull off miracle finish to top Arizona." *The UW Daily*, 11 October 2009.

—Condotta, Bob. "Huskies win in a miraculous finish." *The Seattle Times*, 11 October 2009.

45. A Season to Forget

—Brewer, Jerry. "How low can they go? Huskies sink even further." *The Seattle Times*, 23 November 2008.

—Brewer, Jerry. "The bad ride is mercifully over for Huskies." *The Seattle Times*, 7 December 2008.

—Condotta, Bob. "On his way out." *The Seattle Times*, 28 October 2008.

—Condotta, Bob. "Cougars down the Huskies in two overtimes." *The Seattle Times*, 23 November 2008.

—"Washington finishes 0–12 season with loss to Cal." The Associated Press, 6 December 2008.

46. Lawyer Milloy

—Kelley, Steve. "Seahawks' Lawyer Milloy bucks youth-centric NFL trend." *The Seattle Times*, 22 September 2010.

—Kugiya, Hugo. "It's clear: Husky star Milloy set for NFL." *The Seattle Times*, 6 January 1996.

—Kugiya, Hugo. "Courting able Lawyer: Lincoln's Milloy seen as gritty survivor." *The Seattle Times*, 12 September 1991.

—Milles, Todd. "Night to honor 'greatest athlete' to ever come out of Tacoma—Lawyer Milloy." *The News Tribune*, 20 September 2012.

—Smith, Craig. "NFL Draft: Milloy could get an early call." *The Seattle Times*, 15 April 1996.

47. Do the Wave

—Anderson, Rick. "Crazy George says he created The Wave." *The Seattle Times*, 28 September 1991.

—Buck, Jerry. "Robb Weller at home after making waves." *The Washington Post*, 6 August 1989.

—Kossen, Bill. "Saluting the man who gave us The Wave." *The Seattle Times*, 26 September 1999.

48. The Hitman: Dave Hoffmann

—Condotta, Bob. "Catching up with Dave Hoffmann." *The Seattle Times*, 14 November 2003.

—Hoffmann, Dave, and Derek Johnson. "The Husky Hitman." Derek Johnson Books, LLC, 2012.

—Newnham, Blaine. "UW Turns To `Bruise Brothers.'" *The Seattle Times*, 19 August 1992.

— Rockne, Dick. "Putting a stop to any doubts — Hoffman, UW's top tackler, rewards coach's early faith." 3 October 1991.

49. 2003 Apple Cup Upset

—Condotta, Bob. "Sweet redemption." *The Seattle Times*, 23 November 2003.

—Newnham, Blaine. "Huskies' defense turns tide against Cougars." 23 November 2003.

50. Don McKeta

—Meyers, Georg N. "Huskies rally, edge Oregon, 7-6." *The Seattle Times*, 30 October 1960.

—Meyers, Georg N. "The 'new' McKeta." *The Seattle Times*, 6 August 1964.

—Stark, Chuck. "Don McKeta is one proud Husky." *Kitsap Sun*, 16 October 2011.

51. Man of Steele

—Ringer, Sandy. "Blanchet's Steele still rates No. 1." *The Seattle Times*, 13 November 1998.

—Rockne, Dick. "Man of Steele." *The Seattle Times*, 31 August 1979.

—Rockne, Dick. "Huskies rain TDs on Cowboys." *The Seattle Times*, 9 September 1979.

52. Cody Pickett

—Befidi, Jeannine. "Pickett pens own final script at home." 23 November 2003.

—Condotta, Bob. "Cody Pickett looks back after retirement from football." *The Seattle Times*, 24 March 2011.

—Miller, Ted. "Pickett displays 'Tui' qualities." *Seattle Post-Intelligencer*, 22 October 2001.

—Newnham, Blaine. "Newest hero ignores pain, carries team on injured shoulder." *The Seattle Times*, 21 October 2001.

—Sherwin, Bob. "Learning the ropes of cowhide and pigskin." *The New York Times*, 4 November 2005.

—Taylor, Phil. "On Saturdays He's No Cowboy." *Sports Illustrated*, 1 September 2003.

53. Who's the Best QB?

—Jude, Adam. "What makes a great UW quarterback? Chris Petersen hopes to find out." *The Seattle Times*, 30 August 2015.

54. Browning's Breakthrough

—Jude, Adam. "UW Huskies quarterback Jake Browning: 'I'm not a robot.'" *The Seattle Times*, 23 November 2016.

55. 2011 Alamo Bowl

—"Baylor wins Alamo Bowl shootout." The Associated Press, 30 December 2011.

—Condotta, Bob. "Huskies score 56 points, but still can't beat Baylor." *The Seattle Times*, 30 December 2011.

—Condotta, Bob. "Huskies fire defensive coordinator Nick Holt, two other defensive assistant coaches." *The Seattle Times*, 31 December 2011.

56. The Helmet Car

—Jude, Adam. "UW retiring the Husky Helmet Car." *The Seattle Times*, 8 August 2013.

57. 2012 Upset of Stanford

—Brewer, Jerry. "Bigger upset is that Huskies won with defense." *The Seattle Times*, 28 September 2012.

—Condotta, Bob. "Huskies use big plays, and big defense, to stop No. 8 Stanford." *The Seattle Times*, 28 September 2012.

—Gemmell, Kevin. "Huskies shock Stanford, not themselves." ESPN.com, 28 September 2012.

58. Greg Lewis

—Nelson, Glenn. "Heir to a king: Lewis rivals McElhenny as UW's greatest." *The Seattle Times*, 27 December 1990.

—Newnham, Blaine. "UW rose to the occasion: 'Cool' Lewis exemplifies Husky spirit." 28 October 1990.

—Rockne, Dick. "UW's Greg Lewis running to daylight." *The Seattle Times*, 19 August 1990.

59. Ross' Speedy Return

—Allen, Percy. "Fastest Husky John Ross says he needs to slow down." *The Seattle Times*, 9 August 2016.

—Jude, Adam. "Healthy again, John Ross III optimistic about a breakthrough for UW offense." *The Seattle Times*, 25 April 2016.

—Jude, Adam. "Huskies make a bold opening statement in routing Rutgers." *The Seattle Times*, 3 September 2016.

—Jude, Adam. "Huskies' John Ross to skip senior season, enter NFL draft." 2 January 2017.

60. Jacque Robinson

—Ashmun, Chuck. "Familiar faces keep pressure on Robinson." *The Seattle Times*, 4 April 1982.

—Meyers, Georg N. "Robinson? He's set to give UW fans a start." 15 October 1982.

—Rockne, Dick. "Weighting game nearly over for Jacque." 27 December 1984.

—Rockne, Dick. "Jacque Robinson Back At UW To Earn Counseling Degree." 27 December 1992

—Kelley, Steve. "Fall from grace. Jacque Robinson, age 20, acts as if he's having time of his life." *The Seattle Times*, 27 October 1983.

61. Nate Robinson

—Condotta, Bob. "Seahawks give former Huskies star Nate Robinson a tryout." *The Seattle Times*, 14 June 2016.

—Raley, Dan. "UW freshman Nate Robinson excels on the floor and the field." *Seattle Post-Intelligencer*, 19 February 2003.

—Brewer, Jerry. "Nate Robinson at 30: still having lots of fun." *The Seattle Times*, 6 July 2014.

—Newnham, Blaine. "Nate's got game, but just one sport now." *The Seattle Times*, 6 November 2003

62. 1981 Win Against USC

—Ashmun, Chuck. "Blowout! Huskies in bowl battle." *The Seattle Times*, 16 November 1981.

—Lyons, Gil. "Husky loss most disappointing of his career — by far, says Allen." *The Seattle Times*, 16 November 1981.

—Schwarzmann, Bob. "On a wet windy day, Huskies think sun." *The Seattle Times*, 16 November 1981.

63. The Dawgmother

—Jude, Adam. "Still the Dawgmother." *The Seattle Times,* 16 October 2016.

64. The Thursday Speeches

—Tormey, Peter. *The Thursday Speeches: Lessons in Life, Leadership, and Football from Coach Don James.* Self published, 2014.

65. Jim Lambright

—Kugiya, Hugo. "Labor of love: Lambright dives into dream." *The Seattle Times,* 1 September 1993.

—Newnham, Blaine. "Huskies make their point — Lambright's energy, emotion will replace James' experience." *The Seattle Times,* 5 September 1993.

—Raley, Dan. "Where Are They Now? Jim Lambright comes to grips." *Seattle Post-Intelligencer,* 25 September 2007.

—Rockne, Dick. "Dream job lands amid nightmare." *The Seattle Times,* 23 August 1993.

66. Bark for Sark

—Brewer, Jerry. "Coach revives promise of UW program." *The Seattle Times,* 9 December 2008.

—Condotta, Bob. "A fresh start: New coach's youthful enthusiasm is matched with festive reception." *The Seattle Times,* 9 December 2008.

—Jude, Adam. "Steve Sarkisian set to meet Washington for first time since leaving Huskies." *The Seattle Times,* 3 October 2015.

—Jude, Adam. "Huskies upset USC 17–12 and beat Steve Sarkisian, their former coach." *The Seattle Times,* 8 October 2015.

67. Keith Price

—Condotta, Bob. "Huskies make changes to their spring practices; remains starter as two-part schedule includes break." *The Seattle Times,* 5 March 2013.

—Jude, Adam. "Keith Price eager to bounce back in his senior year at UW." *The Seattle Times,* 3 August 2013.

—Jude, Adam. "Washington routs Boise State in first game at renovated Husky Stadium." *The Seattle Times,* 1 September 2013.

—Kelley, Steve. "Huskies' life after Locker in good hands with Price, Montana." *The Seattle Times,* 1 May 2011.

68. Shaq: A Do-It-All Star

—Jude, Adam. "Shaq Thompson returns home to face Cal." *The Seattle Times*, 8 October 2014.

—Kaplan, Emily. "The linebacker who couldn't hit." The Monday Morning Quarterback/*Sports Illustrated*, 11 February 2015.

69. Budda Baker

—Jude, Adam. "Huskies' star recruit Budda Baker will have to earn playing time." *The Seattle Times*, 8 August 2014.

—Jude, Adam. "Budda Baker leads Huskies' deep and talented secondary." *The Seattle Times*, 25 August 2016.

—Jude, Adam. "UW's Budda Baker recognized as 'consensus' All-American by NCAA." *The Seattle Times*, 15 December 2016.

70. Three Dawg Night

—Jude, Adam. "Three Huskies taken in first round of NFL draft." *The Seattle Times*, 30 April 2015.

71. Happy Sack King

—Jude, Adam. "Huskies' Hau'oli Kikaha back on the field with new name, perspective." *The Seattle Times*, 25 September 2013.

—Jude, Adam. "UW sack king Hau'oli Kikaha drafted in second round by New Orleans Saints." *The Seattle Times*, 1 May 2015.

72. Huskies Shut Down Desmond Howard

—Farrey, Tom. "UW defense shoots down Heisman winner Desmond Howard." *The Seattle Times*, 2 January 1992.

—Newnham, Blaine. "James engineers split national title." *The Seattle Times*, 2 January 1992.

73. Huskies in the Hall

—National Football Foundation: footballfoundation.org.

74. Randy Hart

—Jude, Adam. "Ex-Husky and ex-Stanford assistant Randy Hart has conflicting emotions about Friday's game." *The Seattle Times*, 28 September 2016.

—Maisel, Ivan. "For the first time in 50 years, spring football begins without Randy Hart." ESPN.com, 10 March 2016.

75. Marshawn's Joy Ride

—Condotta, Bob. "Ecstasy and agony." *The Seattle Times*, 22 October 2016.

—Condotta, Bob. "Wrong place, but right time." *The Seattle Times*, 22 October 2016.

—Jude, Adam. "Marshawn Lynch goes cart mode during entrance before Cal-UW game." *The Seattle Times*, 5 November 2016.

—Miller, Ted. "Hey, remember that time Marshawn Lynch took an injury-cart joyride?" ESPN.com, 1 November 2016.

76. Reggie Williams

—Condotta, Bob. "Apple Cup: End of the line?" *The Seattle Times*, 20 November 2003.

—Miller, Ted. "Star from the start: UW's Williams seems destined for greatness." *Seattle Post-Intelligencer*, 22 November 2011.

—Newnham, Blaine. "Reggie Williams heads to NFL." *The Seattle Times*, 16 December 2003.

—Newnham, Blaine. "Reggie Williams was quite the catch." *The Seattle Times*, 18 November 2001.

—Romero, Jose Miguel. "Prize catch: Reggie Williams." *The Seattle Times*, 6 September 2000.

77. Pettis' Historic Punt Return

—Jude, Adam. "Dante Pettis' punt return, late defensive stand give Huskies a 31–24 win over Utah." *The Seattle Times*, 29 October 2016.

—Jude, Adam. "UW's Dante Pettis has perfected Chris Petersen's art of the punt return." *The Seattle Times*, 3 November 2016.

78. Simply Marv-elous

—Eskenazi, David; Steve Rudman. "Wayback machine: Marv Harshman's athletic life." SportsPressNW.com, 20 March 2012.

—Lund, Rick. "Simply Marv-elous: Harshman's most talented Husky team." *The Seattle Times*, 11 May 2013.

—Withers, Bud. "Marv Harshman deserved his reputation as a college basketball coaching legend." *The Seattle Times*, 12 April 2013.

—Withers, Bud. "Harshman remembered at public memorial service." *The Seattle Times*, 11 May 2013.

79. Bicentennial Breakthrough

—Condotta, Bob. "Cracking top 10: 1975–76 team went 22–6." *The Seattle Times*, 21 January 2005.

—Raley, Dan. "Where Are They Now: Chester Dorsey, former UW guard." *Seattle Post-Intelligencer*, 15 February 2005.

—Schwarzmann, Bob. "Huskies' campaign ends painfully." *The Seattle Times*, 14 March 1976.

80. Washington's Wunderkinds: Schrempf and Welp

—Meyers, Georg N. "Coaching German dribblers a bearable ordeal for Marv." *The Seattle Times*, 29 November 1983.

—Newnham, Blaine. "Husky Big Man is here." *The Seattle Times*, 15 February 1983.

—Raley, Dan. "Where are they now: Christian Welp." *Seattle Post-Intelligencer*, 6 January 2004.

—Reid, Scott M. "Christian Welp blazed trails, created cherished memories." *The Orange County Register*, 6 March 2015.

—Schwarzmann, Bob. "Long wait over: UW Pac-10 champion." *The Seattle Times*, 9 March 1984.

—Wolff, Alexander. "Two Bits, Four Bits, Six Bits, A Deutsche Mark!" *Sports Illustrated*, 12 March 1984.

81. Todd MacCulloch

—Allen, Percy. "Another UW escape act; MacCulloch saves Huskies again." *The Seattle Times*, 19 January 1997.

—Caple, Jim. "Todd MacCulloch: NBA alum, pinball wizard." ESPN.com, 8 June 2012.

—Carpenter, Les. "Center's career derailed by his feet." *The Washington Post*, 28 December 2008.

—Kelley, Steve. "Todd MacCulloch hosts pinball world championship at his Bainbridge home." *The Seattle Times*, 9 June 2012.

—Newnham, Blaine. "UW's MacCulloch comes of age." *The Seattle Times*, 12 January 1997.

—Sherwin, Bob. "A very mellow MacCulloch will try to turn it up a notch." *The Seattle Times*, 13 January 1999.

82. 1953 Final Four

—Newnham, Blaine. "Until this team makes Final Four, Houbregs' Huskies best." *The Seattle Times*, 24 March 2005.

—Russell, Eugene N. "Huskies have edge." *The Seattle Times*, 12 March 1953.
—Russell, Eugene N. "Husky defense sets Chiefs down, 92–70." *The Seattle Times*, 14 March 1953.
—Russell, Eugene N. "Headed for the top." *The Seattle Times*, 16 March 1953.
—Russell, Eugene N. "Huskies suffer worst loss in Dye's three-year reign." *The Seattle Times*, 18 March 1953.
—Russell, Eugene N. "Kansas outclassed, outlucked Huskies." *The Seattle Times*, 24 March 1953.

83. Bob Rondeau

—Allen. Percy. "Voices of the Game: UW broadcaster Bob Rondeau found his calling in sports." *The Seattle Times*, 28 July 2009.
—Belt, Derek. "Bob Rondeau is 'The Voice of the Huskies.'" *Column Magazine*, December 2003.
—Jude, Adam. "Longtime UW broadcaster Bob Rondeau honored by National Football Foundation." *The Seattle Times*, 5 May 2016.
—Shelton, Don. "Husky Stadium memorable moments: Bob Rondeau's personal milestones." *The Seattle Times*, 2 November 2011.
—Stone, Larry. "Craig Heyamoto, Bob Rondeau's stat man, makes his mark in his own way for UW football." *The Seattle Times*, 20 October 2016.

84. Messin' with Texas

—Condotta, Bob. "Mackey in the field of his dreams off the field." *The Seattle Times*, 27 December 2002.
—Rockne, Dick. "Huskies enjoy those Texas turnovers." *The Seattle Times*, 23 December 1979.
—Rockne, Dick. "Freshmen's feats make Huskies' future look bright." *The Seattle Times,* 23 December 1979.

85. Chris Polk

—Condotta, Bob. "Washington's Chris Polk will leave for NFL." *The Seattle Times*, 2 January 2012.
—Kelly, Steve. "Running back Chris Polk glad he stayed at Washington." *The Seattle Times*, 19 August 2009.
—Kelley, Steve. "Chris Polk is UW's best running back ever." *The Seattle Times*, 31 October 2011.

86. Get in line

—Jude, Adam. "'Line U': Huskies trying to reignite their lineage of strong offensive line play." *The Seattle Times*, 22 September 2016.

87. Skansi's Miracle Catch

—Jude, Adam. "Paul Skansi returns to help the Huskies, 35 years after his miracle catch in Apple Cup."

88. Jennifer Cohen

—Jude, Adam. "Jennifer Cohen, UW's interim athletic director, was inspired by Don James." *The Seattle Times*, 30 January 2016.

—Jude, Adam. "New Huskies athletic director Jen Cohen: 'We're going to get this place rockin' again.'" *The Seattle Times*, 25 May 2016.

89. Sing "Bow Down"

—"Daily Song Contest Yields Peppy Chant." *The University of Washington Daily*, 1 November 1915.

—"Bow Down To Washington." University of Washington Library website.

90. A Defensive Renaissance

—Allen, Percy. "Washington faces challenge of replacing defensive stars." *The Seattle Times*, 28 August 2015.

—Allen, Percy. "Washington Huskies are leading the nation in fumble recoveries and turnover margin." *The Seattle Times*, 18 October 2016.

—Jude, Adam. "Alabama's Nick Saban compares Huskies' defensive secondary to Seattle Seahawks' secondary." *The Seattle Times*, 26 December 2016.

—Stone, Larry. "Coordinator Pete Kwiatkowski has a new concern for UW defense." *The Seattle Times*, 30 August 2016.

91. UW's All-Time Team

No sources used.

92. Read *The Boys in the Boat*

—Brown, Daniel James. *The Boys in the Boat*. Penguin Books, 2013.

—Gwinn, Mary Ann. "Riding a wave: How 'Boys in the Boat' became a best-seller." *The Seattle Times*, 13 July 2014.

—Hamilton, Kevin J. "'The Boys in the Boat': UW team vanquishes Hitler's crew." *The Seattle Times*, 2 June 2013.

93. Kelsey Plum

—Allen, Percy. "UW's Kelsey Plum breaks Jackie Stiles' NCAA all-time scoring record in 57-point performance vs. Utah." *The Seattle Times*, 25 February 2017.

—Jude, Adam. "Here's what's made UW's Kelsey Plum one of the most prolific scorers in Pac-12 basketball history." *The Seattle Times*, 12 March 2016.

—Schnell, Lindsay. "Leader of the Pack." *Sports Illustrated*, 7 November 2016.

94. Women's Final Four

—Jude, Adam. "Chantel Osahor, UW women advance to first-ever Final Four, knock out Stanford." *The Seattle Times*, 27 March 2016.

—Jude, Adam. "UW women move on to Elite 8 after easy win over Kentucky." *The Seattle Times*, 25 March 2016.

—Jude, Adam. "UW women soaking up the spotlight as they prepare for first Final Four trip." *The Seattle Times*, 30 March 2016.

—Jude, Adam. "UW women fall to Syracuse, 80-59, in Final Four despite Talia Walton's 29 points." *The Seattle Times*, 3 April 2016.

—Quillen, Ian. "UW women stun Maryland, reach Sweet 16 of NCAA tournament." *The Seattle Times*, 21 March 2016.

95. Uncle Hec

—"Tribute to a gallant coach: 'My boys' mattered most to Uncle Hec." *The Seattle Times*, 7 August 1964.

—"Uncle Hec Edmundson will retire." *The Seattle Times*, 21 March 1954.

—Eskenazi, David. "Wayback machine: Ace coach Hec Edmundson." SportsPressNW.com, 15 November 2011.

96. Down Goes Gonzaga

—Condotta, Bob. "Zags' run grows to 7." *The Seattle Times*, 2 December 2004.

—Condotta. Bob. "UW wins dogfight." *The Seattle Times*, 5 December 2005.

—Kelley, Steve. "As good as college hoops gets." *The Seattle Times*, 5 December 2005.

—"Huskies edge out Zags 99-95." The Associated Press, 4 December 2005.

97. Washington Stuns UCLA

—Dougherty, Gary. "Three of Washington's finest moments at Hec Ed came against UCLA." *The Seattle Times*, 2 March 2011.

—Schwarzmann, Ben. "Huskies upset Bruins, 103–81." *The Seattle Times*, 23 February 1975.

—Schwarzmann, Ben. "3 seconds left, Huskies stun Bruins." *The Seattle Times*, 23 February 1979.

98. Lorenzo Romar

—Condotta, Bob. "Huskies gain faith from savior." *The Seattle Times*, 27 January 2015.

—Condotta, Bob. "Huskies best in show." *The Seattle Times*, 13 March 2005.

—Condotta, Bob. "Time to dance." *The Seattle Times*, 14 March 2005.

—Raley, Dan. "The Romar Way: It's the only way for the Huskies." *Seattle Post-Intelligencer*, 30 January 2003.

—Schwarzmann, Bob. "Romar guides Huskies past 'Cats." *The Seattle Times*, 10 December 1978.

—Sherwin, Bob. "1st for UW, fit for Romar." *The Seattle Times*, 5 April 2002.

—Stone, Larry. "UW's Lorenzo Romar preaches patience, but it's getting harder to buy in." *The Seattle Times*, 31 January 2017.

99. Freshmen Phenoms Chriss and Murray

—Allen, Percy. "Washington's Dejounte Murray and Marquese Chriss declare for NBA draft." *The Seattle Times*, 23 March 2016.

—Allen, Percy. "Former Washington star Marquise Chriss soaring up NBA draft boards." *The Seattle Times*, 6 June 2016.

—Caple, Christian. "Lorenzo Romar on the departures of Murray and Chriss, offseason recruiting and more." *The News Tribune*, 24 March 2016.

100. Markelle Fultz

—Allen, Percy. "Highly touted Markelle Fultz has been better than advertised for Huskies." *The Seattle Times*, 24 January 2017.

—Auerbach, Nicole. "No trick shot: Markelle Fultz rises from JV team to national star." *USA TODAY*, 19 January 2017.

—Calkins, Matt. "Markelle Fultz likely a star that leaves Husky basketball fans in awe." *The Seattle Times*, 12 October 2016.

—Caple, Christian. "The making of Markelle Fultz, the most coveted recruit in UW history." *The News Tribune*, 9 November 2016.